Conserving the Railway Heritag

Conserving the Railway Heritage

Edited by

Peter Burman and Michael Stratton

Centre for Conservation Studies,
Institute of Advanced Architectural Studies,
The University of York, UK

E & FN SPON
An Imprint of Chapman & Hall

London · Weinheim · New York · Tokyo · Melbourne · Madras

Published by E & FN Spon, an imprint of Chapman & Hall,
2–6 Boundary Row, London SE1 8HN, UK

Chapman & Hall, 2–6 Boundary Row, London SE1 8HN, UK

Chapman & Hall GmbH, Pappelallee 3, 69469 Weinheim, Germany

Chapman & Hall USA, 115 Fifth Avenue, New York, NY 10003, USA

Chapman & Hall Japan, ITP-Japan, Kyowa Building, 3F, 2–2–1 Hirakawacho, Chiyoda-ku, Tokyo 102, Japan

Chapman & Hall Australia, 102 Dodds Street, South Melbourne, Victoria 3205, Australia

Chapman & Hall India, R. Seshadri, 32 Second Main Road, CIT East, Madras 600 035, India

First edition 1997

© 1997 E & FN Spon
    pp 75–88 © Adrian Vaughan

Typeset in 10/12 pt Times by Photoprint, Torquay
Printed in Great Britain by the Alden Press, Osney Mead, Oxford

ISBN   0 419 21280 9

A catalogue record for this book is available from the British Library

Contents

Contributors

Gregory Beecroft
Senior Project Surveyor, British Rail
Property Board

Gordon Biddle
Railway historian

Charles Blackett-Ord
Blackett-Ord Consulting Engineers

Peter Burman
Director, Centre for Conservation Studies,
Institute of Advanced Architectural
Studies, The University of York

John Cattell
Royal Commission on the Historical
Monuments of England

Sir Neil Cossons
Director, National Museum of Science &
Industry

Nick Derbyshire
Nick Derbyshire Design Associates

Keith Falconer
Royal Commission on the Historical
Monuments of England

John Hume
Chief Inspector of Historic Buildings,
Historic Scotland

Barrie Jones
Royal Commission on the Historical
Monuments of England

David Lawrence
Railway historian

Steve Pilcher
London Division, English Heritage

Leslie Soane
Executive Director, Railway Heritage Trust

Dr Michael Stratton
Lecturer in Conservation Studies, Institute
of Advanced Architectural Studies,
The University of York

Robert Thorne
Associate, Alan Baxter & Associates

Richard Threlfall
Department of Transport

Adrian Vaughan
Railway historian

John Yates
Inspector, Conservation for the West
Midlands and the North, English Heritage

Preface and acknowledgements

The railway heritage is all too often taken for granted – by travellers, enthusiasts and conservation professionals alike – as a solid and safe aspect of our inheritance from the Victorian period. But its future has never been secure. Railway companies, and British Railways during its early years, had little compunction about clearing old structures for modern facilities, an up-to-date image or faster line speeds. The major losses of the 1960s – symbolized by the demolition of the Euston Arch – prompted a change of heart. Indeed there is now the possibility that the recent discovery of much of the masonry from the Doric gateway dumped in a water channel in east London may permit its re-erection in central London. During the 1980s Manchester Central was converted to an exhibition centre. Over the past decade the Railway Heritage Trust has encouraged British Rail to conserve decayed stations and find alternative uses for those larger than can be justified by current levels of operation. Interest has spread from fine examples of station architecture to embrace viaducts – strongly featured in the chapters of this book – warehouses, workshops, signal boxes and railway housing.

There is much to celebrate but, as the chapters of this book demonstrate, the railway heritage is still vulnerable. Privatization has introduced an atmosphere of uncertainty, though most would be relieved that operational stations and structures have passed to one agency, Railtrack, rather than being dispersed to a multitude of franchisees. The revival of railways across western Europe has brought new, vibrant ideas into the world of station architecture. The true test of the new international yet privatized world of Britain's railways will be the standards of conservation and quality of new design achieved when St Pancras becomes the terminus for the high-speed link to the Channel Tunnel. This is already a matter of concern to the Victorian Society and other amenity societies, though few would begrudge the potential offered by Britain's greatest historic terminus at last gaining a status fitting to the grandeur of its overall roof and hotel frontage.

The last few years have seen lively debates as to the nature of the railway heritage and over the contributions of those involved in its study and preservation. The three-day event held at the King's Manor, York, between 11 and 13 May 1994 was deliberately called a 'consultation'. It brought together a group of men and women, speakers and delegates, who all for various reasons share a passionate interest in the past, present and future of the railway system. They came together, in a spirit of mutual consultation, to consider two broad areas of concern: how to define and establish the nature of the railway heritage; and how to set priorities for conservation in the broadest sense. The consultation owed much to the joint goodwill and support of Sir Neil Cossons, Director of the National Museum of Science & Industry, within whose responsibilities the National Railway Museum at York also falls, and the Vice-Chancellor of the University of York, Professor Ron Cooke. The Vice-Chancellor opened the consultation with some stirring words about the value of cross-cutting disciplines, architectural conservation undoubtedly being one of these; and pointing to the consultation as a valuable catalyst, bringing together key people at a critical moment in the development of the railway system in Britain.

Sir Neil Cossons, in his keynote address, announced the decision to establish jointly, between the National Museum of Science & Industry and the University of York, an Institute of Railway Studies. Since then, the Institute has become strongly established, with its own professor, Colin Divall, research students and a lively programme of research workshops. Certificate and MA courses in railway studies are being planned.

The papers from this consultation were developed into the chapters of a book with close support from the Institute of Railway Studies and the National Railway Museum, in particular from Philip Atkins, Ed Bartholemew, Neil Cossons, Colin Divall, Dieter Hopkin and Andrew Scott.

Gordon Biddle and Barrie Trinder provided additional entries for the bibliographical chapter. All of the contributors responded positively to the idea of the consultation papers being developed into a book, and went to great efforts to update their contributions and provide a rich variety of illustrations. Thanks are also due to Pamela Hodgson, Academic Secretary at the Centre for Conservation Studies, for her help in bringing this project together, and to Caroline Mallinder, Architecture Editor at E & FN Spon, for her enthusiasm and guidance.

Credits
Illustrations are individually credited to the photographer or archive. Particular thanks are due to the Royal Commission on Historical Monuments of England, the Railway Heritage Trust and the National Railway Museum for supplying a series of high quality images.

Peter Burman
Michael Stratton
Institute of Advanced Architectural Studies, The University of York

Part One
Overview

Neil Cossons

An agenda for the railway heritage

The railway revolution

The emergence of the steam railway in the first quarter of the nineteenth century was a phenomenon of extraordinary importance, not only in the development of industrialization worldwide but as one of the key new technologies without which much of nineteenth-century civilization as we came to know it could not have come about. From primeval origins to a fully fledged form of transport took less than 25 years: from, say, 1802 and Richard Trevithick's early experiments in Coalbrookdale and later Penydarren to the opening of the Stockton and Darlington Railway in 1825. In less than another 20 years the era of the railway was with us, and the new technologies and the systems that supported them were being adopted in countries throughout Europe and in North America.

The nineteenth century was the age of the railway; it had no significant competitor until the second decade of the twentieth, and today, nearly 200 years after its birth, it is to the railway – steel wheels on steel rails, with the prime mover travelling with the load – that all over Europe we are again turning to satisfy our needs for high-speed city-centre to city-centre travel, and for efficient and environment-friendly passenger transport inside cities themselves. If the middle years of the nineteenth century represented the era of the railway revolution then there seems every likelihood that the dawn of the new millennium will see the age of the railway renaissance. It is particularly apposite therefore to be considering the future of the railway heritage, so soon after the opening of the Channel Tunnel, perhaps the most significant railway development in Europe this century.

The whole of the formative development of the railway took place, and only could have taken place, in Britain. Only in this country were the essential technologies all together in one place, backed by engineers, innovators and entrepreneurs capable of developing them rapidly and effectively. Combine these qualities with the economic and social circumstances of a nation that was already well advanced on its path towards industrialization, and with the ready and expanding markets of a growing empire, then the conditions for the spread of the railway could not have been more auspicious.

The railway, throughout its existence, has in the main been a force for good. The benefits it has brought vastly outweigh the disbenefits. Unlike the ship, the internal-combustion-engined road vehicle or the aircraft, the railway in its own right has hardly ever been the engine of war – the instrument of slaughter – although railways have of course contributed vastly to the ability of nations to make war one with another. The railway holds a position of profound but largely overlooked importance in the culture of us all, and a place of affection for many who spend their spare time engaged in one way or another in its worship.

Fig. 1.1 Limstone quarries at Pant, south of Oswestry, Shropshire, were linked in 1797 to the Montgomeryshire Canal by a self-acting incline. This wooden winding drum stands west of the A483 at the head of the incline. (Neil Cossons)

The conservation challenge

In some respects it is this nostalgia for the railway, and especially the steam railway, that prevents us as a nation from taking sufficiently seriously the recording and preservation of its history and heritage. The material evidence of the origins and subsequent development of the railway is not properly regarded by the population at large in the same context as those aspects of our past that we commonly perceive and value as heritage. Nor are the standards of scholarship or conservation that would be taken for granted in the fields of, say, Roman archaeology or the care of historic buildings applied with similar rigour in the case of the railway.

That is changing, as the chapters in this book amply demonstrate. But there is still much to be done to ensure that the railway, in the country of its birth, is accorded the same recognition and the same quality of protection as the rest of the man-made environment, so that our successors in a century or more will be able to appreciate, understand and value this most extraordinary achievement of

Fig. 1.2 Bridge across the A514 in Ticknall, Derbyshire completed in 1802 to carry the Ashby & Ticknall Tramway to local limestone quarries. (Neil Cossons)

Fig. 1.3 The standard Midland Railway signal box once common from St Pancras to Carlisle and Lincoln to Avonmouth is now scarce in original use and unaltered form. (Neil Cossons)

our forebears. A primary purpose of this book might, I suggest, be to set an agenda for how this might be achieved.

It is a complex area: much more difficult to handle than in the more conventional and already well-accepted areas of the heritage. Many of the sites of primary importance are still in use, in the main for the purpose for which they were originally designed and built. This places very special responsibilities on their owners, an issue even more critical in the context of privatization. Others, which have become redundant, occupy high-value urban sites, where pressure to redevelop may be acute. Adaptation to new uses is clearly an option in some cases, but I cannot help feeling that if these were, for example, ecclesiastical buildings or great country houses that were under such universal threat they would be the subject of a Royal Commission. Elsewhere there are the imponderable problems of what to do with redundant railway viaducts. Often of immense aesthetic and landscape value, they nevertheless represent a continuing maintenance burden, which at the very minimum must satisfy basic standards of safety. For some structures – for example, the iron viaducts at Bennerley across the Erewash Valley on the Nottinghamshire and Derbyshire border or Meldon in Devon – the scale of this maintenance commitment will be immense.

Why should we preserve the railway heritage? Part of that question I hope has already been answered. The overwhelming historical importance of the railway, in all its various manifestations, is such that it must form part of the past that we choose to take forward into the future. And what we take forward with us must be in a sufficient state of completeness and authenticity, supported by proper levels of knowledge and understanding, and accorded appropriate standards of professional care, so that our successors may gain some tangible comprehension of its extraordinary impact upon humanity.

In this country our responsibilities are unique, for two reasons. First, and most obvious, the steam railway began here; and second, the material evidence of the railway – its prehistory, history and subsequent development – still survives in profusion. That record is unique and sufficiently complete to represent an outstanding archaeological, historical and – perhaps more important – cultural asset that we can ill afford to lose.

There is also perhaps a third reason why we should preserve the remains of the railway, which also has implications for what we should keep. Not only did Britain export the concept and technological formula of the railway to the rest of the world, but she became a major provider of railways too. Almost every nation has some evidence of Britain's contribution, if only in the gauge of the track. But many have more tangible remains: the great Retiro terminus in Buenos Aires or the typical English country stations in the outskirts of that city – at San Isidro, for example – that look as if they would be more at home in

Fig. 1.4 At Ashby-de-la-Zouch, Leicestershire, the redundant station building (Midland Railway, 1849) has been converted to new use. In the foreground is the track of the Burton & Ashby Light Railway. (Neil Cossons)

Fig. 1.5 Harringworth Viaduct (Midland Railway, probably by J. Underwood, 1879), with its 82 brick arches across the valley of the River Welland on the Midland line from Kettering via Melton Mowbray to Nottingham. (Neil Cossons)

Dorset, all designed by British engineers and architects and many built by British contracting companies. And the locomotives and rolling-stock often survive too, although usually now mainly in museums. Here again the evidence is often of primary importance; think for example of the unique collection of British equipment in the railway museum at Gavle in Sweden. We have I believe a very special obligation, much as we do in the broader field of industrial archaeology, where similar relationships between Britain as the first industrial nation and the rest of the world apply. That obligation is to ensure that this overseas evidence survives, by encouraging those who, increasingly, recognize that the railway is also a part of their heritage.

Scholarship

In order to have a responsible policy for the future of the railway heritage it is essential that we have a sound knowledge and understanding of it. Here I have major concerns, for despite the enormous amount of energy and enthusiasm generated by the railway as a subject of popular interest and appreciation, and the huge output of publications, serious high-quality study and research of the railway is in a decline. This may lead to extinction in the-not-too-distant future. That is not to say that here and there first-class work is not going on, but when one looks at the output overall, nowhere is it possible to see programmes of planned and systematic study and research dedicated to expanding our knowledge and understanding of the railway. And much of what is going on is tightly focused. There are no authoritative business histories of any of the 'big four' companies that ran Britain's railways from 1923 to 1947, let alone of British Railways itself. Nowhere has the history of the railway as such been the special area of concern of any academic or conservation agency, with the possible exception of the National Railway Museum in York.

If a broader understanding of the railway and its role is in itself a worthwhile objective – and I believe it is – then we must expand our own knowledge at a scholarly level. If we believe a broader public understanding is the key to a widening of the acceptability of the railway, as an essential part of the nation's heritage, as well as a fundamentally important form of transport for the future (and I most certainly do), then again we must base the case upon sound knowledge derived from first-class study and research.

Priorities for conservation

The future policies and subsequent progress of the conservation of the railway heritage must, as with all other areas of the heritage, be based on a foundation of sound and evolving scholarship. If we look for example at the outstanding success of British archaeology in the last 40 years we can see a strong academic base pushing forward the boundaries of knowledge on the one hand and that new knowledge being translated directly into popular understanding on the

Fig. 1.6 Meldon Viaduct, built by the London & South Western Railway in 1874. (Neil Cossons)

9

other. Think of *Animal, Vegetable and Mineral* in the 1950s and 1960s, and of *Chronicle* a few years later. The ability of archaeologists to use their new knowledge to capture the imagination of the public and use that as a route towards widespread public support for their cause offers lessons from which we can learn a lot. Again, in a somewhat different context, consider the highly successful visitor attraction, *Yorvik*, and the pioneering work of the York Archaeological Trust. To see that support turned into sustained funding, much of it from the public purse, is salutary. Within the next year or two it is by no means beyond the bounds of possibility that Stonehenge and its environs – a World Heritage Site of immense archaeological and cultural significance – will be financed to the tune of hundreds of millions of pounds in order to ensure its survival for the future. And so it should be. But I suggest too that the symbols by which we as the first industrial society are going to be recognized in a thousand years' time, including the primary physical evidence of the railway revolution, need the same thoughtful care and attention, the same scholarly understanding and the same broad recognition and public support if they are to have a future too.

Now let me turn to some of what I think we should be preserving. This is not by any means a definitive or prescriptive list, but provides I hope a few exemplars of the sorts of issues that still confront us if we intend seriously as a nation to ensure the survival of a truly representative railway heritage portfolio. Let me try on you a few areas that I believe are worthy of special consideration.

I shall take them in a broadly chronological sequence. First, I think we need a national survey of the surviving evidence of the tramways and tramroads that preceded, and in part overlapped, the arrival of the steam railway nearly two centuries ago. That legacy is prolific, unique and worthy of systematic attention and subsequent care. Many of the key monuments are scheduled or listed, but beyond that formal care is minimal. We need a scale of priorities; to achieve that a survey is an essential prerequisite. Out of that survey might come a published synoptic study of the iron tramway and its immediate predecessors equal in historical weight and authority to Michael Lewis's outstanding *Early Wooden Railways* (Lewis, 1970) but with the addition of the archaeological evidence.

Next, and on a completely different front, the surviving locomotives of the period from 1813 to, say, 1845 – the formative years – are in need of proper historical and archaeological study. What has been done has been piecemeal, and much of it so long ago as to be without the benefits of modern research techniques. Most of these locomotives are in the National Railway Collection, and those that are not – both in Britain and overseas – are well known and reasonably safe. Some have been in public ownership for well over a century; it is worth remembering that the Science Museum in London, as the National Museum of Science & Industry, has been collecting railway locomotives since the early 1860s. But our overall knowledge of this primordial genre is lamentably thin and much of it dated. (In this context it is sad to note that a notable engineer whose own practical knowledge and understanding of the early steam locomotive was beyond compare – Mike Satow – has recently been lost to us.)

My next objective would be to see the whole of the old Great Western main line, from Bristol to Paddington, designated as a World Heritage Site. It is reasonable, I suggest, to say that the railway came of age with the opening of the first major inter-city routes in the late 1830s and early 1840s. These are monuments in their own right, evidence of the innovative new system of transport at the stage where its true and overwhelming significance first came to be recognized. One could argue with some persuasion that the Stockton & Darlington and the Liverpool & Manchester had equal if not greater claims to this sort of recognition. But then consider, in both cases, the extent of the surviving material evidence and the argument becomes less convincing. Clearly there are individual structures of immense significance. One thinks for example of Liverpool Road Station, Manchester, the Sankey Viaduct or the skew bridge at Rainhill, not to mention the Grade II listed memorial to William Huskisson, now sadly in a seriously vandalized condition. But, overall, the evidence of the original lines, dating from the 1820s and 1830s is intermittent.

When it comes to the two prime candidates, the London & Birmingham and the Great Western, then again the former – despite a fine range of individual buildings and civil engineering works of immense importance – has been so altered over the years, not least by electrification in the 1960s, that designation of the line in its entirety would be difficult to sustain. The Great Western, however, despite the fact that it originally included the unusual and eccentric feature of the broad gauge, still contains substantially intact the civil engineering and architectural features of a first-generation inter-city main line. It is in essence a prototype main line, essentially Stephensonian in concept, and built at a time when the engineer's word was gospel. From Temple Meads, the world's oldest surviving train shed terminus – and surely the most precious railway building in this country – to the spectacle of Paddington, with *en route* the works through Bath, the tunnels at Box, the railway village at Swindon, the crossing of the Thames at Maidenhead, Wharncliffe Viaduct at Hanwell, and innumerable occupation arches and other original details, the line combines completeness and authenticity with spectacular landscape quality.

World Heritage Site designation does not, in Britain, confer any additional legislative protection or financial provision. What it does, however, is give a quality of recognition and identity, essential in the building up of a broader base of public support for the protection of the railway heritage. Of our existing World Heritage Sites only one reflects Britain's emergence in the eighteenth century as the first industrial nation: the Ironbridge Gorge. It is, I believe, both appropriate and essential that the nation's early contribution to the development of the railway is similarly recognized through what should become a great linear site, a new form of National Park. There are precedents. Hadrian's Wall is a World Heritage Site, and so too is the Great Wall of China.

Appreciation and interpretation

Let me now move to something of an entirely different nature. As I have suggested, a wider public appreciation of the railway heritage is essential if proper regard, protection and funding are to be achieved. What I should like to see is a system throughout the country in which key structures and buildings are identified and interpreted to the public. I am not suggesting a blue plaque

Fig. 1.7 Beams of the six Cornish engines installed at Sudbrook, Gloucestershire, in 1886 to drain the Severn Tunnel. Demolished in the early 1970s. (Neil Cossons)

scheme of the type initiated by the old London County Council and now continued by English Heritage. What I have in mind is a panel, perhaps the size of a standard railway poster – a museum label, if you like – which would be used to say something of the history, architectural and structural details of the key railway monuments. Passengers through the Great London termini, like King's Cross, Paddington or St Pancras, would find panels including illustrative material, a few brief paragraphs of information and a note on where more details could be obtained. In the countryside, similarly, there would be well-designed panels fixed on or near outstanding structures, providing authoritative and consistently presented interpretative information.

My final item on the menu is different again. One of the great manifestations of popular interest in the railway is the movement that has led to the preservation of numerous locomotives and items of rolling-stock that operate on restored branch lines. This is what might be called the 'voluntary sector' of the railway preservation business, and it has a substantial following not only in terms of those who, in their spare time, have brought these railways into existence, form their shareholders and staff and operate them, often to high standards of professionalism, but also in the people who as passengers enjoy what they have to offer and provide the bulk of their income. Some of these

12

railways are simply small lines on which a locomotive and a few carriages run up and down. Others are well-established quasi-commercial operations working, to all intents and purposes, like the original railway company they replaced. Some attempt in the conservation of their railway estate to recreate history, if not in the entire operation of the railway then certainly in the presentation of individual buildings or indeed whole stations. Some come pretty close to being complete replica railways recreating the authentic experience of a railway of the past.

My plea is that here and there might be one or two of these preserved lines whose *primary* objective is to recreate in as accurate a manner as possible the historical and operational detail of a railway from the past. By this I mean that a passenger could arrive at a station that was, to all intents and purposes, as it might have been in its heyday. A train with the right locomotives and rolling-stock would arrive at that station and the journey would be as authentic a railway experience as possible. In other words I am suggesting that there is an opportunity – perhaps several opportunities – for one or two of the best-preserved railways, where conditions are especially favourable, and in particular where authentic estates can be matched with the right sort of locomotives and rolling-stock, to operate in effect as open-air museums.

Recreated history is, as we all know, slightly suspect theologically. We have all visited those museums in Scandinavia or North America that attempt to recreate life from the distant past. And we all know that today's interpreters do not have the marks of smallpox, nor do they suffer from rickets, and rarely can they recreate the language of, for example, seventeenth-century England. But, where these museums are run with a foundation of sound scholarship and rigorous policies of conservation and operation, they can, I believe, form a highly effective means of evoking the past and creating, for many people, a view of history that otherwise they would not have or might be of no interest to them.

The opportunity to do this for a typical small English branch line is, I believe, available. There might well be arguments by the railway preservation movement that such an activity would be financially impossible. My counter-argument would be that to dedicate oneself to such a laudable objective would generate a real following from people whose interests stretched way beyond the straightforward day out on a branch line; and the educational value could be immense. Furthermore, I believe that such a venture should be a recipient of public funds. Just as museums and heritage sites in the care of the state receive public funding so too could an operational railway dedicated primarily – and I emphasize the 'primarily' – to encapsulating in as accurate a manner as possible the operational details and flavour of a railway of the past. If, as seems increasingly probable, Heritage Lottery funds were to be used for creating endowments (and the precedent already exists in the Arts Lottery endowment for the Dulwich Picture Gallery), then an underwriting of the museum costs of an historically authentic railway would represent a marvellous investment for the future.

If this was not a keynote chapter I could continue with many other proposals whereby the railway heritage could be protected, not in an exhaustive manner, because we cannot and should not keep everything, but in order that the key sites and monuments, and operational features, of the railway in its heyday could be preserved for posterity. Before we take such a list as mine and expand it we need some clearer priorities and sense of direction, otherwise efforts will be dissipated and resources wasted. That seems to me to be the cue for contemplating how the issues of managing the future of the railway heritage might be addressed.

A future for the railway heritage
There are a variety of existing players in the railway heritage business. The National Railway Museum is one of the most important. But few of these bodies – and the National Railway Museum is one of the exceptions – are dedicated primarily to the conservation and interpretation of the railway heritage. Others, such as English Heritage and its Welsh and Scottish equivalents, and the Royal Commissions, have a broad remit, of which railways represent a small and sometimes insignificant part. Then there is the railway enthusiast movement, a part of which is or believes itself to be primarily concerned with preservation. Finally, I identify the Railway Heritage Trust, a body with an extraordinary record of achievement. It is, I believe, unique as an organization; its accomplishments have been outstanding, and Leslie Soane will relate in a subsequent chapter something of what he and the Trust have done.

How might the efforts of these various agencies be best applied? Here I must return to one of the points I made earlier. In order to have responsible policies for the future of the railway heritage it is essential that our knowledge and understanding continue to develop. It is easy to look at the railway past through rose-coloured spectacles, providing us with a nostalgic view of those aspects of the railway for which as architectural historians, enthusiasts for civil engineering, or railway buffs, we have some form of affection, perhaps originating from our childhoods or the memories of our fathers. That is not good enough. The railway heritage deserves the same quality of treatment as the rest of our past. It does not at present enjoy well-set foundations in study and research.

Let me now set out how, here in York, we are remedying that deficiency. The National Museum of Science & Industry, of which the National Railway Museum is a key component, and the University of York have joined together to foster study and research into the railway. As the result of discussions between the Vice-Chancellor and myself the University and the Museum have established as a joint venture the Institute of Railway Studies. We believe that the immense contribution of the railway to our national life – past, present and future – and the serious study of its economic, social, geographical and technological significance (and this of course includes its architectural and engineering qualities), deserve a national research and teaching centre. The principal purpose of the Institute is to advance the study and understanding of the railway in all its aspects. It will focus initially on high-quality research and postgraduate training. Its resources include the outstanding collections of the National Railway Museum itself, and its initiatives are based on the support of the University and the academic standing and impetus that this provides, together with the existing curatorial and archival staff of the National Railway Museum. The newly appointed Head of the Institute, with the status of

Fig. 1.8 Gravestones in Bromsgrove churchyard, Worcestershire, of two engineers on the Birmingham & Gloucester Railway, killed by a boiler explosion in 1840. Damaged by vandals. (Neil Cossons)

Professor of Railway Studies in the University and Head of Research in the Museum, is Colin Divall, who joins us from Manchester. Our objective is not only to stimulate and encourage study and research within the orbit of the museum and the university but to encourage others outside these institutions to use our respective resources – and in particular our collections – for furthering the understanding of the railway. The fruits of that study and research we wish to see applied not only at a scholarly level but as a foundation for broadening public interest and appeal. The role of a national museum is not only to hold collections but also to know about them. The value of our collections derives, in the main, from the knowledge and information that they contain. It is our job to release that knowledge so that it may be applied through, for example, exhibitions, publications, radio and television.

A further and very important aim in promoting that study and research should be to help the statutory agencies in the fields of conservation and recording, and perhaps the voluntary sector too, with their priorities and agendas. We should be looking for the broad works of synthesis that will enable these bodies to put their own specific objectives and activities into context. I have no doubt that English Heritage and the Royal Commissions would be enthusiastic clients of the Institute of Railway Studies. Indeed, the English Royal Commission has, in its own way, recently become a railway heritage organization by transferring its offices and archives from Savile Row to the converted drawing-offices of the Great Western Railway at Swindon. Similarly, the newly formed Railway Heritage Committee, set up to assist with the identification and designation of railway material for preservation, will we hope be able to draw on the accumulated expertise of the Institute.

Let me conclude briefly by addressing the issue of for whom the railway heritage exists. I suggested at the outset that the railway heritage was not adequately regarded by the public at large. For many, an expression of interest in railways evokes the inevitable and now somewhat hackneyed picture of trainspotters in anoraks. There is, I believe, a natural tendency that dictates that each aspect of the heritage is regarded – socially and culturally – as much by how we perceive its adherents as by the stuff of heritage itself. When we visit a National Trust property part of its flavour is imparted by the people who greet us. It is different from, say, an English Heritage site or a country house opened on Sunday afternoons by its owner. But we take seriously what these organizations and the people that support them do and how they do it. They, in their turn, have gone to great efforts to be taken seriously, by promoting professionalism in all that they do and in generating an image of being well run. They have also gone to great lengths to keep the issues of cultural value and funding – especially public funding – high on the nation's agenda.

Paradoxically, it has been the railway preservation movement's often perverse view that its independence is one of its greatest virtues, together with its extraordinary ability to generate significant funding from within its own membership, that has led to its isolation from the mainstream of cultural heritage preservation. Marginalization from within as well as patronizing public perception from without work strongly against it. Even a debate on the railway heritage in Parliament does not start from the premise of historical or cultural significance so much as from childhood memories of steam trains. This is not helpful. It is partly a reflection of a popular view that people who are interested in railways are not to be taken seriously. They are trainspotters or railway buffs, for whom a weekend of 'playing trains' is what turns them on. This socio-cultural dimension is widespread. It was described recently in an article in the *Sunday Times* by Jonathan Margolis. He said:

> Trainspotters are our worst nightmare. As harmless as it is possible for *Homo sapiens* to be, they still set something alight in us. The compulsion to collect and to order, we reason, is clearly an attempt by powerless individuals to control what little they can save of their world. We are obviously talking anal retention as an Olympic event here . . . It is not just that they are hobbyists, with the sniff of smelly socks obsessionism which that conveys; fishing or golf or pigeon-fancying most of us can live with. But the sheer passivity of trainspotting, the time-wasting idiocy of writing train numbers down in a book for no purpose is, like infinity, too much to contemplate. (Margolis, 1993)

That is the voice of prejudice, but it is a view widely held, and one that, like it or not, we have to live with. Our objective must be to lift the sights and raise the aspirations of those with a serious strategic interest in the future of the railway heritage. That is why the museum and university here in York have established our joint institute. That is also why we need, between us all, to establish the credentials for the railway heritage. The people for whom we are doing it are the public at large, whose heritage it is. We must not lose sight, through our interests, our passions and our obsessions for the railway and all it represents, of the fact that it is one of the most important dimensions in our cultural history, its heritage is noble and significant, and the future of that heritage should be the concern of us all.

Select bibliography
Lewis, M.J.T. (1970) *Early Wooden Railways*, Routledge & Kegan Paul, London.
Margolis, J. (1993) Platform souls. *Sunday Times* (*The Culture*), 16 May.

Peter Burman

Philosophies for conserving the railway heritage

Introduction

My own interest in railways was fostered and encouraged by being a trustee of SAVE Britain's Heritage. SAVE was established in European Architectural Heritage Year 1975 to campaign for threatened aspects of the built environment, and to promote study, research into and awareness of the nation's built heritage. Our earliest major project, some 18 months after our establishment, was the organization of an exhibition to draw attention to the plight of one signally important aspect of railway culture, namely its buildings. The exhibition, which was held at the RIBA Heinz Gallery from January to March 1977, was called *Off the Rails: Saving Railway Heritage*. Looking back on it I realize that one of the reasons why the exhibition was such a landmark was that it examined railway buildings with the same seriousness with which other categories of buildings were already for the most part being treated, and it promoted an understanding of them that acknowledged their value in architectural, historical, technical and social contexts. Understandably enough, the exhibition and the publications that accompanied it aroused a good deal of ire in certain circles: that is to say, those more committed to an efficient running of the railway system than to maintaining structures that were perceived in a good many cases to have outrun their useful life. However, we also demonstrated the enormous potential of railway structures to be adapted for new uses, without necessarily losing thereby their associational or cultural values in the process.

Establishing a philosophical approach

Against this background it may now surely be asked whether, and if so to what extent, we can identify appropriate philosophies for conserving the railway heritage: whether, in fact, railway structures should be seen as part of the

18

mainstream of historic buildings – albeit of a variety that in various countries and cultures causes them to be considered as 'technical monuments' – or whether different and separate considerations apply. It is curious that appreciation of the railway heritage has been slow in coming, and that there have been few attempts to see and understand it and its problems in a holistic way. If asked to define the 'railway heritage' it ought to be possible to reply in the same robust terms as William Morris's SPAB Manifesto of 1877, and define it as

> anything which can be looked on as artistic, picturesque, historical, antique, or substantial: any work, in short, over which educated, artistic people would think it worth while to argue at all. (Morris, 1877)

In terms of railway heritage this must surely embrace the rich treasuries of railway archives, buildings such as railway stations and engine sheds and railway works, lesser structures such as signal boxes, technical equipment of many kinds (much of it innovative and the product of highly original minds), major structures in the landscape such as bridges and viaducts, and minor artefacts that nevertheless convey the local distinctiveness of the various companies, such as clocks, benches and other furniture.

The British contribution to the development of the railways was an important one: the idea of metal wheels on metal track was so attractive to the vision of those who in the nineteenth century were trying to create more efficient means of transport, so robust, and so long lasting, that it quickly spread from Britain to other countries. There is therefore about the railway heritage a universal aspect that is immensely appealing. What has not survived in some countries, such as unaltered examples of particular building types or particular classes of locomotives still in use, may well be found in another. Moreover, as the great cities of the world developed during the course of the nineteenth century, railway stations came often to occupy a symbolic central location: one has only to think of Paris, Hamburg, Leipzig or Prague for examples of superb railway termini in Europe. Or, to go further afield, one of the best-loved and most spectacular buildings in Bombay is the Victoria Terminus (affectionately known locally as the 'VT'), designed by the English architect F.W. Stevens, and opened in 1888, which is very obviously one of the key buildings in a city that Gavin Stamp has described as 'the finest Gothic Revival city in the world' (Dwivedi and Mehrotra, 1995).

Symbolically, the Victoria Terminus features a high dome surmounted by a figure of Progress as the most arresting element in its composition, while the gables of the side wings on the west side are surmounted by groups representing Engineering and Commerce. It would scarcely be possible to imagine a richer symbolism of nineteenth-century urban ideals, all focused on a railway station. Moreover, the interior is made splendid by the use of the choicest Italian marbles and polished India-blue stone, and the carved stone and ornamental ironwork were designed by Stevens but executed by the talented students of the J.J. School of Art. In any measured evaluation of nineteenth-century architecture, the Victoria Terminus would surely now – as seen from the perspective of the late twentieth century – have to be counted as one of the major monuments of world architecture.

19

Fig. 2.1 The roof of Leipzig Station spanning 26 tracks, completed to designs by Kühne & Lossow in 1915. (M.J. Stratton)

Background to the philosophical debate

In considering a philosophy for railway heritage, we are perhaps hampered by the fact that conservation philosophy has been evolving since the early nineteenth century up to the present-day debate about 'authenticity'; and the railway heritage has become appreciated at virtually the same time. The evolution of conservation philosophy was, to a considerable degree, backward looking in that writers and thinkers from Karl-Friedrich Schinkel in Germany to

Fig. 2.2 The frontage of the Victoria Terminus, Bombay, by F.W. Stevens, opened 1888. (M.J. Stratton)

Fig. 2.3 The central domed tower of the Victoria Terminus. (M.J. Stratton)

Morris in England were clearly thinking principally of the venerable monuments of the more distant past, and particularly ecclesiastical monuments and (in Morris's case) vernacular buildings as well. His definition, quoted above, of what constituted value was clearly intended to embrace the cottage and the farmhouse as well as the castle or cathedral, but it is difficult to apply his thinking to railway heritage except in one significant respect. Following John Ruskin in *The Seven Lamps of Architecture*, published in 1849, Morris put tremendous emphasis on good maintenance:

> to stave off decay by daily care, to prop a perilous wall or mend a leaky roof by such means as are obviously meant for support or covering, and show no pretense of other art, and otherwise to resist all tampering with either the fabric or ornament of the building as it stands. (Morris, 1877)

All the conservation manuals and eloquent exhortations since, from Sir John Marshall's admirable handbook in early twentieth-century India to Sir Bernard Feilden's classic statement in late twentieth-century England, have built on Morris's passionate plea. There are indeed two points here, the first being the strong emphasis on maintenance in good order, and the second relating to authenticity, to which we shall have to return.

William Morris's philosophy was not only directed towards preservation and conservation of monuments of the past; he was an equally passionate advocate of the revival of true craftsmanship (though equally he had an understanding of the value of machinery in its proper place, as demonstrated by the adoption of labour-saving mechanical methods in the workshops of his firm), and his ideas about authenticity are linked with his passionate conviction that architecture should move away from copyism to a fresh, natural and non-stylistic approach to designing: hence, probably, his advocacy of the idea that repairs, changes or additions should be 'wrought in the unmistakable fashion of the time', though probably even he would admit of such exceptions as the fifteenth-century continuation of the nave of Westminster Abbey in the style established in the early thirteenth century.

William Morris had effective co-workers and influential successors. In the following generation came W.R. Lethaby, first Principal of the Central School of Arts & Crafts in London, who around the turn of the century became a most effective protagonist of the SPAB point of view, consciously following in the footsteps of Morris and of Philip Webb. His writings repay much study in this context, and moreover – like Webb – he was not opposed to the introduction of new building materials and exciting constructional techniques such as the development of railway architecture had made much more possible and much more general. He, in turn, helped to nurture the next generation, which included the man who was Secretary of the SPAB from 1911 to 1936, A.R. Powys. The significance of Powys in this particular context is that he was one of the two British delegates to the Athens Conference of October 1931 (the other being Sir Cecil Harcourt-Smith, Director of the Victoria & Albert Museum), whose deliberations produced substantial Conclusions and the Athens Charter, which has become one of the foundations for later twentieth-century thinking.

Again, it must be admitted that it is quite difficult to apply the advice of the Athens documents to railway buildings, except in a general sense: Powys's handiwork may be found in the advice to initiate 'a system of regular and permanent maintenance', which is clearly one of the most striking needs for railway buildings, particularly those that are under-used or which have fallen into an unacknowledged 'waiting period' (to borrow a phrase used in the late twentieth century to describe redundant churches and chapels that are still looking for a new use) (Powys, 1929, pp. 3–16). At such times, maintenance can be crucial to survival.

Another general sentiment in the Athens documents refers to international collaboration, and this too is something that is greatly needed in the railway heritage field. Tentative steps have been taken, it is true; and informally lessons derived in one country are gratefully applied in another. But there is lacking a true international forum for the discussion of and dissemination of solutions in the railway heritage field. Some other recommendations in the Athens documents strike a useful and still relevant note: for instance, the importance of education, and the value of international documentation.

The true successor of the Athens documents was the Venice Charter of 1964. The opening idea is that historic monuments or buildings are 'imbued with a message from the past' and are 'living witnesses', and it can surely be argued that this is as true of, say, E.W. Elmslie's railway station of 1863 in Great Malvern as it is, for instance, of St Paul's Cathedral or Conway Castle. Moreover, the two key definitions can readily be applied to railway architecture, where there is a real danger of seeing it too much in isolation even when it is valued for itself. The Venice Charter says that the concept of such a building or monument embraces

> not only the single architectural work but also the urban or rural setting in which is found the evidence of a particular civilization, a significant development or an historic event. This applies not only to great works of art but also to more modest works of the past which have acquired cultural significance with the passing of time.

It is useful to ponder this definition with some of Britain's most significant railway structures in mind: St Pancras Station (J. O'Connor's famous painting of 1881, *Pentonville Road and St Pancras Station*, actually shows it in its context); the Royal Border Bridge, at Berwick-upon-Tweed; the Royal Albert Bridge, at Saltash; the wooden Barmouth Bridge; the Esk Valley Viaduct, near Whitby; the surviving buildings of the workshops at Swindon; the iron viaduct at Bennerley, near Ilkeston in Derbyshire; and the Leaderfoot Viaduct, near Melrose, in the Scottish Borders.

The second definition says that

> The conservation and restoration of monuments must have recourse to all the sciences and techniques which can contribute to the study and safeguarding of the architectural heritage.

Perhaps the most readily available example in England of a case where state-of-the-art investigation, documentation, and painstaking conservation and repair work have been carried out to the highest modern standards is the Grand Midland Hotel, St Pancras, by The Conservation Practice.

Just as Morris's Manifesto can be more clearly understood by examining it against the background of the restoration controversies of the 1860s and 1870s, so the Venice Charter is very much a document of its time. The early 1960s was a time of terrible danger for the historic buildings of Europe, especially as the 'cult of the new' took a grip on countries recovering from the cataclysm of the Second World War. Hence it is understandable that the Charter should declare that the 'conservation of monuments is always facilitated by making use of them for some socially useful purpose' (ICOMOS, 1964). If we think of a redundant building type at that time – a country house, a water-mill or windmill, or indeed a railway station – it makes perfectly good sense. But the same article goes on to say 'Such use is therefore desirable but it must not change the layout or decoration of the building', and that now seems far too limiting.

There are indeed examples, and the eighteenth-century grist mill at Owlpen Manor comes to mind, where a new use – in this case, as a holiday cottage – has been brought about through sympathetic conversion, while retaining all the eighteenth-century wooden mill machinery; but that is rare. Much more likely is the kind of conversion to new use that, while respecting the original fabric and character as far as possible, involves a certain or even radical degree of change. Let us take redundant signal boxes, and we will find that one at Coxwold in North Yorkshire, on the Pilmoor to Malton line, has been adapted to serve as a garden shed with no alteration to speak of at all; while at York station the signal box has been adapted by the retailer W.H. Smith to serve as a shop, with total evisceration of the ground floor, and only the sharp-eyed would probably recognize on looking at it that it had once been the signal box.

Fig. 2.4 Coxwold signal box, North Yorkshire, on the North Eastern Railway branch line to Ampleforth and Malton, reused as a garden shed. (M.J. Stratton)

In one case, the value has been retained to a considerable degree (of course the technically and culturally important technical equipment has been lost), but in the other case the value has been retained only to a superficial degree; yet we are glad that the structure has been retained and reused and could be capable of further reuse into the future. Redundant termini, from Manchester to Madrid, have been adapted to house exhibitions and tropical gardens. Some still languish, especially in the USA, where huge central stations were built in the early decades of this century, shortly before the rise of the automobile and the airliner led to drastic cutbacks in rail services. The grand station of the Michigan Central Railroad in Detroit, built in 1913, stands empty and unused, most of the windows of its 16 storeys having been smashed. The city's other great terminus, the Union Depot, was demolished in 1974.

As with Ruskin and Morris, strong stress is laid upon maintenance 'on a permanent basis', and proper emphasis is given to 'preserving a setting which is not out of scale' and that 'Wherever the traditional setting exists, it must be kept'. Again, the Venice Charter is in harmony with William Morris's and the SPAB's thinking when it urges against the moving of an historic building 'except where the safeguarding of that monument demands it or where it is justified by national or international interest of paramount importance'; and Article 8 urges that sculpture, painting or decoration 'which form an integral part of a monument may only be removed from it if this is the sole means of

Fig. 2.5 The interior of York Station, North Eastern Railway, by T. Prosser and W. Peachey, 1877. A view across to platform 3, showing the signal box converted into the station supervisor's office. (M.J. Stratton)

Fig. 2.6 Detroit Station, Michigan Central Railroad, by Warren & Wetmore, 1913; the city's last surviving station, closed, vacant and vandalized. (M.J. Stratton)

ensuring their preservation'. In the recent conservation process undergone by the Grand Midland Station at St Pancras, evidence has been revealed of extensive schemes of painted decoration and, in the Grand Coffee Room, evidence of a rich scheme of mural decoration and polychromy, as well as decorative metalwork and tiles. In such a case as this, where the cultural value has been properly defined, it has been accepted, if not without question at least after appropriate debate, that all such essential features should be retained, respected and conserved, now or later.

Following the Athens documents, the Venice Charter gives proper due to documentation and publication. These are important considerations. It is greatly to the credit of the Royal Commission on the Historical Monuments of England (RCHME) that, in 1995, it published an authoritative and attractive book, by John Cattell and Keith Falconer, on *Swindon: The Legacy of a Railway Town*, and that this has treated the architectural legacy of the Great Western Railway's works and village at Swindon with the same seriousness as any other significant aspect of architecture or architectural history (Cattell and Falconer, 1995). The works were drastically reduced in size during the last two decades of their operational life. Moreover, the Royal Commission has not simply studied the surviving buildings and the wealth of associated documentation, it has even converted the former general offices of the Great Western Railway into a state-of-the-art National Monument Record Centre, England's primary source of information on the architectural and archaeological heritage. The study traces the history of the works and their associated railway village from a greenfield site in 1841 through the gradual evolution of the complex structure of the works and the parallel development of the village, to the provision of a church, schools and parsonage (such as might have been provided elsewhere by an

26

enlightened and benevolent squire), and numerous buildings for social benefit.

Establishing cultural significance

It is arguable that, although the signatories included experts from at least one
other continent, the Venice Charter is essentially European in its cultural
assumptions; and, moreover, its concept of the 'monument' or historic building
is essentially still looking far backwards into the past. So it was a particularly
welcome development that, in the 1980s, the Florence Charter first tackled the
question of preserving historic gardens, and then the Washington Charter
tackled 'historic urban areas, large and small, including cities, towns and
historic centres or quarters, together with their natural and man-made environ-
ments'; but at the end of the decade we have both the Charter of Lausanne
(taking a broad view of the archaeological heritage as constituting 'the basic
record of past human activities', whatever they may have been) and the Burra
Charter, evolved out of discussion by members of the International Council on
Monuments and Sites (ICOMOS) of Australia, first formulated and adopted in
August 1979, but then with important revisions and additions in 1981 and 1988.
As with the Venice Charter, the Burra Charter starts with definitions, but this
time there are not two but ten, and as they are all important it is almost
invidious to single out some of them. But, nevertheless, a big step forward in
understanding is achieved by the definition of the word 'place', which means
'site, area, building or other work, group of buildings or other works together
with associated contents and surrounds', which is a much richer and helpful
definition than any thus far achieved (ICOMOS, 1979). If we apply this, for
instance, to St Pancras Station in London we can understand that in this case
'place' means not only Sir George Gilbert Scott's Grand Midland Hotel and
William Barlow's train shed but also the forecourt, the platforms, the booking
office, and the installations that are an integral part of the original fabric, not a
few of which –perhaps even a little surprisingly – survive. Then the next
definition is indeed crucial, for it is of 'cultural significance', which is defined
as meaning the 'aesthetic, historic, scientific or social value for past, present or
future generations'.

What, we may ask, is then the 'cultural significance' of St Pancras Station?
David Cole in his 1980 study of *The Works of Sir Gilbert Scott* (which has
O'Connor's painting on the dustjacket) says of it:

> The completed building resembles no English Medieval work: perhaps it
> is most similar to a Flemish *hotel de ville* . . . but the result of Scott's
> careful design, looked at in the perspective of a hundred years, is a
> building which, were it his only major work, would at once place him
> among the first half dozen of Victorian architects. (Cole, 1980)

More recently (1995), Gavin Stamp has written, in his introduction to the
new scholarly edition of Scott's *Personal and Professional Recollections*:

> His major secular works seem less constrained by precedent than his too
> numerous ecclesiastical commissions and the Albert Memorial and the

Midland Grand Hotel at St Pancras must be regarded as amongst the finest works of the Victorian Gothic Revival. (Scott, 1879, 1995)

These quotations, powerful as they are, do not adequately represent a Statement of Cultural Significance, but a crucial set of guidelines adopted in 1984, and revised in 1988, explain the importance of this concept, what is included within the meaning of the terms 'aesthetic, historic, scientific or social value', and how by a step-by-step approach the cultural significance can be teased out and incorporated in a brief but authoritative Statement of Cultural Significance. There seems no reasonable doubt that all work to historic or landmark buildings, including all work proposed to buildings or structures that can be considered to be part of the railway heritage, would benefit enormously by the 'taking stock' of patient research, definition, and analysis leading to such a Statement of Cultural Significance as is advocated here; and I can speak from personal experience of applying it, as a committee member, to such structures as the west front of Lincoln Cathedral and Sir John Soane's severely damaged masterpiece, Pell Wall Hall.

Armed with this statement, we can then go on to decide what are the appropriate conservation processes, which, in the Burra Charter's definition, mean 'all the processes of looking after a place so as to retain its cultural significance' including maintenance and, according to circumstances, 'preservation, restoration, reconstruction and adaptation and . . . commonly a combination of more than one of these'. Buttressing this definition of conservation are two conservation principles, namely that the 'aim of conservation is to retain the cultural significance of a place and must include provision for its security, its maintenance and its future', and that conservation is 'based on a respect for the existing fabric and should involve the least possible physical intervention', and should not 'distort the evidence provided by the fabric'.

It may perhaps be fruitful to consider to what extent, whether consciously or unconsciously, these considerations may have applied to the redevelopment of Liverpool Street Station, London. As it had come down to us, and as I knew it well from the mid-1960s to the mid-1980s, it was essentially a creation of the 1870s, being brought into use in 1874–75. The style has been described as a 'restrained Gothic', the responsibility of Edward Wilson. To it in 1884 was added the Great Eastern Hotel, designed by Charles Barry (son of Sir Charles Barry, architect of the Houses of Parliament) in a loosely Dutch Renaissance style. The station was extended in 1892, the hotel in 1901 by Colonel Robert Edis. It was a very confusing station to use, and – though that was not its fault – was much compromised over the years, and seemingly rather neglected.

The story leading to its eventual transformation, including some demolition and some new building, is a complex one and derived from an original intention in the mid-1970s to demolish both the Broad Street Station and the Liverpool Street Station and replace them with one greatly enlarged station. Instead, Broad Street Station has indeed gone, and the Broadgate development (which has many good features) is there instead; following a planning inquiry, British Rail was required to retain the western train shed of Liverpool Street Station but was able to demolish the later eastern train shed and the original station office buildings and to carry out a comprehensive reorganization and remodelling, which has arguably given London something fresh and exciting of considerable cultural value. Not only the western train shed but also the Great Eastern Hotel have both been retained; the redevelopment has provided for all platforms, existing and new, to terminate at the same point; and right across them all, from east to west, a vast new concourse has been built (which required the demolition of the Grade II listed railway offices).

What has been novel, and which perhaps arose out of a careful analysis of the cultural significance of the surviving structures, is that the new work has been carried out in the same style and materials (yellow stock brick) as the original, thereby giving a sense of unity, fitness of purpose, monumentality and strength to the whole. The new west wall, with its great triplets of lancet lights under brick revealing arches, marches vigorously from one end of the station to the other, and is a thrilling visual experience. The new entrance from Liverpool Street is also a buttress for the roof structure, and is framed by two towers (one a clock tower) with lively profiles, and discernible echoes of the Arts and Crafts Movement. Close by this entrance is the new block of replacement offices, built in the same vigorous early thirteenth-century style as its predecessor. It is wholly convincing.

Of the concourse, Marcus Binney wrote in 1992:

> I have seen it matched in smartness only by Washington's Union Station. What both these projects share is a desire to make the most of the drama and grandeur of the historic structure. The result is an extraordinary mixture of restoration, replica, reinstatement and pastiche (not meant in any derogatory sense), combined with high-tech elements that are still very much in the tradition of iron and glass. It takes a while to appreciate just how much of the magnificent vaulted structure that greets you is brand new. The dividing line is some way down the platforms, distinguished by the bright colours of the new work.

By contrast, Robert Thorne in his review of the station in the *Architects' Journal* describes the concourse as being

> choked with shops, barriers, plant boxes and indicator boards – the whole sleight of hand by which British Rail tries to pretend that stations are for everything but trains. The airport aesthetic has triumphed, creating a muddled and directionless concourse. Because of the levels in relation to the street, upper level walkways form logical and delightful routes through and around the station, but to put shops on the most prominent part of them, directly above the platform barrier line, dissects the train shed exactly where it should be most open. Smartly detailed though they are, the shops cannot hope to be any more diaphanous than their high street brethren.

I incline more to agree with British Rail's architect for the project, Nick Derbyshire, who has argued that the shops created the false wall of the concourse. Without them the concourse would not exist as a place in its own right; it would simply be one end of the train shed. They also perform some of the same function as the organ loft in a typical cathedral, adding to the sense of space beyond.

And as Steve Pilcher has remarked of the shops, too (Pilcher, 1993), they are

quite well designed in their own right; they represent an attractive use of modern materials, with their curved glass screens and bold stainless steel bracing. One's eye is drawn to them and is then tempted with the view of the train shed beyond.

The serviceableness of a consistent philosophical approach

What is being advocated here is that, consciously *rather* than unconsciously, a determined attempt should be made both nationally and internationally to have a consistent, defensible philosophical approach to the preservation and transformation of railway architecture. Other contributors to this volume have given their own suggestions and placed their own different emphases, but for my part I would advocate the following as a checklist for further consideration and action:

- Maintenance, advocated with strength and wisdom from Ruskin to the Burra Charter, has to be encouraged, both for railway buildings remaining in operational use at present (but some of which may well be redundant in the future), and for buildings that have already ceased to be in practice or in actuality part of the railway heritage. For railway structures remaining in operational use, the drawing up and honouring of a maintenance manual would be a great help; and it would also be helpful if the grant-aiding bodies would reconsider their present criteria, and be prepared to make grants for maintenance as well as for repairs. In this way the delicate balance of carrots and sticks that is an essential part of the legislation governing historic buildings, in virtually every country, would be made to work in the interests of sound maintenance – thus obviating many repair works, often destructive to a greater or lesser degree in themselves, which could have been avoided if regular maintenance had been carried out.
- Gradually, for every railway structure – whether listed or unlisted – of substantial character, a Statement of Cultural Significance should be drawn up. Railway stations, and other railway buildings, no longer in operational use are often very apt for adaptation as living accommodation, and this would often be preferable to offices. Smaller stations, for instance, make very attractive private homes; larger stations might be used to provide secure sheltered housing. Many stations could be subdivided, providing holiday accommodation, for example; and, as with all conversion works of this kind, the work can be carried out either well or ill. It is far more likely to be carried out well if there is a clear understanding, written down and appreciated by all involved, of precisely where the cultural significance of that building lies.

- It may be found in a particular case that, on drawing up a Statement of Cultural Significance, it would be singularly difficult or perhaps inappropriate to adapt that particular station or group of buildings to an alternative use, however sensitively. We already have the admirable example of the private preserved railways (and how remarkable it is that in Tony Hall-Patch's book *The Great British Railway: A Living History*, 12 pages are needed to provide information on the railway museums or preserved railways in the United Kingdom), but it seems highly desirable that the Railway Heritage Trust or the National Trust, or the National Trust for Scotland, should between them seek out one or more stations and treat them with the same degree of care, research, and seriousness with which they would approach any other significant historic building, and open it and interpret it to the visiting public (Hall-Patch, 1992).
- Publicity and publication are required. The general public, as well as the scholar, need more information about what exists in terms of the railway heritage, where it is, and why it is significant. One possibility would be to research and publish a *Domesday Book* – in effect a thematic survey of the railway heritage – and this would be surely both widely welcomed and make a highly successful publication.
- The production of a railway heritage map, attractively designed and made widely available, would be a tremendous asset in making the railway heritage more widely known and appreciated.
- Research and publication are required at all levels, and at the more scholarly end of the spectrum the new Institute of Railway Studies established jointly in York between the University of York and the National Railway Museum clearly has an important task.
- Computerization of listed buildings is already under way. But information held by the British Rail Property Board, relating to the railway heritage, should be made much more widely known.
- When railway architecture becomes redundant, experience already shows that there could be a variety of excellent new uses. But in order to achieve this, much more vigorous marketing is needed.
- In the area of public relations and publicity, so much good work has been done, is being done, and could be done for the railway heritage. But it deserves to be given wider publicity, and for example the excellent work of the Railway Heritage Trust is scarcely known about outside preservationist circles. Altogether, much more deserves to be done to 'win hearts and minds' for the cause of railway heritage.

Conclusion

Placing all this in the context of the Burra Charter once again, Article 20 suggests that

> Adaptation is acceptable where the conservation of the place cannot otherwise be achieved, and where the adaptation does not substantially detract from its cultural significance.

This seems worth pondering. Every official encouragement, and probably the majority of economic indicators, suggest that imaginative reuse (and imaginative can be simple and straightforward, as well as innovative or high-tech) is often the answer to preserving railway heritage, and giving it a long-term future. But this can be done without impairing significantly its cultural value, and hence the significance of the word 'substantially' in Article 20. Here we come back to the question of a proper evaluation of the building or structures in the first place, and Article 23 lays down that

> Work on a place must be preceded by professionally prepared studies of the physical, documentary and other evidence, and the existing fabric recorded before any intervention in the place.

Article 24 deals with study and investigation of a place; Article 25 urges that a written 'statement of conservation policy' must be professionally prepared setting out the cultural significance and proposed conservation procedure 'together with justification and supporting evidence, including photographs, drawings and all appropriate samples'.

The Burra Charter commends itself by its clarity, its logic, and the track record of experience. Not being limited to a European-based culture, it has been found acceptable and usable in many different countries, in many different circumstances. No doubt it has its drawbacks, and even at this very moment it is undergoing a further revision reflecting the insights of the final decade of the twentieth century; but it provides perhaps the best and most helpful tool we have yet, relevant to buildings of all cultures and periods – and hence also useful for the wise handling and future preservation and use of the railway heritage, for the benefit of us all.

Select Bibliography

Biddle, G. (1973) *Victorian Stations*, David & Charles, Newton Abbot.

Biddle, G. and Nock, O.S. (eds) (1993) *The Railway Heritage of Britain*, Michael Joseph, London.

Burman, P. (1979) Small town stations, in *Railway Architecture* (eds M. Binney and D. Pearce), Orbis Publishing, London, pp. 68–87.

Cattell, J. and Falconer, K. (1995) *Swindon: The Legacy of a Railway Town*, HMSO, London.

Cole, D. (1980) *The Works of Sir Gilbert Scott*, Architectural Press, London.

Dwivedi, S. and Mehrotra, R (1995) *Bombay: The Cities Within*, Eminence Designs, Bombay.

Hall-Patch, T. (1992) *The Great British Railway: A Living History*, David & Charles, Newton Abbot.

ICOMOS (1964) *Venice Charter*, ICOMOS, Venice.

ICOMOS (1979, rev 1988) *Burra Charter*, Australian National Committee, ICOMOS, Burra.

Morris, M. (1877) *SPAB Manifesto*, SPAB, London. The Society for the Protection of Ancient Buildings was founded by William Morris and others in March 1877. He, Philip Webb and George Wardle were deputed to draw up the Manifesto, which was thereupon adopted as the foundation document of the Society, and is one of the most celebrated prose passages dealing with historic preservation in the English language.

Pilcher, S. (1993) *Changing Attitudes to the Conservation of England's Railway Heritage*. Architectural Association dissertation, London.

Powys, A.R. (1929) *Repair of Ancient Buildings*, J.M. Dent, London.

Scott, G.G. (1879) *Personal and Professional Recollections*. Reprinted 1995 in facsimile with an introduction by Gavin Stamp, Paul Watkins, Stamford.

Michael Stratton

A bibliographical overview of the railway heritage

Introduction

The railway heritage is typically studied with 'railway' and built 'heritage' as separate strands. This chapter introduces the key publications from both approaches, juxtaposing the work of railway historians and those devoted to architectural history and conservation. It also embraces writings on structures essential to the operation of trains – bridges, warehouses, workshops and engine sheds – that have suffered neglect through a preoccupation with the more fanciful architecture of Victorian stations.

The literature will be reviewed according to building type. By looking chronologically under each heading, one can sense the changing attitudes of railway companies to their estate. Different types of structure and even individual buildings have been celebrated, forgotten and even derided – and then appreciated again in response to threatened destruction or refurbishment. Most railway bodies have had an ambivalent attitude to their buildings. In the

Fig. 3.1 The statue of Robert Stephenson being removed from the great hall of Euston Station, London, prior to demolition, 1963. (NRM 1601/21/63)

34

early decades of passenger carrying in the 1830s and 1840s, companies that evolved out of carrying freight viewed stations in a pragmatic light. A century later, many structures were so shrouded in soot as to be a source of shame rather than corporate pride. Even great engineering achievements were likely to be forgotten soon after their opening, apart from anniversary junketings.

This short essay is best seen as a modest adjunct to the definitive bibliography of railway history in general (Ottley, 1965, 1983) and augmented by a supplement of Ottley (1988). Entries on 'Architecture and design' are in section E5, but useful books and articles are also listed under 'Stations and architecture' within the sections devoted to individual companies. Railway-oriented journals, such as *Railway Magazine*, are invaluable. More general titles such as the *Illustrated London News, Builder* and *Engineer* offer useful information. An index for the *Engineer* from 1856 to 1959 (Prockter, 1964) provides an entrée to this under-used source. There are references to engineers, locomotive builders and railway companies, and to building types and structures including stations, water towers and even creosoting works. There is no full guide to the archives relating to railway structures across the country, but Ottley (1973) lists the key collections in libraries and archives relating to railway history. This volume predates the transfer of the National Railway Museum to York, and the first point of contact for books or photographs must now be the indices of the Library and Archive in Leeman Road.

Most of the vast literature on railways is too preoccupied with steam and, more recently, diesel locomotives to give much attention to buildings and other infrastructure. However, there are now serious histories of most of the major companies, which put architecture and engineering in a commercial context. An early but model work is the three-volume study of the Great Central by Dow (1959–65).

Railway construction

Early, horse-drawn railways had no prestigious stations, being built to carry minerals and other freight. They were modest in length, and might have contour-hugging curves and cable-hauled inclines to avoid the need for large viaducts or tunnels. They are recorded by contemporary artists in a matter-of-fact way, though some of the more impressive bridges, such as the Causey Arch in County Durham, did become recognized as heralding the achievements of the great railway engineers of the nineteenth century. Pictures of primitive railways were first presented in the context of an evolving tradition of industrial art by Klingender (1972). Their track beds have subsequently been the subject of archaeological study, presented in the writings of Lewis (1970), which emphasized the regional variations between Shropshire and the North-East of England. The more recent volume by Hughes (1991) drew upon the meticulous study by the Welsh Royal Commission of the embankments, bridges and inclines that carried the Brecon Forest Tramroad.

The nature of early nineteenth-century railways, hybrids between mineral tracks and mainlines, is presented in one of the few contemporary studies of the period, *A Practical Treatise on Railroads* by Wood (1825). A historian's overview, in the broad context of industrial landscapes, is provided by Trinder (1982). The first generation of passenger-carrying railways has generated surprisingly few publications. One of the most useful, *Railway Practice* by Brees (1837), illustrates structures on the first long-distance main lines, such as the London & Birmingham, the Great Western, the Midland Counties and the Grand Junction. Working drawings for bridges, viaducts and tunnels are accompanied by brief descriptions showing how iron became used for smaller bridge spans. The adoption of Egyptian or Gothic styles is recommended as a way of ensuring that railway lines improve rather than desecrate landed estates through which they may have to be built. A remarkably comprehensive study of the lines built up to the end of the 1830s, covering their construction, engineering features and locomotives, is provided by Whishaw (1840). Guides to Victorian railway engineering are provided by Baker (1848) and Day (1860).

The dramatic engineering works for these main lines were, as with canals, largely dependent on hand labour aided by pick and wheelbarrow. Their scale, and the human effort in creating them, is wonderfully conveyed in the drawings of John Cook Bourne, recording Camden Bank and Tring Cutting on the London & Birmingham Railway (Bourne, 1839) and Maidenhead Bridge and Box Tunnel on the Great Western main line from Paddington to Bristol (Bourne, 1846).

The parallel challenge of erecting large and essentially new building types such as stations and engine houses is presented in the fine drawings reproduced in Dempsey (1850) and Dempsey (1856). His compilation volume (Dempsey, 1855), aimed at the practical railway engineer and dedicated to Robert Stephenson, progresses from explaining the engineering of track curves and retaining walls to bridges as well as buildings.

Later texts, written when railways were no longer viewed with a sense of wonder, are more educational than celebratory in tone. An introduction to levelling, setting out curves and earthworks is provided by Stewart (1908), just at the time when large-scale railway works in this country had ended. Turn-of-the-century engineering projects, such as the extension of the Great Central to London, are, however, recorded by photography, a technology not available in the 1830s. The National Railway Museum photographic collection has photographs showing track laying, for example at Bolton, but the most prized source is their album portraying the engineering works needed to bring the Midland main line into London at St Pancras.

There is no broad-based historical study of the impact of the railway on the British landscape, but Kellett (1979) provides a perceptive analysis of the changes wrought across many Victorian cities. He shows how companies tried to locate their termini in slum areas where land was cheapest, and explains why most were so slow to invest in services and stations in the suburbs.

The cult of the engineer

The feat of creating a national railway network in just a quarter of a century has traditionally been credited to a small engineering elite, to be numbered on the fingers of one hand. Samuel Smiles wrote a biography of George Stephenson (Smiles, 1857). In this volume and his compilation *The Lives of the Engineers* (Smiles, 1862) he honoured them as heroic leaders of gangs of navvies (labourers), and for overcoming great engineering and political odds through

Herculean efforts and a self-motivation derived, in the case of Stephenson, from a modest cottage background. Biography was mingled with fiction in another account of his life by Stebbing (1896), half written in Geordie (Tyneside dialect) and full of tales to demonstrate his humility amidst fame and prosperity. The great Victorian engineers retained their high status in the early twentieth century, at a time when Victorian architects were the subject of wide ridicule. The Great Western latched onto Brunel in the period between the two World Wars, to help advertise the distinctiveness of the railway.

Interest in the great canal and railway engineers was rekindled by L.T.C. Rolt's biographies of Isambard Kingdom Brunel (Rolt, 1957) and George and Robert Stephenson (Rolt, 1960), which combine an explanation of their technological achievements with a vivid evocation of their characters. Subsequent research and publication, such as Pugsley (1976) on Brunel, draw upon newly discovered archives, and it is now in vogue to offer a revisionist viewpoint, emphasizing the role of lesser-known engineers and assistants.

Railway contractors have only recently gained their due attention. Joby (1983) progresses from examining canal builders to the figureheads of railway contracting – Thomas Brassey and Samuel Morton Peto – and then lesser-known late-Victorian firms. More recent studies of the key railway contractors are provided by Burton (1992, 1994). Most recently, Chrimes *et al.* (1994) have written on Mackenzie and other early railway contractors. Lesser contractors were of great significance in filling out the network that covered most of lowland England by the end of the century. A study focusing on the North of England, by Popplewell (1985), demonstrates the local origins of many of the contractors of the post-Stockton & Darlington period, and provides useful archival and secondary references. A volume on railway surveyors by Biddle (1990) looks at the broad issue of property management over a period of almost two centuries.

Britain's railways were largely built by manual labour. *The Railway Navvies* by Coleman (1968) opened up the migrating world of navvies, truck payment, and shanty settlements, giving particular attention to such epic feats as the construction of the Woodhead Tunnel in the Peak District. This subject has also been covered by Burton (1992), in the particularly rich study by Brooke (1983), and in a local case study by Mitchell (1975), who presents a guide to the evidence of shanties around the Pennine settlement of Dent on the Settle and Carlisle line.

Railway stations
The opening ceremony for a major new station would be followed by accounts of its architectural decoration and any bold engineering features, local newspapers giving them lengthy write-ups as symbols of civic pride. Many drawings survive as part of the national rail archive at Kew Record Office, while some county record offices or local libraries also hold large-scale plans, which show the original track layouts, or deposited building plans showing the plans and elevations of the key buildings. The official railway guides written by George Measom provide the first broad commentary on railway stations, as well as highlighting the key industries in cities en route. His volume on the Great Northern Railway (Measom, 1861), for example, covers not only King's Cross

and the goods station and hotel, but major stations, viaducts and tunnels as far north as Halifax. The second half of the volume embraces features from York to Oban and Aberdeen. Architectural journals showed a diminishing interest in railway architecture from the late nineteenth century, partly because there was less to report on, but also as their editors tended to focus on more elevated building types such as churches, country houses and art galleries.

By the period between the two World Wars the railway companies themselves concentrated on promoting images of efficiency and speed through streamlined locomotives or electric services. Both the LMS and GWR saw their plans to rebuild stations in a modern style frustrated by the Second World War. Some glimmerings of renewed pride emerged in centenary celebrations, such as at Paddington in 1954. The only organization that made stations central to a progressive identity was the London Underground. During the 1930s the London Passenger Transport Board sought a visual continuity, from sleek tube trains to Holden's sweeping station canopies and modern typefaces for signage. However, the London Underground almost ignored its modernist stations in its posters, preferring to show pastoral images to lure Londoners to the suburbs and beyond.

The railway companies built up fine collections of drawings of their stations, but few seem to have made any systematic photographic record. The Midland Railway is one exception; a fine collection of images dating from the Edwardian period is held by the National Railway Museum. Enthusiasts and historians were relatively slow to turn their lenses away from steam locomotives to architecture, but the NRM does also hold a full record of North Staffordshire Railway stations taken by an amateur in the 1950s.

A pioneering and possibly the first historical study of British railway stations was produced by Clark (1947–8), covering south-west England, North Wales and south-east England in three volumes. *An Introduction to Railway Architecture*, written by Barman (1950), sets out an agenda for analysing this building type in terms of their contradictory needs to 'fit in and belong' and yet demonstrate a 'sense of conquest over nature's forces'. The first major volume on railway stations, and arguably still the most broad-ranging and perceptive, was written by Caroll Meeks. *The Railway Station: An Architectural History* (Meeks, 1957) looks at the evolving functional requirements of railway stations and their design in terms of 'creative eclecticism', rather than being essentially an inventory or preoccupied by specific architects and styles. No other publication gives such a richly international coverage to the subject of termini or analyses their plans so meticulously. A book by Holland (1971), built on Meeks's interest in aspects of circulation, examines the operation of railway stations in the context of public transport facilities, from roadside inns to airport terminals.

Jack Simmons, the grand master of railway history, has further developed this broad-brush approach in his *The Railway in Town and Country 1830–1914* (Simmons, 1986), and *The Victorian Railway* (Simmons, 1991) shows how railways contributed to and drew from the growth of towns and cities, how commercial requirements and design values interrelated, and how stations, hotels and warehouses were all part of the same empire developed by the companies.

It is worth noting that most of Britain's major stations are analysed briefly in the regional survey of British architecture, the *Buildings of England, Scotland and Wales*, initiated by Nikolaus Pevsner and now being revised and extended. The recent second editions give fuller coverage to railway buildings. Volumes within the *Batsford Guide to the Industrial Archaeology of the British Isles*, published in the late 1970s but never completed, always give due reference to railway structures. Some of the gazetteers published over the preceding decade by David & Charles as their *Industrial Archaeology of the British Isles* are of even greater value, because they record structures now heavily altered or completely lost. The *Civil Engineering Heritage* series produced in recent years by the Panel for Historical Engineering Works of the Institution of Civil Engineers embraces stations, bridges and tunnels, and provides valuable information on the engineers and architects involved. The volume covering northern England is edited by Barbey (1981). Meanwhile the 15 volumes in the *Regional History of the Railways of Great Britain*, published by David St John Thomas, approach the subject from a different standpoint. They focus on the creation, operation and closure of railway lines, and are of particular value in unravelling the multiplicity of companies involved in building stations, whether separate or joint, and associated facilities in a particular area. Another key source is the *Pre-Grouping Atlas* (Conolly, 1976), with lines operated by differing companies and their stations marked in contrasting colours.

The majority of writings on railway stations have been in the form of gazetteers. A relatively early study is provided by Denton (1965). The first comprehensive survey of British stations was provided by Biddle (1973), his analysis being aided by a detailed index referring to virtually every significant station in the country. Writing in the mid-1960s, David Lloyd and Donald Insall presented a list of 60 stations large and small that should be protected, as well as examining the problems of modernization and finding future uses for the 1000 stations being closed under the Beeching plan (Lloyd and Insall, 1967). Concern at the loss of station buildings following closure or through replacement by bus shelter accommodation deepened in the 1970s. The companion to the exhibition *Off the Rails* organized by SAVE Britain's Heritage (1977) told a sorry tale of neglect both by British Rail and by local authorities, and of the derelict condition of land cleared of tracks or workshops. A larger but equally indicting volume (Binney and Pearce, 1979) provided chapters on every type of station, and on engine sheds and railway towns. It attacked the lack of sympathy within British Rail for its inheritance, and suggested positive ways of adapting buildings as opposed to neglecting, demolishing or mutilating them. Particular attention was given to the inflexible imposition of the British Rail corporate identity over facades through heavy-handed restoration schemes, as undertaken at Cambridge and Drayton Park.

The appointment of Peter Parker as Chairman of British Rail in 1976 heralded a change in heart. The major volume *The Railway Heritage of Britain* edited by Biddle and Nock (1983) provides a national gazetteer covering over 500 historic railway structures. This book was an initiative led by Bernard Kaukas, who had been appointed Director – Environment of British Rail in 1977. Its publication was followed up by a conference on *The Future of the*

Railway Heritage organized by the Royal Society of Arts and the Cubitt Trust Panel, and held in October 1984. The published report of the proceedings (RSA Cubitt Trust Panel, 1985) presents a more positive outlook. Not only did the British Railways Board use the forum to announce the formation of the Railway Heritage Trust with initial funding of £1 million, but the chairman, Sir Robert Reid, strongly expressed pride in the railway heritage:

> Business and conservation can go hand in hand. A renovated station gives
> BR a better image and draws in customers.

The conference recorded conservation achievements at operating stations – York and Hebden Bridge – and schemes of conversion such as at Brunel's Temple Meads and Central Station at Manchester. An exhibition shown at the conference toured the country, and was largely reproduced as a catalogue of photographs entitled *Aspects of Railway Architecture* (Clarke *et al.*, 1985), drawing on the photographic collections of the National Railway Museum and embracing such neglected themes as signalling and company offices. A year later Gordon Biddle produced his volume *Great Railway Stations of Britain* (Biddle, 1986), while Richards and MacKenzie (1986) provided the first historical analysis of the facilities provided by stations and their representation in literature, painting, postcard and film.

The London Underground is of particular interest for the quality of the stations built in the 1930s, when Frank Pick was the vice-president of London Transport. See Menear (1983) and Green and Rewse-Davies (1995) for a more in-depth study of underground station architecture, and Barman (1974) for a biography of Frank Pick.

Great termini

Historians of differing hue turned to examining the great London termini, just at the time when the end of steam, the rebuilding of Euston and plans to demolish St Pancras threatened their atmosphere combining soaring arches, chaotic bustle and smoke. The first general study (Jackson, 1969) considered London termini from an operational as well as architectural viewpoint, giving particular attention to the problems of congestion at the end of the nineteenth century, which resulted in major rebuilding programmes by many of the companies. A wonderful eulogy for the soot-begrimed splendour of un-refurbished termini was penned by Betjeman (1972), ending with a scathing attack on the new Euston, 'a mini-version of London Airport'. The text is complemented by the contrast of grime and shafts of sunlight in John Gay's evocative photographs.

The masterly study of St Pancras by Simmons (1968) not only analysed the complex design history and construction of both William Henry Barlow's shed and George Gilbert Scott's hotel but also looked at the services in and out of the station over a century and the controversy that raged when its closure was suggested in 1966. An historical study has now been produced on the adjacent King's Cross Station by Hunter and Thorne (1990). The recent studies of King's Cross by Hawkins (1990) and of Euston by Ellaway (1994) present a rich range of illustrative material, in the latter case showing the first London terminus before its demolition in the 1960s. The only provincial terminus that

Fig. 3.2 The train shed of St Pancras Station, London, nearing completion, by W.H. Barlow, c.1868. (NRM 280/85)

has been the subject of its own book is the earliest: the world's oldest surviving purpose-built railway station, Liverpool Road, Manchester, is analysed by Fitzgerald (1980) through an archaeological approach and a series of building plans. Glasgow's stations, from the major termini to the suburbs, the underground and freight depots, are analysed in Johnston and Hume (1979).

The Ian Allan series on *Rail Centres* and *Super Centres* analyses the development and adaptation of railway termini and in some cases freight facilities in the context of railway development across the major conurbations. The volume on Nottingham by Vanns (1993) unravels the roles of the Midland and Great Central in Nottingham. The volume on Birmingham by Collins (1992) presents a detailed analysis of the Great Western, Midland and LNWR; contemporary illustrations unravel the chronology of rebuilding of Birmingham New Street in the 1960s.

Railway hotels were typically located at the head of terminus sheds; Carter (1990) recounts the development of this opulent building type from the Crewe Arms Hotel built by Lord Crewe in 1836 through to the palace-like buildings erected in city centres and resorts. He also covers the ways in which they were managed and publicized, and their decline, up to the sale of the last hotel from railway ownership in 1983. British termini and their hotels have featured in international studies. See the exhibition catalogue *All Stations* (Dethier, 1981) and the superbly illustrated volume *Great Railway Stations of Europe* by Binney *et al.* (1984).

Stations round the regions

Many provincial stations have now been the subject of volumes focusing on the structures built by or inherited by the 'big four' railway companies. They often

41

consider both passenger and freight facilities, and may provide detailed track and even signalling plans. A relatively early example of this genre (Anderson and Fox, 1981) examined stations of the LMS, including its Scottish constituents. The Oxford Publishing Company has published the majority of the large-format surveys. Track plans as well as photographs of selected LMS stations are provided by Hendry and Hendry (1982). Examples range in size from a tiny halt to Liverpool Exchange terminus. Some, built in modernist concrete, opened as late as the 1930s. A comparable exercise for the Southern Region was undertaken by Pryer and Bowring (1980), particular emphasis being given to minor termini and junctions and to providing detailed signalling diagrams. A photographic study of railway stations in the Southern Region was produced by Wikeley and Middleton (1971). The Great Western was covered by Clark (1976) and Vaughan (1977). Other regional volumes to note include Hoole (1985) on north-east stations and Biddle (1981) on those of the North-West.

Interest in small rural stations grew from the 1970s, partly in response to closures but also due to rationalization, which reduced many survivors to the status of unstaffed halts. A major inventory of closed stations is provided by Clinker and Firth (1971) in the form of a list of 25 815 dates running from

Fig. 3.3 Bakewell Station, showing the ridge-and-furrow canopies typical of the Midland Railway, 1860s. Photographed in 1903. (NRM DY 2461)

Abbey & West Dereham to Ystrad. A recent publication by Butt (1995) lists every station, halt, platform and stopping place on the British passenger network, giving, most valuably, the opening as well as the closing date. Renamings and relocations are also dated. There have been numerous regionally based studies. The Great Western has received lavish attention, partly because of the popularity of its branch lines among modellers. See, for example, Vaughan (1988). Stations taken over by the Southern Region are presented in Anstell (1984), and those inherited or built by the LNER by Brodribb (1988). Private stations, built by an estate owner or industry, have been studied by Croughton *et al.* (1982).

Railway warehouses and freight yards

Huge, gaunt brick warehouses and their surrounding yards arguably had a greater impact on the fabric of the Victorian town and city than did the adjoining passenger stations. These once bustling but now often derelict or partly redeveloped areas have been neglected by both railway and architectural historians. They had few prestigious overtones for the Victorian or Edwardian writers or artists. Companies did use photography to record their goods depots, especially those developed from the 1870s. Images held at the National

Fig. 3.4 Lawley Street warehouse, Birmingham, Midland Railway, photographed in 1922. Note the combination of horse-drawn and motor wagons, and that the negative was 'doctored' to show LMS rather than 'Midland' on the warehouse. (NRM DY 2748)

Fig. 3.5 GNR warehouse, Deansgate, Manchester, by W.T. Foxlee, photographed in 1897, showing the innovative steel-framed warehouse under construction. It is currently used as a car park, but is the subject of controversial proposals. (NRM DON N50)

Railway Museum show, for example, the Midland Railway's yard adjacent to St Pancras at Euston Road, and the GNR warehouse at Manchester, built 1895–99 as one of the most advanced goods exchanges in the country, linked to canal and road and designed with a steel frame.

A manual on the organization of goods depots, staff, and handling of goods from cattle to masts for battleships is provided by West (1912), drawing upon his experience as goods agent with the LNWR and as superintendent with the SECR. Warehouses were sometimes featured in railway magazines during the inter-war period, with photographs emphasizing the apparent chaos of horse-drawn carts weaving their way round piles of barrels and crates.

There are no books devoted entirely to the subject of railway warehouses but two previously mentioned volumes on stations (Fitzgerald, 1980; Hunter and Thorne, 1990) cover warehouses at Liverpool Road, Manchester and above King's Cross in minute detail. The latter volume provides a building-by-building study of the surviving coal drops and warehouses built by the Great Northern and Midland railways close to the Regents Canal. Such buildings have been rendered surplus to railway use by a revolution in goods traffic. The shift to bulk-handling and containerization is covered by Munns (1986) in his *Milk Churns to Merry-Go-Rounds*, an especially useful volume on the development of modern coal-carrying systems and other aspects of contemporary practice.

Marshalling yards have been the largest and most ill-starred investment in freight of the twentieth century. The story of their laying-out, operation and decline is told by Rhodes (1988). The major yards in London and the provinces are analysed, starting with the Edge Hill Grid Iron Yard in Liverpool which pioneered the use of gravity to sort trains, and progressing to Bescot, Carlisle and Tinsley. The text is supported by track diagrams as well as photographs.

Fig. 3.6 Toton marshalling yard, showing rakes of private-owner wagons, 1927. (NRM DY 14427)

Railway works

The major railway workshops are a newly favoured subject for historians and industrial archaeologists, again in response to swingeing cut-backs, demolitions and alterations. From the establishment of the first major company works, such as Swindon and Derby c.1840, groups of sheds and foundries evolved into huge locomotive and rolling-stock building complexes. They first became of interest as the seat of empire of the great locomotive engineers, where their locomotive designs were developed and realized. The first systematic study of railway works, by Bowen Cooke (1893), provides contemporary descriptions of Crewe, Derby, Doncaster, Stratford, Cowlairs and Swindon as well as of the key locomotive designs that emerged from their erecting shops.

The richest insight into the highly segregated world of a major railway works at the turn of the century is provided by the account of 23 years' work at the Great Western Railway's Works at Swindon in Williams (1915). Railway workshops became more widely known to the public in the inter-war period through open days; the *Railway Magazine* recorded visits by groups of Crusaders organized by Cecil J. Allen, while pictures of Swindon featured in books produced by the GWR.

The earliest historical study, by Bulleid (1963), focused on engineering figureheads such as H.N. Gresley, G.J. Churchward and W.A. Stanier, covering the way in which they developed designs and put them into production. It was only following cutbacks and closures associated with dieselization and electrification that historians became more directly interested in the works where A4s, Kings and Duchesse were created. The first general, historically orientated studies were by Lowe (1975, 1979). The fullest analysis of the main railway works, from Ashford to Cowlairs, has been provided by Larkin (1988). His *The Railway Workshops of Britain 1823–1986* examines in detail the relationship between locomotive, carriage and wagon building, and issues of shop organization and modernization and cutbacks in the twentieth century. It is complemented by his lighter and more richly illustrated volume (Larkin, 1992). Huntriss (1994) and Johnson (1995) also examine the major railway workshops in a popular way, drawing on the rich collections of company photographs that have been preserved. *Building Britain's Locomotives* by Lowe (1979) progresses through the stages of building steam locomotives, from the drawing-office to the erecting-shop and testbeds, illustrated by photographs of Swindon, Derby and some private builders such as Bagnall's of Stafford. Many of the same works are examined by Marsden (1990), though he concentrates on the construction of diesels and multiple units since the 1950s.

For detailed accounts of individual works see Radford (1971) on Derby, and Reed (1982) and Drummond (1995) on Crewe. The study of North Road Locomotive Works in Darlington by Hoole (1967) concentrates on the different designs of locomotive and the engineers responsible. The study of Doncaster by Woods and Tuffrey (1987) uses maps and plans to outline the physical development of the carriage shops close to the station and the locomotive-erecting shop to the west, supplemented by a tremendous range of well-captioned photographs of newly completed locomotives and carriages including, of course, Gresley's Pacifics and LNER teak carriages. Every department of Swindon is described and magnificently illustrated by Peck (1983). The 'home' of the Great Western has just been the subject of one of the first in-depth studies of railway works by the Royal Commission, published as Cattell and Falconer (1995).

Private locomotive builders have rarely received their due attention. The mighty firms of Glasgow, including Sharp, Stewart, Neilson, Dubs and the North British, are analysed in Nicolson and O'Neill (1987), showing exotic-looking locomotives for export being hauled through the streets of the city and dangling from cranes. *Beardmore Built* by Johnston (1993) is of particular interest for showing how a Clydeside shipyard diversified into locomotive construction primarily for the LNWR and East Indian Railway, to make use of spare capacity after the end of the First World War.

Coaling depots and sheds

Engine sheds were places of hard, filthy work; there was little that railway companies could exploit for publicity. Apart from the most grandiose round-house, at Camden just up the bank from Euston, few were presented in books or articles until interest was roused by the demise of steam and ensuing closures. Probably the earliest historical study is by Beavor (1974). As cutbacks in diesel motive power have caused further demolitions, so a number of highly detailed regional gazetteers have been published. Chris Hawkins launched the concept with a study of sheds inherited from the Southern Railway in Hawkins and Reeve (1979), then progressed to the LMS in Hawkins and Reeve (1981, 1982, 1984, 1987a) and Hawkins *et al.* (1989a, 1990), the Great Eastern (Hawkins and Reeve, 1986, 1987b), the Great Western (Hawkins and Reeve, 1987c), and the LNER (Hawkins *et al.*, 1988). Taking one volume as an example, *Great Eastern Railway Engine Sheds* covers the huge depot of Stratford and tiny East Anglian out-stations, with detailed trackplans. The

LNER volume shows how, in 1923, the company inherited a collection of neglected and inadequate sheds. New coaling plants were provided to improve efficiency, while the buildings themselves were patched up. The Southern and the LMS, in contrast, embarked on major schemes of renewal, the use of concrete by the Southern being illustrated in Hawkins (1987). Recent books have concentrated on the history of engine sheds in the British Railways period, those within the Southern Region being covered by Hawkins and Reeve (1989) and in the Midland Region in Hawkins *et al.* (1989b), those within ex-LSWR territory in Hawkins and Reeve (1990), and diesel depots in general in Hawkins *et al.* (1989c).

The pace of research and publication by Chris Hawkins is rivalled by the six volumes produced by P. Bolger on motive power depots, such as on the North Eastern Railway (Bolger, 1984) and the LMS (Bolger, 1981), and giving allocations of locomotives towards the end of the steam era. A third series launched in the 1980s covers the country in four volumes, Volume 2, by Smith (1989), covering central England, East Anglia and Wales. These studies tend to concentrate on the sheds themselves, which may survive in alternative use but give less attention to other features such as turntables and the massive concrete coal drops erected in the inter-war period at most large depots. They combine

Fig. 3.7 Holbeck locomotive shed, Leeds, viewed from the coaling stage. Photographed in 1939. (NRM DY 25981)

47

to demonstrate that British Railways instigated an impressive building campaign, erecting concrete coalers and ash disposal plants and steel and asbestos sheds, to be followed by the erection of new types of shed to house diesels. A relatively up-to-date schedule of over 300 depots, workshops and stabling points, giving a summary of the types of locomotives and units stabled at each, is provided by Webster *et al.* (1987).

Signal boxes

Interest in signal boxes has also been given added urgency by threats to their survival. Enthusiasts and railway historians have unravelled the different types that were developed from the 1840s by companies such as Saxby and Farmer, and recorded survivors, especially those about to be closed and cleared. An early historical overview is provided by Day and Cooper (1958). Their *Railway Signalling Systems* briefly covered semaphore signals before focusing on the nature of electrical systems and track circuits and relays, aided by cutaway and cross-section diagrams.

A pioneering and highly detailed study of Great Western signalling was written by Vaughan (1973) covering not only different types of signal but signal boxes, level crossings and tail lamps for passenger and freight trains. Southern signalling is covered by Pryer (1977). *An Album of Pre-Grouping Signal Boxes*, by King (1976), illustrates many types of pre-grouping box with photographs taken in the 1960s and 1970s, and themselves now of historical interest. Another broad study is *The Signal Box: A Pictorial History* produced by the Signalling Study Group (1986). The *Signal Box Directory* by Kay (1992) constitutes the most detailed gazetteer, evolving out of lists published in the newsletter of the Signalling Record Society from 1981. The list gives the date of each box, its design type, frame design, date and frame size, as well as the

Fig. 3.8 The pastoral image in the suburbs: Sydenham Hill signal box, London & Dover Railway, c.1900. The warning bell notified locals when a train left Penge (East) Station. (NRM 697/2/56)

type of locking currently in use, including even London Underground boxes and those disused and preserved. The human story of manning a signal box is related in *Railway Lines and Levers* by Bradshaw (1993), who recounts his experiences in working for the LMS in Lancashire and the Great Western. Further reminiscences are provided by Vaughan (1981, 1983). A concise insight into current signalling systems used by British Rail is given by Hall (1992), working from the principles of absolute block signalling systems to automatic train protection and even hot axle box detectors.

Bridges and viaducts

Engineering features provided some of the most enduring symbols of the railway age. They were celebrated in paintings and engravings, many of the finest portrayals being in the collection accumulated by Sir Arthur Elton, and now held by the Ironbridge Gorge Museum. A sample are reproduced in Klingender (1972). Such awe-inspiring views contrast with the more down-to-earth engineering manuals, for example by Nicholson (1839). Numerous further manuals were published. The theoretical and practical merits of different types of rail bridge – such as lattice girders, arched rib and suspended girders – were examined by Baker (1873), who also compared the weight of wrought iron or steel required for particular designs. The effect of vibrations set up by locomotives running at speed, largely in the form of hammer-blows due to balance-weights on the driving wheels of steam locomotives, was researched by a Bridge Stress Committee, the findings being published in Inglis (1934).

The large-span bridges, soaring over river or estuary, have justified more lavish publications, both contemporary and historical in perspective. The Britannia and Conway bridges in North Wales were recorded by Clark (1850). A clutch of major structures, including the Britannia Bridge, the High Level Bridge in Newcastle and the Crumlin Viaduct in the South Wales valleys, are covered by Jenkin (1878). The drama of designing and building great railway bridges came to focus on Scotland. The massive steel structure of the Forth Bridge was reproduced in Phillips (1888), while a marvellous range of photographs was taken by R.D. Stevens around the period of the grouping in the early 1920s.

The sweeping grandeur of railway bridges meant that they never passed out of aesthetic fashion. *The Bridges of Britain* by de Maré (1954) places railway structures in the context of traditional masonry construction and modern reinforced concrete and steel road bridges. An early work purely on railway bridges was produced by Walters (1963), combining a broad historical survey with detailed drawings of 27 examples. Studies of individual bridges have followed. The tragic saga of the Tay Bridge and its collapse was recounted by Prebble (1956), though engineering historians have repeatedly worked over this ground to condemn or partially exonerate its engineer, Thomas Bouch. Hammond (1964) provides a detailed study of the Forth Bridge, including the lessons drawn from the Tay Bridge disaster, the role of Sir John Fowler and Sir Benjamin Baker, and details of the construction of the foundations and superstructure. The Britannia Bridge over the Menai Straits has been researched and written up by Rosenberg and Vincenti (1978). The study of Brunel's Saltash Bridge by Bowden (1983) considers the challenge of floating and lifting

Fig. 3.9 Midland Railway record photograph of Avonside Wharf, Bristol, 1922. Note the barges and wagons of the Midland Railway and the glass cone in the background. (NRM DY 12629)

the two huge trusses and the subsequent history of this link between Devon and Cornwall, including signalling arrangements for the section of single track over the deck.

There is just one national study on the subject of railway viaducts: Arlette (1983) illustrates the major examples in Britain, from Ais Gill to Yarm, including those built for narrow-gauge lines. The remarkable timber viaducts of Cornwall built by the Great Western to designs by Brunel are studied in great detail in Binding (1993).

Tunnels

Railway tunnels, like viaducts, had a precedent in canal engineering. John Cooke Bourne recorded the epic feat of boring the Kilsby Tunnel on the London & Birmingham and the grand portals of Box Tunnel on the Great Western, but little was written on the subject until the less than heroically titled *The Severn Tunnel: Its Construction and Difficulties*. Walker (1888) recounts the problems suffered in creating this link between England and Wales during 1879–86, including flooding by a 'tidal wave', and a smallpox epidemic, which necessitated construction of a fever hospital. The key historical study of this subject is *British Railway Tunnels* by Blower (1964), which surveys over 70 tunnels in Britain, giving their dimensions and a brief account of their construction and any subsequent modifications.

The Channel Tunnel has become the subject of several books. The failed projects of over two centuries are documented by Bonavia (1987). On the tunnel itself and the associated infrastructure in terms of trains, track, and signalling, see Semmens and Machefert-Tassin (1994).

Docks

Docks were a major area of investment for railway companies, but Harwich, Grimsby, Immingham, Bristol and Swansea, for example, have been studied primarily by maritime historians or industrial archaeologists. For a broad context on this subject it is worth reading Simmons (1986, 1991), who considers the role of railways in developing liner ports, coal docks, naval dockyards and packet stations. There are, however, fine photographs taken by the railway companies typically during the Edwardian and inter-war periods, Holyhead Harbour being documented by the LNWR c.1905 and Avonside, Bristol by the Midland Railway in the 1920s. Railway companies produced richly illustrated brochures to advertise their dock facilities; see for example LNER (1932) for photographs and plans from Harwich to Tyne Dock and Tayport.

Select bibliography

Anderson, V.R. and Fox, G.K. (1981) *A Pictorial Record of LMS Architecture*, Oxford Publishing, Oxford.

Anstell, R. (1984) *Southern Country Stations*, Vol. 1, *LSWR*, Ian Allan, Shepperton.

Arlette, D.J. (1983) *Railway Viaducts of the British Isles*, JED Publications, Par.

Baker, B. (1873) *Long-Span Railway Bridges and Short-Span Railway Bridges*, Spon, London.

Baker, T. (1848) *Railway Engineering, or Field Work Preparatory to the Construction of Railways*, Longman, Brown, Green & Longmans, London.

Barbey, M.F. (1981) *Civil Engineering Heritage: Northern England*, Thomas Telford, London.

Barman, C. (1950) *An Introduction to Railway Architecture*, Art and Technics, London.

Barman, C. (1974) *The Man who Built London Transport: a Biography of Frank Pick*, David & Charles, Newton Abbot.

Beavor, E.S. (1974) *Steam Motive Power Depots*, Ian Allan, Shepperton

Betjeman, J. (1972) *London's Historic Railway Stations*, John Murray, London.

Biddle, G. (1973) *Victorian Stations*, David & Charles, Newton Abbot.

Biddle, G. (1981) *Railway Stations in the North West: a Pictorial History*, Dalesman, Clapham.

Biddle, G. (1986) *Great Railway Stations of Britain: Their Architecture, Growth and Development*, David & Charles, Newton Abbot.

Biddle, G. (1990) *The Railway Surveyors: The Story of Railway Property Management 1800–1990*, British Rail Property Board, London.

Biddle, G. and Nock, O.S. (1983) *The Railway Heritage of Britain*, Michael Joseph, London.

Binding, J. (1993) *Brunel's Cornish Viaducts*, Pendragon, Penryn.

Binney, M. and Pearce, D. (1979) *Railway Architecture*, Orbis, London.

Binney, M., Hamm, M. and Föhl, A. (1984) *Great Railway Stations of Europe*, Thames & Hudson, London.

Blower, A. (1964) *British Railway Tunnels*, Ian Allan, London.

Bolger, P. (1981) *Motive Power Depots: LMS*, Ian Allan, Shepperton.

Bolger, P. (1984) *Motive Power Depots: NER*, Ian Allan, Shepperton.

Bonavia, M.R. (1987) *The Channel Tunnel Story*, David & Charles, Newton Abbot.

Bourne, J.C. (1839) *Drawings on the London and Birmingham Railway ... with an Historical and Descriptive Account by John Britton, FSA*, Ackerman, London.

Bourne, J.C. (1846) *The History and Description of the Great Western Railway*, Bogue, London.

Bowden, T.N. (1983) *Brunel's Royal Albert Bridge, Saltash*, Peter Watts, Gloucester.

Bowen Cooke, C.J. (1893) *Round the Works of our Great Railways*, Edward Arnold, London.

Bradshaw, R. (1993) *Railway Lines and Levers*, Unicorn Books, Paddock Wood.

Brees, S.C. (1837) *Railway Practice: A Collection of Working Plans and Practical Details of Construction in the Public Works of the Most Celebrated Engineers*, John Williams, London.

Brodribb, J. (1988) *LNER Country Stations*, Ian Allan, Shepperton.

Brooke, D. (1983) *The Railway Navvy*, David & Charles, Newton Abbot.

Bulleid, H.A.V. (1963) *Master Builders of Steam*, Ian Allan, London.

Burton, A. (1992) *The Railway Builders*, John Murray, London.

Burton, A. (1994) *The Railway Empire*, John Murray, London.

Butt, R.V.J. (1995) *The Directory of Railway Stations*, Patrick Stephens, Sparkford.

Carter, O. (1990) *An Illustrated History of British Railway Hotels 1838–1983*, Silver Link, St Michael's.

Cattell, J. and Falconer, K. (1995) *Swindon: The Legacy of a Railway Town*, HMSO, London.

Chrimes, M.M., Murphy, M.K. and Ribeill, G. (1994) *Mackenzie – Giant of the Railways*, Railtrack, London.

Clark, E. (1850) *The Britannia and Conway Tubular Bridges*, 2 vols, Day & Son, London.

Clark, R.H. (1947, 1948) *British Railway Stations*, Railway & Technical Press, South Merstham.

Clark, R.H. (1976) *An Historical Survey of Selected Great Western Stations*, 2 vols, Oxford Publishing Company.

Clarke, L., Ives, J., Rankin, S. and Simons, P. (1985) *Aspects of Railway Architecture*, Bristol Marketing Board, Bristol.

Clinker, C.R. and Firth, J.M. (1971) *Clinker's Register of Closed Passenger Stations and Goods Depots in England, Scotland and Wales 1830–1970*, C.R. Clinker, Padstow.

Coleman, T. (1968) *The Railway Navvies*, Penguin, Harmondsworth.

Collins, P. (1992) *Rail Super Centres: Birmingham*, Ian Allan, Shepperton.

Conder, F.R., ed. Simmons, J. (1983) *The Men who Built Railways*, Thomas Telford, London.

Conolly, W. P. (1976) *British Railways Pre-Grouping Atlas and Gazetteer*, Ian Allan, London.

Croughton, G., Kidner, R.W. and Young, A. (1982) *Private and Untimetabled Railway Stations*, Oakwood Press, Salisbury.

Day, J. (1860) *A Practical Treatise on the Construction and Formation of Railways*, Simpkin, Marshall & Co, London.

Day, J.R. and Cooper, B.K. (1958) *Railway Signalling Systems*, Frederick Muller, London.

de Maré, E. (1954) *The Bridges of Britain*, Batsford, London.

Dempsey, G.D. (1850) *Iron Roofs: A Series of Examples, illustrating Various Combinations of Iron, both Malleable and Cast, in the Construction of Roofs for Warehouses, Factories, Railway Stations and other Buildings*, Atchley, London.

Dempsey, G.D. (1855) *The Practical Railway Engineer*, John Weale, London.

Dempsey, G.D. (1856) *Engineering Examples: Working Drawings of Stations, Engine-houses, manufactories, Warehouses, Workshops, etc., etc.*, Atchley, London.

Denton, J.H., (1965) *British Railway Stations*, Ian Allan, London.

Dethier, J. (1981) *All Stations: A Journey through 150 Years*, Thames & Hudson, London.

Dow, G. (1959, 1962) *Great Central Vols 1 & 2*, Locomotive Publishing Company, London.

Dow, G. (1965) *Great Central: Vol. 3*, Ian Allan, London.

Drummond, D.K. (1995) *Crewe: Railway Town, Company and People 1840–1914*, Scolar Press, Aldershot.

Ellaway, K.J. (1994) *The Great British Railway Station: Euston*, Irwell, Oldham.

Fitzgerald, R.S. (1980) *Liverpool Road Station, Manchester: An Historical and Architectural Survey*, Manchester University Press.

Green, O. and Rewse-Davies, J. (1995) *Designed for London: 150 Years of Transport Design*, King, London.

Hall, S. (1992) *BR Signalling Handbook*, Ian Allan, Shepperton.

Hammond, R. (1964) *The Forth Bridge and its Builders*, Eyre & Spottiswoode, London.

Hawkins, C. (1987) *Southern Nouveau*, Wild Swan, Upper Bucklebury.

Hawkins, C. (1990) *The Great British Railway Station: Kings Cross*, Irwell, Oldham.

Hawkins, C. and Reeve, G. (1979) *An Historical Survey of Southern Sheds*, Oxford Publishing Company, Oxford.

Hawkins, C. and Reeve, G. (1981, 1982, 1984, 1987a) *LMS Engine Sheds: their History and Development*, 4 vols, Wild Swan, Upper Bucklebury.

Hawkins, C. and Reeve, G. (1986, 1987b) *Great Eastern Railway Engine Sheds*, Wild Swan, Didcot and Upper Bucklebury.

Hawkins, C. and Reeve, G. (1987c) *An Illustrated History of Great Western Railway Engine Sheds. 1: London Division*, Wild Swan, Upper Bucklebury.

Hawkins, C. and Reeve, G. (1989) *British Railways Engine Sheds No. 2 – A Southern Style*, Irwell, Oldham.

Hawkins, C. and Reeve, G. (1990) *LSWR Sheds*, Irwell Press, Oldham.

Hawkins, C., Hooper, J. and Reeve, G. (1988) *British Railway Engine Sheds: an LNER Inheritance*, Irwell, Pinner.

Hawkins, C., Reeve, G. and Stevenson, J. (1989a, 1990) *LMS Engine Sheds*, Vols 6 and 7, Irwell Press, Oldham.

Hawkins, C., Hooper, J. and Reeve, J. (1989b) *British Railways Engine Sheds: London Midland Matters*, Irwell, Oldham.

Hawkins, C., Hooper, J. and Reeve, J. (1989c) *Diesel Depots: the Early Years*, Irwell, Oldham.

Hendry, R.P. and Hendry, R.P. (1982) *An Historical Survey of Selected LMS Stations*, Oxford Publishing Company, Poole.

Holland, H. (1971) *Travellers' Architecture*, George Harrap, London.

Hoole, K. (1967) *North Road Locomotive Works, Darlington*, Roundhouse, Hatch End.

Hoole, K. (1985) *Railway Stations of the North East*, David & Charles, Newton Abbot.

Hughes, S.R.H. (1991) *The Brecon Forest Tramroads*, RCAHM Wales, Aberystwyth.

Hunter, M. and Thorne, R. (1990) *Change at King's Cross*, Historical Publications, London.

Huntriss, D. (1994) *Steam Works: BR Locomotives and Workshops in the Age of Steam*, Ian Allan, Shepperton.

Inglis, C.E. (1934) *A Mathematical Treatise on Vibrations in Railway Bridges*, Cambridge University Press.

Jackson, A.A. (1969) *London's Termini*, David & Charles, Newton Abbot.

Jenkin, F. (1878) *Bridges: An Elementary Treatise on their Construction and History*, A. & C. Black, Edinburgh.

Joby, R.S. (1983) *The Railway Builders*, David & Charles, Newton Abbot.

Johnson, B. (1995) *British Railway Locomotive Works in the Days of Steam*, Challenge, Oldham.

Johnston, C. and Hume, J.R. (1979) *Glasgow Stations*, David & Charles, London.

Johnston, I. (1993) *Beardmore Built*, Clydebank District Libraries & Museums Department, Glasgow.

Kay, P. (1992) *Signal Box Directory*, P. Kay, Teignmouth.

Kellett, J.R. (1979) *Railways and Victorian Cities*, Routledge & Kegan Paul, London.

King, M.A. (1976) *An Album of Pre-Grouping Signal Boxes*, Turntable Publications, Sheffield.

Klingender, F.D., ed. Elton, A. (1972) *Art and the Industrial Revolution*, Paladin, St Albans.

Larkin, E. (1988) *The Railway Workshops of Britain 1823–1986*, Macmillan, Basingstoke.

Larkin, E. (1992) *An Illustrated History of British Railways Workshops*, Oxford Publishing Company, Sparkford.

Lewis, M.J.T. (1970) *Early Wooden Railways*, Routledge & Kegan Paul, London.

Lloyd, D. and Insall, D. (1967, reprint 1978) *Railway Station Architecture*, David & Charles, Newton Abbot.

LNER (1932) *Ports of the London & North Eastern Railway*, LNER, London.

Lowe, J.W. (1975) *British Steam Locomotive Builders*, Goose & Son, Cambridge.

Lowe, J.W. (1979) *Building Britain's Locomotives*, Moorland Publishing, Ashbourne.

Marsden, C.J. (1990) *British Rail Engineering Ltd*, Foulis, OPC, Yeovil.

Measom, G. (1861) *The Official Illustrated Guide to the Great Northern Railway*, Griffin, Bohn & Co, London.

Meeks, C.V.S. (1957) *The Railway Station: An Architectural History*, Architectural Press, London.

Menear, L. (1983) *London's Underground Stations*, Midas, Tunbridge Wells.

Mitchell, W.R. (1975) *The Railway Shanties*, Settle and District Civic Society, Settle.

Munns, R.T. (1986) *Milk Churns to Merry-Go-Rounds: A Centenary of Train Operation*, David & Charles, Newton Abbot.

Nicholson, P. (1839) *The Guide to Railway Masonry*, John Weale, London.

Nicolson, M. & O'Neill, M. (1987) *Glasgow: Locomotive Builder to the World*, Polygon, Glasgow.

Ottley, G. (1965) *A Bibliography of British Railway History*, George Allen & Unwin, London.

Ottley, G. (1973) *Railway History: a Guide to 61 Collections in Libraries and Archives in Great Britain*, Library Association, London.

Ottley, G. (1983) *A Bibliography of British Railway History*, HMSO, London.

Ottley, G. (1988) *A Bibliography of British Railway History*, Supplement, HMSO, London.

Peck, A.S. (1983) *The Great Western at Swindon Works*, Oxford Publishing Company, Poole.

Phillips, P. (1888) *The Forth Bridge in its Various Stages of Construction*, Grant & Son, Edinburgh.

Popplewell, L. (1985) *A Gazetteer of the Railway Contractors and Engineers of Northern England 1830–1914*, Melledgen Press, Bournemouth.

Prebble, J. (1956) *The High Girders*, Secker & Warburg, London.

Prockter, C.E. (1964) *'The Engineer' Index 1856–1959*, Morgan, London.

Pryer, G.A. (1977) *A Pictorial Record of Southern Signals*, Oxford Publishing Company, Oxford.

Pryer, G.A. and Bowring, G.J. (1980) *An Historical Survey of Selected Southern Stations*, Vol. 1, Oxford Publishing Company, Oxford.

Pugsley, A. (1976) *The Works of Isambard Kingdom Brunel: An Engineering Appreciation*, Institution of Civil Engineers, London.

Radford, J.B. (1971) *Derby Works and Midland Locomotives*, Ian Allan, London.

Reed, B. (1982) *Crewe Locomotive Works and its Men*, David & Charles, Newton Abbot.

Rhodes, M. (1988) *The Illustrated History of British Marshalling-yards*, Oxford Publishing Company, Sparkford.

Richards, J. & MacKenzie, J.M. (1986) *The Railway Station: A Social History*, Oxford University Press.

Rolt, L.T.C. (1957) *Isambard Kingdom Brunel: A Biography*, Longman, London.

Rolt, L.T.C. (1960) *George and Robert Stephenson: the Railway Revolution*, Longman, London.

Rosenberg, N and Vincenti, W. (1978) *The Britannia Bridge: The Generation and Diffusion of Technical Knowledge*, MIT, Boston.

RSA Cubitt Trust Panel (1985) *The Future of the Railway Heritage*, Royal Society of Arts Cubitt Trust Panel, London.

SAVE, ed. Pearce, D. and Binney, M. (1977) *Off the Rails*, SAVE Britain's Heritage, London.

Semmens, P. and Machefert-Tassin, Y. (1994) *Channel Tunnel Trains*, Eurotunnel, Folkestone.

Signalling Study Group (1986) *The Signal Box: A Pictorial History*, Oxford Publishing Company, Poole.

Simmons, J. (1968) *St Pancras Station*, George Allen & Unwin, London.

Simmons, J. (1986) *The Railway in Town and Country 1830–1914*, David & Charles, Newton Abbot.

Simmons, J. (1991) *The Victorian Railway*, Thames & Hudson, London.

Smiles, S. (1857) *The Story of the Life of George Stephenson*, John Murray, London.

Smiles, S. (1862) *The Lives of the Engineers*, 2 vols, John Murray, London

Smith, P. (1989) *The Handbook of Steam Motive Power Depots, Vol. 2: Central England, East Anglia and Wales*, Platform 5, Sheffield.

Stebbing, G. (1896) *Beating the Record: A Story of the Life and Times of George Stephenson*, Shaw, London.

Stewart, B. (1908) *Handbook of Railway Surveying*, Spon, London.

Trinder, B. (1982) *Making of the Industrial Landscape*, J. M. Dent, London.

Vanns, M. (1993) *Rail Centres: Nottingham*, Ian Allan, Shepperton.

Vaughan, A. (1973) *A Pictorial Record of Great Western Signalling*, Oxford Publishing Company, Oxford.

Vaughan, A. (1977) *A Pictorial Record of Great Western Architecture*, Oxford Publishing Company, Oxford.

Vaughan, A. (1981) *Signalman's Morning*, John Murray, London.

Vaughan, A. (1983) *Signalman's Twilight*, John Murray, London.

Vaughan, A. (1988) *GWR Junction Stations*, Ian Allan, Shepperton.

Walker, T. (1888) *The Severn Tunnel: Its Construction and Difficulties*, Bentley & Son, London.

Walters, D. (1963) *British Railway Bridges*, Ian Allan, London.

Webster, N., Greengrass, R. and Greaves, S. (1987) *British Rail Depot Directory*, Metro Enterprises, Shipley.

West, F.W. (1912) *The Railway Goods Station*, Spon, London.

Whishaw, F. (1840) *The Railways of Great Britain and Ireland*, Simpkin, Marshall, London.

Wikeley, N. and Middleton, J. (1971) *Railway Stations: Southern Region*, Peco, Seaton.

Williams, A. (1915, reprint 1986) *Life in a Railway Factory*, Alan Sutton, Gloucester.

Wood, N. (1825) *A Practical Treatise on Railroads*, Longman, London.

Woods, S.J. and Tuffrey, P. (1987) *Doncaster Plant Works*, Bond Publications, Doncaster.

Part Two
Historic Appraisal

Gordon Biddle

Historic railway structures in Britain: *a continuing appraisal*

The growing appreciation of historic railway structures over the last 25 years or so has not been driven solely by their intrinsic architectural qualities. A key factor is their contribution to the landscape and townscape, which is where many would argue their main value – or otherwise – lies. It certainly represents one of the principal reasons for giving them statutory protection. Here are a few representative examples.

Viaducts and tunnels

Viaducts, more than any other feature, express the early railway builders' supreme self-confidence. They believed they were building 'for ever', as many railway Acts of Parliament stated, and their massive structures testify to that belief. Let us take four viaducts, each very different in construction and setting, but each making a very positive impact on the landscape. The dramatic Ouse Valley Viaduct at Balcombe, Sussex, 1840, has 37 red-brick arches, and is somewhat unusually decorated with elegant balustrades that have a charming little pavilion at each end. These embellishments were specially commissioned from the architect David Mocatta. Near Peebles in the Borders of Scotland, the six elliptical arches of the Neidpath Viaduct, 1864, cross the River Tweed in a wooded valley, the pale grey stone graced by a delicate iron openwork parapet and making a very positive contribution to the setting. On the Settle & Carlisle line, the lofty Dent Head Viaduct, 1875, in rock-faced stone, adds grandeur to the rugged Pennine scenery in which it sits so well. Lastly among rural viaducts is Barmouth, 1867: the longest wooden railway bridge in Britain and one of only three survivors. It strides for nearly half a mile across the Mawddach estuary as a reminder of the widespread use of timber by the railway builders in just as daring a fashion as stone, brick, iron and steel.

In towns, the opposite happened: viaducts quickly created linear slums and urban blight, which in many places is still prevalent. The part of Birmingham that is overshadowed by Bordesley Viaduct, 1852, still conjures up the images created by Dore and Dickens. Nowhere was this more pronounced than in south London, criss-crossed by a bewildering pattern of viaducts, although there, as elsewhere, their role is now being reversed as they are steadily undergoing refurbishment to form the focus of urban regeneration projects, such as Spa Road business park in Bermondsey, one of a number of excellent schemes of this kind.

In some places railway viaducts formed barriers: in Brighton, for instance, where London Road viaduct, 1846, for long stopped the spread of housing up the valley; and particularly in Manchester and Salford, where the centre is almost entirely ringed. But in a number of urban areas the dramatic dominance of a viaduct is now looked on as a valuable part of the local environment, enhanced by cleaning and, at Stockport and Accrington, emphasized by floodlighting at night.

Tunnels, by contrast, are much less visible. But their builders still gave them massive portals, deliberately designed to imply great strength in order to allay the fears of early railway travellers as they were plunged into the depths of the earth. Frequently the entrances were decorated. I.K. Brunel favoured a classical theme for the western portal of Box Tunnel in Wiltshire, 1841; further west he chose Gothic turrets and crenellations between Bath and Bristol – a widely used idiom, because Gothic was regarded as particularly appropriate to the awesome excitement that tunnels engendered in those incurable romantics, the early Victorians.

Stations

Station design took a different course. A homely cottage style, or the resemblance to the gate lodge on a country estate, was felt appropriate in rural areas, in an effort to provide something familiar to country folk that would encourage them to travel, or to appease a landowner: hence the amazing variety in railway stations built during the first 30 years or so, from the half-timbering of Fenny Stratford in Buckinghamshire, 1846, and others on the same line, to the modest, typically Scottish wayside station in local stone at Errol in Perthshire, 1847, and the gentle Italianate styling of Appledore in Kent, 1851.

Stations in small towns provoked equal efforts to harmonize, such as the quiet classicism of Canterbury West, 1846. Ideas of harmony could provide contrasts too, notably at Lincoln where the Midland Railway's St Marks Station, 1846, was classical; but not far away, two years later John Taylor designed a Tudor Central Station for the Great Northern, complete with a crenellated tower. But occasionally there might be an extraordinary outburst, as at the market town of Ulverston in south Cumbria, where the small Furness Railway commissioned Austin & Paley of Lancaster to design a large elaborate Italianate station, 1873, which is arguably the most imposing building in the town.

Frequently, designers left a readily identifiable stamp on a line, or on a number of lines in various parts of the country. Brunel's small stations, in several styles, were very distinctive, to be found on most of the railways he

Fig. 4.1 Lincoln Central Station, Great Northern Railway, by J. Taylor, 1848. Photographed in 1966. (G. Biddle)

Fig. 4.2 Lichfield Drive Bridge, Shugborough, Staffordshire, Trent Valley Railway, by J. W. Livock, 1847; showing the insignia of the Earl of Lichfield. (G. Biddle)

Fig. 4.3 Charing Station, London, Chatham & Dover Railway, 1884. Photographed in 1967. (G. Biddle)

Fig. 4.4 Cottages, Strathpeffer, Highland Railway. (G. Biddle)

Fig. 4.5 Houses, Rowsley, Midland Railway. Re-roofed with modern tiles. (G. Biddle)

Fig. 4.6 South terrace, Tebay, South Durham & Lancashire Union Railway. Note the slate walling, characteristic of the Lake District. (G. Biddle)

63

built. Francis Thompson produced some of our most delicately designed stations for the North Midland Railway, 1840, of which only Wingfield remains, now privately owned and sadly neglected despite listing. He went on to work for the Chester & Holyhead company, where in addition to Chester itself he built a long string of stations to a common theme. Flint is a good surviving example of one of the larger ones. The same basic pattern was later copied by other designers in East Anglia, such as at Wrabness on the Harwich branch, 1854.

The influence or patronage of prominent landowners and important share-holders is also clearly implanted on the railway at a number of places. Bridges and tunnel mouths might be specially designed or decorated to satisfy a landowner whose support for the line – or, at least, his agreement not to oppose it – was vital in planning the route: the underbridge and tunnel portals in Shugborough Park, Staffordshire, 1847, for the Earl of Lichfield, for instance; different coats of arms on two bridges between Coventry and Leamington, 1844; arms on a bridge at the foot of the Falls of Cruachan on the Callander & Oban line in Scotland, 1880; Lord Braybrooke's arms on the south portals of Audley End and Littlebury Tunnels in Essex, 1845. Specially designed or embellished stations were not uncommon either: Brocklesby, Humberside, 1848, for the Earl of Yarborough, chairman of the Manchester Sheffield & Lincolnshire Railway; Sandon, Staffordshire, 1849, for the Earl of Harrowby, who was on the North Staffordshire Railway board; Audley End again, where Lord Braybrooke exacted further favours; and for the Duke of Sutherland, an Italianate station at Trentham, Staffordshire, 1848, by Sir Charles Barry, who designed the hall close by.

A common element in all these structures was the use of local building materials, particularly stone. It was later, from the 1860s onwards, that railways themselves brought about the spread of brick as a building material throughout much of England, and the demise of the vernacular, including on their own structures and often accompanied by standardization of design. Charing in Kent, 1884, is a good example of a late-Victorian standard red-brick station on the South Eastern Railway; Goring & Streatley, Oxfordshire, is a familiar Great Western example of 1893. The railways were also responsible for spreading certain types of brick far beyond their natural localities. The Great Northern used buff 'London stocks', and Flettons from the Peterborough brickfields; the Lancashire & Yorkshire took fiery red Accrington 'plastic' bricks throughout the north-west; the Great Western 'Ruabon reds'. Many companies used the very durable 'Staffordshire blue' engineering bricks for tunnels, bridges and cutting walls in districts where there was high atmospheric pollution. The Oxford Worcester & Wolverhampton Railway used them for stations, too, and – very unfeelingly – on some rural viaducts, like the prominent one at Hoo Brook, near Kidderminster. This period also saw much mutilation of earlier work, by unsympathetic alterations, extensions and repairs.

Most railways provided houses for their employees, and by 1920 owned some 27 000 across the country. A few blended well, like the Highland Railway's cottages at Strathpeffer, but mostly they represented standard build-ings erected regardless of the local vernacular style. The Midland Railway built an entire village at Rowsley, where terraces of tile-hung houses were quite out of keeping in mid-Derbyshire. The London & North Western Railway had a particularly poor record. Its raw, red houses, built of Crewe brick, can still be seen from London to Carlisle and Swansea to Leeds.

Turning now to the big cities, early stations were often more sophisticated, expressing with grand buildings the railways' desire to impress, and their pride in achievement. None was more so than the Doric Arch at Euston, 1838, which was originally fronted by a square. Sadly, the arch was demolished in 1961. But its counterpart in Birmingham remains, restored and put to good use, although it has always looked out of place in an area of canal wharves, back streets and small industries.

City stations in Britain seldom formed the focal point of a town planning or new streets scheme, unlike many in Europe and North America. The pattern of development was quite different, so that many of our fine stations do not receive their due prominence in the townscape. The long, magnificent classical facade of Huddersfield station, 1841, for instance, can only be fully appreciated from the side; the square fronting it is rather too small, yet it was part of a development plan by the Ramsden family trustees, who owned most of Huddersfield at the time. Intended as a focal point, the station is monumental, as the trustees required, but curiously was not given its full due. The noble frontage at Newcastle Central is a similar case. It just misses forming a grand termination to the view down Grainger Street, which turns slightly at its foot, obscuring all but a corner of the magnificent portico. Yet here again it was part of a grand plan for Newcastle.

On occasions a new street was built to the station, as happened at Brighton and Norwich. Here and there the railway was required to build one itself, as at Bath, where the prospect along Manvers Street is satisfactorily terminated by Brunel's Jacobean station facade – which explains why it is assymmetrical.

Often the railway was dreadfully intrusive in towns: witness the 'ruthlessness' (Pevsner's word) of the bowstring girder bridge across the end of Regency Bath Street at Leamington Spa; or worse, the blocking of the 1654

Fig. 4.7 Frontage and portico of Huddersfield Station, by J.P. Pritchett, 1847. (G. Biddle)

65

Fig. 4.8 Heaton Norris Warehouse, Stockport, built by the LNWR. (G. Biddle)

Tolbooth Steeple, one of Glasgow's oldest buildings, by an iron viaduct. In industrial towns vast, lofty warehouses were built, particularly in the north and in Scotland. Heaton Norris warehouse, Stockport, is a good example. Earlier goods sheds, like stations, although more utilitarian, could be more sympathetic to their surroundings, such as the seemly local stone building at Ashbourne in Derbyshire, or might match the passenger station, such as those between Newcastle and Berwick.

Most of the stations mentioned, few among many, have been restored by British Rail or, where they have become redundant, by new owners. Latterly, there has been admirable attention to detail, too. The door and window mouldings at Dunfermline and the fine ticket hall ceiling at Norwich are two typical instances. In the private sector, the charming station building at Ripple, near Tewkesbury in Gloucestershire, has been lovingly restored as living accommodation by its new owner. It is one of a growing number. The private railways, also, have a steadily improving record.

Protection by listing

Most of the Railtrack property discussed so far comprises listed structures, of which there are in total over 1250, quite apart from the many now in other hands. Yet on looking through British Rail's register of statutorily protected structures of January 1993 – the latest edition I have – I am struck by certain inconsistencies, in type and in geographical spread. In saying this I must emphasize that I appreciate the circumstances and procedures surrounding listing and scheduling; the need to try to balance local and national interests (and local ones are important); and the shortcomings of existing legislation.

In England and Wales there seems to be a preponderance of bridges and viaducts, followed at some distance by stations, with other kinds of structure trailing behind. In some cases, of course, like engine sheds, there are very few left anyway. In Scotland, though, the balance is rather better.

Fig. 4.9 Ripple Station, near Tewkesbury, built by the Midland Railway. Photographed in 1958 and now converted to a house. (G. Biddle)

Looking again at listed viaducts, many are operational and therefore not at risk, but a significant number are disused. British Rail sold about 24 and still owns about 50, for which it has a statutory responsibility not easily passed on, representing a considerable potential liability. Most are historically or environmentally important, but some are not, like Martholme Viaduct in north east Lancashire, 1877, an undistinguished structure with little or no landscape value and one of several similar ones, used and disused, in the district. Yet the earlier and very finely detailed viaduct close to the centre of Bury, 1848, is not listed. Appersett, near Hawes in North Yorkshire, is a modest structure of five low arches, which I suspect was included with those on the Settle & Carlisle line (it stands on a branch) when they were listed *en bloc*. There is a similarly undistinguished example at Rowsley, Derbyshire, which is not easy to see. It has recently been sold by British Rail.

On the former Bude branch in north Devon and Cornwall there stand two early examples of reinforced concrete viaducts: Woolstone Mill and Derriton, near Holsworthy. They are only a few miles apart and, saving their size, are identical. Woolstone is barely visible from the nearest road, some distance away, being heavily shrouded by trees; the larger one, Derriton, however, can be fully appreciated from an adjacent road, and one can easily walk beneath it. Early concrete viaducts are important in the history of structural engineering, but here surely only Derriton needs to be kept, particularly as there are also two more much larger ones in the West Country.

Again, in northern Cumbria three identical bridges – all shored up – span the disused track bed of the one-time Port Carlisle Railway, 1854, near Burgh-by-Sands. It started life as a canal in 1823, and the bridges' main historical interest is in the obvious upward extensions of the stone abutments, executed when the wooden swing bridges across the canal were replaced by higher iron spans to give headroom for trains. But is not just one sufficient for retention?

Conversely, near Coventry, three masonry flying arches span the London & Birmingham Railway, 1838, by Robert Stephenson. None is listed, yet they predate Brunel's at Uphill, Somerset, and others of his in the West Country and South Wales, some of which are.

For some time an increasing number of signal boxes have been listed. It is right that a representative number of these disappearing structures should be protected, but there seem to be more from the former North Eastern, Midland and Great Western Railways than any other. For example, the standard Midland wooden box at St Albans South is listed, and has mouldered away for over 10 years, out of use and an eyesore, while the unusual and much more attractive one at Guiseley, near Leeds, was unlisted. It was removed under the recent electrification programme, fortunately for re-erection on a preserved railway.

What are probably the largest two remaining mechanical signal boxes are both listed, although they are both near-identical. The London & North Western Railway built them: Rhyl No 2, and Severn Bridge Junction at Shrewsbury. The former is disused, and stands vandalized at the lineside, so it could be made accessible for other purposes. The Shrewsbury box stands in a triangle of running lines, and access, when it eventually becomes redundant, will be difficult and expensive, assuming a use can be found. Now Rhyl and Shrews-bury are not too far apart, and the reason why both have been listed is probably that Rhyl is in Wales and therefore the interest of Cadw, while Shrewsbury's listing comes under English Heritage. For all that, I question whether we need both. Better, surely, for Cadw to list a Cambrian Railways signal box, which at least would have the merit of having belonged to a Welsh company.

Incidentally, at Oswestry, Shropshire, where there is very little remaining railway these days, a signal post is listed, although whether it includes the semaphore arm as well the register does not say. Surely this is stretching statutory protection too far. I can think of several disused signal posts on abandoned lines up and down the country – one complete with its arm – that presumably were overlooked when the scrap merchants moved in but which, so far as I know, have not been thought suitable for statutory protection. There are, after all, plenty of historic semaphore signals in working order on the preserved railways, even though some are not of the right type in the right place.

There are more anomalies among listed stations. For instance, Aberdeen is listed, but neither of the two main stations at Exeter is. On the line from

Fig. 4.10 Severn Bridge Junction signal box, Shrewsbury, LNWR. Photographed in 1983. (G. Biddle)

Newtown to Machynlleth in Wales, the charming little station at Caersws is listed, but the much more imposing and recently restored one at Machynlleth (both by the same architect, T.M. Penson of Chester) is not. Back at Rhyl, the late-Victorian station, ugly and far too large for present purposes, has been listed, yet the much more important and attractive one at Winchester (1838–40), by the noted architect Sir William Tite, has escaped.

Again, the typical Great Western 1880s station at Wrexham, in stone, with attractive yet characteristic French pavilion roofs, is listed, as is a similar one at Torquay. Here, distance can justify listing them both, although there is another example at Teignmouth, not far from Torquay, made more interesting by the use of variegated stone, which would have been the better candidate of the two in Devon.

Turning to the North-West, the whole of the large station at Preston is listed, justified if for no other reason by its distinctive overall roof, the largest and almost sole survivor of a long dynasty of similar roofs developed by the London & North Western Railway and evolving from the original design for Euston, 1838. But a particularly ugly late-Victorian addition, in buff brick, historically unimportant and now divorced from the station proper, used only for parcels traffic, is also included – quite unnecessarily. Incidentally, there is no need to discuss overall roofs in this context, because all the remaining important train sheds have statutory protection.

Fig. 4.11 Machynlleth Station, Newtown & Machynlleth Railway, by T.M. Penson, 1863. Photographed in 1965 before recent restoration. (G. Biddle)

Fig. 4.12 Lea Hall Station, Birmingham, LMS, by W.H. Hamlyn, 1939. Note cantilevered reinforced concrete canopies. (G. Biddle)

Although once numerous, very few wooden stations now remain in their original state, yet they are an important type. A series between Paddock Wood and Tonbridge in Kent, like Marden and Pluckley, was built in 1842–3. I believe that only Pluckley now remains in this form, well in keeping with the Kentish clapboard tradition, yet it does not appear to be listed. Not long ago an attempt was made to have one of a late-Victorian series on the LNWR Birmingham–Lichfield line listed. They were typical of their kind, little altered, with standard components. Although they were important survivors, listing was turned down, and they have been demolished.

Finally on this topic, a number of 1930s Southern Railway stations are rightly listed, but why are there so few north of the Thames? The pioneer reinforced-concrete station at Apsley, near Watford, or the slightly later Lea Hall, Birmingham, are strong candidates. In the West Country, Newton Abbot station, in 1924–5 'Queen Anne' style, is typical of its day and arguably one of the better buildings in a town not noted for its architecture. It is mentioned in Pevsner, too. In 1995 a number of postwar railway structures, including Coventry and Manchester Oxford Road stations and Birmingham New Street signal box, were listed, so perhaps official thinking is now moving in the right direction.

Let it not be thought that I am making a plea for more listing. Indeed, it may be argued with some logic that there is more than enough already. What I am suggesting is that there is a case for an objective review of existing railway structures, listed and unlisted, regardless of ownership, in terms of type and location. It could turn up justifiable cases for listing and for de-listing. The aim would be to retain a representative stock. In this connection I have recently been pleased to learn that English Heritage hopes soon to be able to carry out thematic reviews of protected buildings, and that railways could well be a candidate. I hope they can be extended to Scotland and Wales as well.

The Lancaster & Carlisle Railway
As an all-embracing illustration of the value of an objective review as it affects a particular stretch of line, I would like to describe a selection of what can be seen on a journey northward along the Lancaster & Carlisle Railway. An important component of the West Coast main line, it was completed in 1847 by a well-known team, which built many railways in Britain and some in France: Joseph Locke and John E. Errington, engineers; Thomas Brassey and William MacKenzie, contractors; and William Tite, architect. It was electrified in 1974, with all that implies in terms of rebuilt overbridges and demolished stations, of which only two intermediate ones are still open. Yet, surprisingly, there is still much to be seen that emphasizes my points. Most of the small stations were built in a common neo-Tudor style and pattern.

- Lancaster Castle station (listed): original Tite building, neo-Tudor, in local stone, with 1858 extension in form of 'keep', to relate to nearby castle – hence the name; 1900 additional buildings, surprisingly harmonious.
- Carnforth: a remarkable set of various railway structures covering the period 1847–1944 by five different companies, all on adjoining or nearby sites:

*Fig. 4.13 Shap Station,
Lancaster & Carlisle
Railway, by Sir W. Tite,
1846–8. Photographed in
1967. (G. Biddle)*

Tite's LCR station building with c.1860 LNWR extension to match, and 1880 LNWR building opposite in sympathetic style, all on main platforms, now disused (none listed). Sharply curved Barrow platforms (still used), one by LMS in 1939 reinforced concrete (not listed). Original stone Furness Railway signal box with coat-of-arms, disused but listed. Later FR standard signal box (not listed). Midland Railway F&M Junction signal box (not listed).

'Steamtown' railway museum – 1944 reinforced-concrete-framed LMS engine shed, coaling tower and ash plant – sole survivors countrywide (listed).

Former Midland Railway stone engine shed, water tower and ancillary buildings, remarkably complete when listing rejected four years ago; recently mutilated.

Several rows of LNWR and Midland Railway workers' houses.

- At the time of writing an urban regeneration plan is being drawn up under the auspices of the Civic Trust Registration Unit which could provide a good opportunity to recognize the importance of these reminders of Carnforth when it was a railway town.
- Yealand: Dockacres underbridge where the building stone changes from gritstone to limestone: an interesting skew arch, with fine ashlar winder courses (not listed).
- Burton & Holme station house, by Tite. Privately owned.
- Milnthorpe station house, by Tite. Privately owned.
- Hincaster Junction: isolated pair of red-brick LNWR houses, formerly for signal box, completely alien in landscape; now privately occupied.
- Oxenholme: junction station, with Tite's station building, 1852 complete, including some original iron-framed windows (not listed). Several rows of LNWR standard red-brick houses once formed the village, which before the railway did not exist (now privately occupied and some altered).
- Rabbit Lane overbridge, limestone, in original condition (listed).

- A685 road overbridge about 1 mile further north, with much more interesting skew arch (not listed).
- Docker Viaduct (listed).
- Tebay: a number of rows of NER and LNWR houses in render, slate and brick, forming a large colony – all that remains of what was an important junction. Several more in village, including a curved stone terrace.
- Shap: station house by Tite (not listed).
- Hugh's Crag or Lowther Viaduct: construction here changes to Eden Valley sandstone (listed).
- Penrith station: by Tite, suitably 'baronial', opposite castle ruins; interesting awning brackets in early 'Euston' style on northbound platform (listed).
- Plumpton: small stone early goods shed; LNWR house, both privately owned.
- Calthwaite: terrace of five LNWR houses, the end one much larger for the station master.
- Southwaite: station house by Tite, privately owned; five LNWR houses in terrace.
- Wreay: station house, in different style, as opened later in 1853; weak gothic, with scalloped bargeboards and stone gable finials; bay window on to platform; privately owned.
- Brisco: station house by Tite; closed in 1852 after only six years, and replaced by Wreay; privately owned.
- Carlisle: Tite's very fine neo-Tudor station building, in small square opposite Smirke's law courts, all very harmonious. Good matching later extensions to original building on opposite platform, beneath ridge-and-furrow overall roof (listed).

Space has precluded more than a brief mention of what remains on this short journey. However, I hope it will indicate something of what can still be seen to

Fig. 4.15 Carlisle Station, by Sir W. Tite, jointly for Lancaster & Carlisle and Caledonian Railways, 1847. (G. Biddle)

the appraising and questioning eye elsewhere, despite changes brought about by modernization of the railway. Lines that have not yet been electrified or extensively altered can reveal even more, much of it still in use for railway purposes.

Elsewhere, Sir Neil Cossons, Director of the Science Museum, has advocated the designation of a 'heritage railway', with the object of preserving as much as possible of the historic infrastructure. He suggests the original Great Western main line from Paddington to Bristol. However, as it is a probable candidate for future electrification, further alteration or removal of original Brunel features would seem inescapable. Professor Jack Simmons has mentioned to me two other possibilities whose future seems reasonably secure, and where there have been fewer changes.

One is older than the GWR: the Newcastle & Carlisle Railway of 1838, still virtually complete with its series of characteristic original stations – nearly all still open – semaphore signals and much North Eastern Railway equipment. There are several viaducts, two tunnels (one now bypassed and disused), and the great Cowran Hills cutting. As on the GWR, there is a handsome station at each end.

The other is the former Midland line from Syston, near Leicester, to Peterborough (exclusive), dating from 1846–48. Here again the stations are nearly all original, with a charming variety, and although some have been closed the main buildings are largely still extant. Here, too, mechanical signalling remains. There may be other equally suitable candidates, and we must not forget Scotland and Wales. But the important point is that Sir Neil's idea should be given serious and immediate consideration before it is too late.

Finally, research. There is still much to be discovered about railway structures, particularly stations, of which there are so many where the designer is unknown. Some valuable short studies of railway architects have appeared of late, but there is a need for more, in greater depth, and with objective analyses of their relationships with the engineers and their terms of employment.

Select bibliography

Biddle, G. (1973) *Victorian Stations*, David & Charles, Newton Abbot.

Biddle, G. (1986) *Great Railway Stations of Britain*, David & Charles, Newton Abbot.

Biddle, G. (1993a) The railway stations of John Livock and T.M. Penson. *Journal of Railway & Canal Historical Society*, Vol. 31, Part 2, No. 154, 61–71.

Biddle, G. (1993b) Railways in Towns, *Journal of Railway & Canal Historical Society*, Vol. 31, Part 4, No. 156, 154–62.

Biddle, G. and Nock, O.S. (1983) *The Railway Heritage of Britain*, Michael Joseph, London.

Binney, M. and Pearce, D. (eds) (1979) *Railway Architecture*, Orbis, London.

Carter, O. (1995) Francis Thompson, 1808–95 – An architectural mystery solved. *BackTrack*, Vol. 9, No. 4, 213–18.

Cole, D. (1958) Mocatta's stations for the Brighton Railway. *Journal of Transport History*, 1st series, Vol. 3, No. 3, 149–57.

Dixey, S.J. (1994) Charles Trubshaw, A Victorian Railway Architect. *Bedside BackTrack*, pp. 65–8.

Lloyd, D. and Insall, D. (1978) *Railway Station Architecture*, David & Charles, Newton Abbot.

Meeks, C.L.V. (1957) *The Railway Station: An Architectural History*, Architectural Press, London.

Minett, H.J. (1965) The railway stations of George Townsend Andrews. *Journal of Transport History*, 1st series, Vol. 7, No. 1, 44–53.

Simmons, J. (1986) *The Railway in Town and Country*, David & Charles, Newton Abbot.

Simmons, J. (1991) *The Victorian Railway*, Thames & Hudson, London.

Adrian Vaughan

Brunel as a creator of environment

Isambard Kingdom Brunel, 1806–59, was unique in the annals of British civil engineering. His nature was a mixture – of the Napoleonic, the artist and the connoisseur of fine art. He grew up under the shadow of his father – Marc – whose mechanically inventive genius was much greater than Isambard's. Marc urged his son into engineering greatness, and the son grew up, in the very impecunious Brunel household, under his father's shadow, bursting with 'great' ideas, dreaming of achieving greatness, full of anxiety in case he should fail.

Commissions were slow to come, but on 16 March 1831 his designs were accepted for a suspension bridge across the Avon. The site consisted of a sheer-sided gorge, about 700 ft (200 m) wide and some 200 ft (60 m) deep. He persuaded the Building Committee that they wanted something *big*, and this included suspension towers 240 ft (73 m) high:

> If the confounded election doesn't come I anticipate a pleasant job, for expenses seem no object provided it is made *grand*. (Rolt, 1957, p. 56)

The towers were to be 'Egyptian', encased in cast-iron plates depicting the processes by which the bridge was made – men at work in the iron foundry, for instance. Brunel discussed his designs with William Beckford, and intended to give the detail design for the decorations to his brother-in-law, the artist John Horsley RA.

Lack of money and political unrest prevented these ideas from being realized, but in the drama of the site, Brunel's bold treatment of it and in his choice of collaborators we see him as he was.

On 5 December 1831 he was travelling on the Liverpool to Manchester Railway. He was not impressed with the actual performance but saw clearly the possibilities of the new form of transport. He drew some very shaky freehand circles on his diary and wrote:

I record this specimen of the shaking on the Manchester Railway. The time is not far off when we shall be able to take our coffee and write whilst going noiselessly and smoothly at 45 mph. Let me try.

Planning the London to Bristol line

A railway from Bristol to London was proposed on 7 May 1832. A committee of businessmen to achieve this met on 21 January 1833 and put the survey out to the cheapest tender. Brunel told them that to give the job to the man who offered to do it for the least money:

> You are simply giving a premium to the man who will make the most flattering promises. The route I will survey will not be the cheapest – but it will be the best. (Vaughan, 1991, p. 46).

In spite of such uncompromising statements, the capitalists who were to put their money into the work employed him as their engineer. As they later discovered to their cost he meant what he said. He viewed the work as a sculptor views a block of marble – an opportunity to make something beautiful. He saw his railway as a luxury (Rolt, 1957, p. 45). He envisaged a railway as a work of art and an engineering *tour de force*, 'the finest work in England', in order to fulfil his ambition to become a byword for excellence – England's finest engineer.

Brunel was not a 'practical' engineer in the manner of the Stephensons or Joseph Locke. Locke's railways were brilliantly utilitarian, his track design becoming the British standard. Brunel's railways were brilliantly non-standard and personal.

He was intent on creating an international transport system on a scale not yet dreamed of – London–Bristol–New York – and it had to be seen to be *his*. In the Bristol to London route he set out deliberately to create a luxurious railway environment of smooth speed, luxury, artistry and strategic importance. Brunel decided on a gauge of 7 ft (2.13 m), carefully planned gradients, long straights and the gentlest possible curves.

His architectural style sometimes used classical or Egyptian or Italian models, rather more Tudor or Jacobean – the latter what one might call 'High Protestant', recalling the days of Britain's first self-made entrepreneurs and adventurers. There are square-headed, mullioned windows but no lancet arches. I do not consider that he ever used Gothic; Gothic was Catholic, and in 1835 to be Catholic was popularly considered to be unBritish.

Brunel had a general's eye for the lie of the land and for strategy. The most direct and most obvious route was that already in use by the stage coaches: from Reading along the Kennet to Newbury and Hungerford, over a summit near Marlborough and down to Devizes, Melksham, and along the Avon valley to Bradford-on-Avon, Bath and Bristol. This would serve locally important market towns but would have passed over a summit at least 500 ft (150 m) above sea and would have been hilly, twisting – and parochial. It would not have been a trunk line and it would not have given access from London and Bristol to South Wales or the Midlands. He took the unconventional – and cleverest – route, north of the Downs up the Thames valley, creating a strategic trunk capable of throwing off vital, secondary trunks.

The practical result of Brunel's perception of what a railway should be was miles of heavy embankments and deep cuttings. The profile of the ground has concentrated the heaviest works from 7 to 47 and from 94 to the $118\frac{1}{2}$ mile posts (11–76 km and 151–191 km). The masonry bridges at river crossings have long, leaping and rather 'flat' spans, and indeed the whole line has a sweeping, streamlined look. Geography supplied a fine route, but it took the eye of an artist–engineer to select it – earlier proposals for a Bristol–London railway saw only the obvious route.

Engineering the route

At Paddington the terminus is about 100 ft (30 m) above sea level. The route runs westwards imperceptibly rising, generally at 1 in 1320, tolerably straight, impatient of any obstacle, whether the Colnbrook swamps or Sonning Hill. The Sonning Hill cutting extended from 32 miles to 34 miles (51–55 km) with a maximum depth of 60 ft (18 m). This would have been partly tunnel to placate Mr Robert Palmer, MP for Berkshire, but the MP refused to remove his opposition even with a tunnel to hide the railway, so the cutting was made.

At Reading, 36 miles (58 km), the line enters the Thames valley proper. The valley is a mile wide but narrowing, the river meandering. Brunel kept to the south side on heavy embankments or clipping through the valley side in a cutting. For $1\frac{1}{2}$ miles (2.4 km) in the vicinity of Tilehurst, $38\frac{1}{2}$ miles (62 km) from London, the river flows at the very foot of the embankment, which has to be built up as a brick wall. At Pangbourne, $41\frac{1}{2}$ miles (67 km), the Berkshire Downs drop steeply, thrusting in from the west against the Chilterns on the east bank. The river valley narrows to a 'throat', with just enough space on the south bank for a road. Brunel took the railway through on the south side slicing through the spur of the Downs by a deep cutting half a mile long. From Pangbourne to Goring, $44\frac{1}{2}$ miles (72 km), is the longest section of level track between Paddington and Bristol.

A mile from Goring the river, heading north, suddenly meanders west to run hard against the foot of the steep Downs. Brunel swung his line across the valley, crossing the Thames at Gatehampton, and swept past the village on the east bank, heading due north as the hills fall back. He had broken out of the gap with the elan of a cavalry charge, preserving his levels and his broad alignment, placing himself perfectly for the westerly sweep around the outriders of the Downs.

The railway crosses the Thames for the last time on the heavily skewed Moulsford bridge, cutting through the valley side to break out onto the plateau giving access to the west-rising Vale of the White Horse.

Brunel planned this splendid course through 'the gap' on two horseback visits to Streatley Down, 21 April and 14 September 1833. The approximate site of his deliberations is reached from 'The Bull', Streatley, up a 1 in 4 hill (Vaughan, 1991, p. 48). The way in which he envisaged the passage of Goring Gap, and the use of land in the transition from the lower valley of the Thames to the rising Vale, seems to me to be a master-stroke. He must also have had the greatest confidence in the skill of the bricklayers who were to build the bridges his conception demanded.

The line crosses the 200 ft (60 m) contour line at Didcot, 53 miles (85 km) from Paddington, and enters the Vale of the White Horse, which 'slopes from the setting sun to the dawn'. Over the 25 miles (40 km) to the summit of the line at Swindon the usual grade was 1 in 754 with a section at 1 in 660. The only earthwork of note is the cutting through Baulking Common, 66 mile post (106 km), with a nice brick arch over the line.

Swindon, 77¼ miles (124 km), was about 320 ft (97 m) above sea level. From Swindon the line fell gently, apart from two short inclines at 1 in 100: Dauntsey Bank, between Wooton Basset and through Box Tunnel between Corsham and Bath. Beyond Bath, 106 miles (170 km), the Avon valley carried the line falling on the Brunellian 1 in 1320 grade, threading seven tunnels to Bristol, 118 miles 28 chains (190.5 km) from Paddington.

Architectural grandeur and sensitivity
A real artist can do no other but consider his materials and the beauty of what he is doing. Brunel used architectural styles and materials in harmony with the district. For his original GWR he appears to have drawn up a set of four standard designs for lesser stations plus a fifth, rather larger, for more deserving cases. There were, as it were, five 'off the peg' silhouettes, but he alternated the choice of standard design along the line and used different, local materials in each to produce apparently endless variety yet with a strong 'family likeness' (Vaughan, 1977, p. 3).

Between Paddington and Didcot, Brunel's expenditure on ambitiously decorative architecture was restrained partly by geography but mainly by the business-like feelings of the GWR's London Committee of Directors. It is fortunate for us that the western half of the line – which had the greater potential for grand designs – was under the control of the Bristol Committee, who were completely under the spell of Brunel's magic – and willing to pay for the privilege.

In the London area, J.C. Bourne states that London 'white' bricks were specified (Bourne, 1842). Whether this colour was used in the great Wharncliffe Viaduct, 7½ miles (12 km) from Paddington, Bourne does not say. Today the bricks are dark coloured, but this may be the result of refacing. The viaduct has Bramley Falls limestone caps on the piers. The viaduct is 300 yards (274 m) long, carrying the rails 65 ft (20 m) above the valley of the River Brent. There are eight arches of 70 ft (21 m) span, springing from large, over-sailing, limestone caps, which sit on massive, brick twin piers or pylons in what Brunel called his 'Egyptian' style. Isambard's father, Marc, records in his diary 'working on Isambard's Brent viaduct' for several weeks commencing in March 1834 (Vaughan, 1991, pp. 126–7).

The Maidenhead Bridge over the Thames, at about 23 miles (37 km), is constructed in red Berkshire brick, with a Bath stone string course the length of the bridge in which sits the brick parapet wall, which is (or was) capped with more Bath stone. The bridge has a short approach viaduct on the east side and crosses the river with two spans of 128 ft (39 m) each, with a rise from springing to crown of 24 ft (7.3 m). This remains the 'flattest' brick arch in the

Fig. 5.1 Maidenhead Bridge, GWR, by I.K. Brunel, 1834. (A. Vaughan)

world, producing a particularly beautiful half-elliptical shape perfected as a full ellipse on calm sunny days, when the arch is reflected in the still water. The particular shape seems to me to be one perfectly in vogue for 1834.

Brunel had four simple, standard designs for wayside stations, the railway equivalent of roadside cottages. The London–Didcot quadrupling of 1870–92 destroyed all the original way-stations. I believe that Southall, 9½ miles (15 km), had a station closely similar to that still standing at Culham (Oxford-shire). Pangbourne was also a 'Culham' type. Ealing Station, 6 miles (10 km), was a 'one off', a tall, rectangular block, similar to a middle-class London 'semi-detached' of the period.

Twyford, 31 miles (50 km), was given a relatively large station, with a main office building in red brick, very similar, if not identical, to that still existing in Bath stone at Bradford-on-Avon, built in 1848. Bradford-on-Avon was a bustling textile manufacturing and market town. Twyford was only a small village, but perhaps Brunel was considering the dignity of the market town of Henley, served by Twyford.

It would seem that Brunel designed a grand station building for Reading, county town and the last large town on the line for 70 miles (113 km). The design was approved by the London Committee, until they saw the cost. They scrapped the plans on 11 April 1839, and sent a letter to their colleagues at Bristol warning them against Brunel's extravagances. What was erected at Reading could hardly have been more crude – a pair of flat-roofed block houses, side by side – Brunel's revenge.

The 'block houses', on the south side of the line, nearest the town, accommodated the booking offices, one dedicated to 'up' trains, the other to 'down' trains. Passengers had access to the offices and the platform without the need to use stairs to cross under or over the line. The 'up' and 'down' platforms were separate, but both ran alongside the south town-side of the line, so again, passengers did not have to use stairs to reach a platform.

It was a Brunellian touch – an intense care for detail, a nice thought for passenger convenience – but it was also typically Brunellian in that it lacked operational practicality. The arrangement created delays, as trains crossed in front of each other as they entered and left the station. The system was also installed at Slough, Taunton, Exeter and Gloucester, and lasted at Reading until 1897.

In the Berkshire and Wiltshire bridges Brunel used the warm red Berkshire brick. The Thames at Reading, 36 miles (58 km), is crossed by a red-brick arch with 60 ft (18 m) span and four side arches. The Thames at Gatehampton, 44 miles (71 km), is crossed on a slight skew by four spans, each 64 ft 4 in (20 m) and at Moulsford, $47\frac{1}{2}$ miles (76 km), with four skew spans, each of 87 ft 8 in (26.7 m). Both bridges are in red brick. The Moulsford bridge is the last major civil engineering construction until the Chippenham viaduct, 95 miles (153 km).

At Didcot, 53 miles (85 km), there was no station until 1844, and that which was built was a miserable, wooden place without style. It was merely an interchange in a lonely, grassy moor when Brunel was preoccupied with the new railways and great, maritime adventures.

Between Didcot and Swindon, through 'the Vale', a great grassy moor, with a scattering of villages, Brunel built three stations. At Steventon, $56\frac{1}{2}$ miles

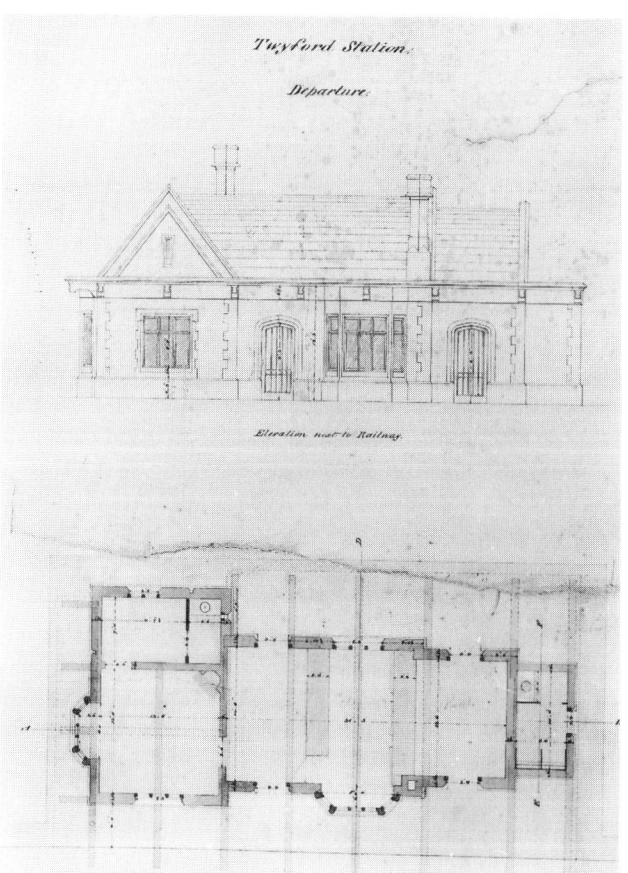

Fig. 5.2 Elevation and plan of Twyford Station, GWR, by I.K. Brunel, 1835. (A. Vaughan)

Elevation towards Rails.

(91 km), the station and goods shed were entirely of timber, and were surely meant to be temporary. The station had a simple, rectangular ground plan, a low, slated roof, with a flat awning extending over the width of the platform to the rails along the length of the building. The awning was supported by very spindly columns, which, coming close to the edge of the platform, must have obstructed movement on and off the trains. All photographs show a simple awning extending a few feet beyond the wall.

Steventon, the halfway point on the railway and beside the main Oxford–Newbury road, was intended to have been the administrative centre of the railway, and was temporarily the station for Oxford until the GWR could overcome university hostility to railways. So while the station building was temporary until the company knew what was going to be required, the administrative offices were going to be permanent.

Brunel supervised the design for a dignified, Bath stone house as the boardroom and offices, a public house, officers' houses and a long row of labourers' cottages – all carefully graded in their degree of space – or pokiness. I say 'supervised' because there is some evidence to suggest that he did not personally design these buildings (Vaughan, 1991, p. 130).

The labourers' cottages were on the downside of the line between the station and Stock's Lane crossing. They consisted of a terrace of nine single-storey dwellings with a two-storey, gabled block at each end. They were built of red brick in the 'Tudor' style, with square-headed windows, blue brick decorations in the walls, under a slated roof topped with tall, rectangular-section chimneys.

The boardroom and office at Steventon remained in use as such for less than six months, although it survives to this day as a dwelling, but the 'temporary' station at Steventon remained in use as a station until demolition in 1965.

The next station was Faringdon Road (Challow from 1864), 64 miles (103 km), near nowhere in particular but serving both Faringdon and Wantage

Fig. 5.3 Elevation of Abingdon Road Station (now Culham), GWR, by I.K. Brunel, 1835. (A. Vaughan)

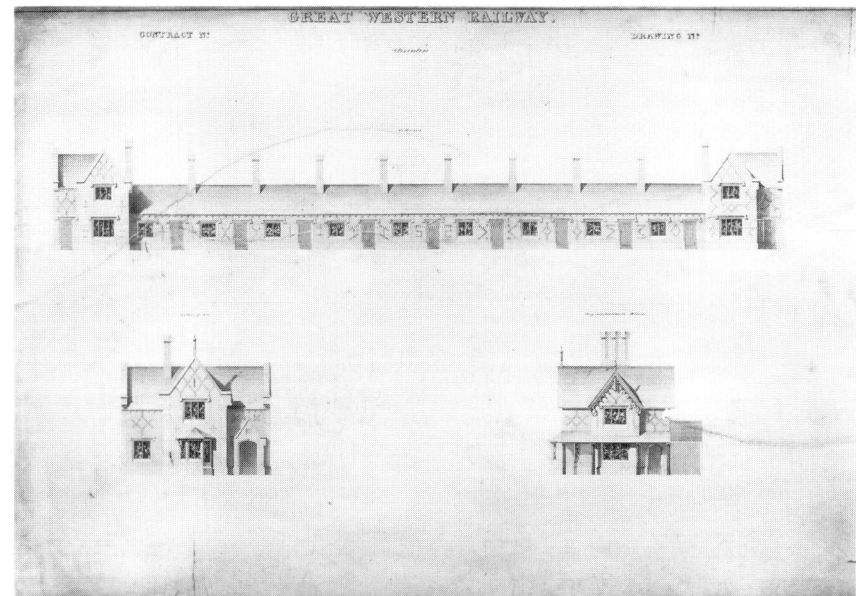

Fig. 5.4 Steventon workmen's cottages on downside of the line, and public house (left) and superintendent's house (right), GWR, by I.K. Brunel. (A. Vaughan)

(Wantage Road station was not built until 1845). It was built to the same design as Steventon, but unlike Steventon it had an enormous red-brick goods shed, somewhat after the style of a Cistercian barn, and at least twice the size of those provided at Shrivenham and Wantage Road. The wooden station was demolished by the GWR, during quadrupling in 1932, but the great goods shed remained until demolition in May 1965.

Shrivenham Station, $71\frac{1}{2}$ miles (115 km), was half a mile south of the village. Brunel provided a standard, wayside design of the type with flint walls, Bath stone quoins and window casings, a wide, all-around canopy and very low-pitched roof. In 1965, protests from Sir John Betjeman against demolition were unsuccessful.

Swindon Junction station, in the jurisdiction of the Bristol Committee, consisted of two island platforms, each with large, two-storey buildings. There were four tracks between the two platforms, the intention obviously being to allow express trains to go dashing through, while other trains and their passengers stood in the 'service area'. The two buildings were connected by a fully enclosed footbridge. Dare I say it? The station was laid out in the same way as certain motorway service stations.

Brunel's buildings, however, were in Bath stone with tall, bay windows in their end walls surmounted by moulded classical pediments. The upper storeys housed a hotel, bedrooms on the south side, dayrooms and a Freemasonic temple on the other. Downstairs there were the usual offices for railway officials and the public – including the famous (or infamous) refreshment rooms.

At Chippenham, high above the main street, Brunel created a delightful, one-off Italian venture. This was a single-storey Bath stone building with a wide, low-pitched roof extending over the platforms. The door and windows had

semicircular heads, the chimneys were actually quite delicate, and there was a simple campanile at one end.

Immediately off the west end of the station's platforms came the absolutely massively solid 'Roman' viaduct. This is followed by a 30 ft (9 m) tall embankment for 2 miles (3 km), into an ever-deepening cutting for 3 miles (5 km), spanned east of Corsham by a magnificent three-arched bridge leading into the Box Tunnel, 3212 yards (2.9 km), commencing at 99 miles (159 km), opening into deep cutting at 101 miles (162 km).

The west end of Box Tunnel, and both ends of the 198 yards (181 m) long Box–Middlehill tunnel that succeeds it, have the most elegant, Bath stone facings, done in Brunellian Roman Imperial style suitable for such a Napoleonic figure as he – three triumphal arches to mark his victory over great odds. With the opening of the Box Tunnel the London to Bristol railway was complete.

There was an additional reason for the triumphalism of Box. A few miles to the south, in the Avon valley, the Kennet & Avon canal crossed the river in a single span. The aqueduct was a major engineering achievement by John Rennie. Brunel had been jealous of the Rennies. He had written of them in his diary in 7 May 1828:

> The young Rennies, *whatever their real merit*, will have built London Bridge . . . while I shall have been engaged on a tunnel which has failed.
> (Vaughan, 1991, p. 31)

Fig. 5.5 Swindon Station, GWR, showing a combination of standard and broad gauge and passenger and freight traffic. Photographed c.1886. (NRM 1238/85)

83

Although he had surpassed John Rennie with the Box Tunnel, the tunnel itself was invisible. He had to make a visible and equal effect to that of the earlier engineer.

Brunel's attitude towards a beautiful landscape is well summed up by his comment to his chief assistant, George Frere, when they came to engineer a railway through the same Avon valley. It was narrow, winding and wooded. Brunel cautioned Frere to be kind to it: 'It is a beautiful valley, it would be a shame to spoil it.'

The Kennet & Avon Canal lay parallel to and above the railway on the down or south side of the proposed line from Bathampton, but at Hampton Row, on the eastern edge of Bath, it swung south as it looped around the lower slope of Bathwick Hill. The railway had to cut through the slope, go under the Warminster Road and avoid the canal. Beyond this road, within the curve of the canal and rising up the hill, were the ornamental Sydney Gardens. These were for the recreation of the inhabitants of the fine terraces of houses stretching to the London (or Poultney) Road. This was a very fashionable area where London courtiers kept their mistresses and lived while attending the pleasures of Bath Spa. When the railway was built it would pass close by the Backs, and the gaze of the plebeian passengers would fall upon the bedroom windows of the Highest in the Land.

Brunel pushed the canal aside, relocating it higher on the hill and levelled the rising ground it had occupied to bring the railway into Bath. He then re-laid Sydney Gardens with grassy walks below great trees. He made the railway part of the park-like garden. The Bath stone concave retaining wall, curving around the hill, buttressed and capped and supporting the cutaway hillside, is a work of art. Bath stone balustrading fringes the track on the gardens' side and a variety of delicate arches, of cast iron and stone, connect the upper and lower levels of

Fig. 5.6 Sydney Gardens, Bath, looking east; iron bridges by I.K. Brunel, 1835. Photographed in 1973. (A. Vaughan)

the gardens. Brunel the landscape gardener is a concept worth pursuing. The entire London to Bristol line was thought out with this in mind.

Bath Station, on a tongue of land within a loop of the River Avon, is approached over the handsome London Road Bridge and St James Viaduct of 37 plain arches. The station has a noble facade in the Jacobean style to face the City. The approach road, Manvers Street, was straightened and realigned, at Brunel's insistence, a couple of feet east, so that the fine building would be exactly central in the vista from the City. The embankment on which the station stands is supported by elegantly turned wing walls; they are indeed like wings, gathering in the travellers to the entrance. The platforms were sheltered by an over-all roof, with a glass windscreen at each end.

Westwards from Bath Station, the Avon was crossed by a twin-arched bridge. The width of the river here is 80 ft (24 m), but the skew of the railway above makes the length of the bridge 164 ft (50 m). Brunel intended an iron bridge, but the contractor failed. In spring 1840 Brunel built a temporary bridge of laminated timber, elliptical ribs decorated with wrought iron tracery in the outermost spandrels. He supervised the work himself, and from starting the design to opening took six months. The work was meant as a stopgap, but was not replaced until 1873.

Beyond the bridge the line runs on a stone viaduct of 73 semicircular arches. In the vicinity of the station this was turreted and crenellated and, where roads or footpaths passed through, pierced with sixteenth-century-style arches.

From Bath to Bristol the style is strongly Tudor or Elizabethan. With the exception of the western bridge over the Avon at Bath, all the under- and over-line bridges, even those just allowing access from field to field, had a sixteenth-

Fig. 5.7 Elevation of Bath Station, GWR, by I.K. Brunel, 1840. (A. Vaughan)

Fig. 5.8 Drawing of the east mouth of Twerton Tunnel, GWR, by I.K. Brunel, c.1840. (A. Vaughan)

Fig. 5.9 Street frontage of Bradford-on-Avon, Wilts, Somerset & Weymouth Railway, Brunel-style design, 1848 and opened 1857. (A. Vaughan)

century-style broad-pointed arch, and were handsomely made in stone, with wing walls also of masonry.

There were seven tunnels between Bath and Bristol: Twerton, 264 yards (241 m); Saltford, 176 yards (161 m); a 53 and a 37 yards long tunnel (48 and 34 m); Fox's Wood No. 3, 1017 yards (930 m); No. 2, 154 yards (141 m); No. 1, 326 yards (298 m). The tunnel portals at Twerton were mock castles complete with twin towers. Fox's Wood No. 2 west end was to have had a mock-castle portal, but heavy rain during construction caused works to collapse. Brunel was very pleased, and gave instructions that it was to be left so that it would become a romantic, ivy-mantled ruin. No. 1 tunnel had a Norman or Romanesque-arched portal.

Shortly after leaving No. 1 tunnel the Avon was crossed by a fine 100 ft (30 m) span masonry arch – flanked by 36 ft (11 m) wide spans; another over the 'Floating Harbour'; and a mile of arches into the terminus. All these arches were in fifteenth-century style.

The station at Bristol Temple Meads had a long 'Tudor' or 'Elizabethan' frontage on the main road. Passenger comfort went to the winds with a long, hard climb to the platforms by a 'Tudor' oak staircase under a sixteenth-century-style ceiling of pendant plasterwork. The wooden platforms were under a roof dressed up to look something like a baronial hall, with mock hammer-beams appearing to support the long, jib-like main beams. Like Steventon, Temple Meads was designed only in part by Brunel. He took a great deal of trouble with the design in general and in detail, but he did it by proxy, corresponding with a resident architect who drew up designs for the great man's approval (Vaughan, 1991, pp. 126–7).

Torquay twilight

Brunel enjoyed the church architecture of Lombardy, which he came to know during his survey work for Italian railways, and at the time he was in advance of general aesthetic fashion in England. The Italian feeling burst out in the warmth and colour of the Devon coast, where he had to provide the stations and buildings to house pumping engines for his atmospheric railway, and they at once recall the churches of Lombardy with their tall campaniles – what elegant chimneys! (Vaughan, 1977, pp. 399–401). He copied from actual churches and wrote regularly to his assistant in Italy, Herschel Babbage, for accurate drawings of this or that detail. Though the 'atmospheric caper' was short-lived, Brunel's remarkable buildings lived on to grace the scene for many years.

In Devon he found the place to create his personal landscape – at Watcombe looking down on Babbacombe Bay, Torquay. He bought the land in parcels from 1849, and spent what spare time he had in planning a country house at the head of the valley, looking down to the bay through carefully landscaped trees. He recruited W.A. Nesfield, adviser on trees to Kew Gardens and the Royal Parks of London, to execute his plans (Vaughan, 1991, p. 203).

Without doubt he intended to set up as a *grand signeur*. He donated funds to rebuild the local church, even though the vicar was very 'High', and he built model housing for his servants. The terraced roads were cut into the hillside; the carefully landscaped groves of trees were planted to give exquisite rides and poignant glimpses of Torbay. The only thing he did not build was his great house.

It was designed, in 1852, by William Burn, in the 'Loire Valley chateau' style. It was so incredibly magnificent that it might be misconstrued as megalomania in stone. The foundations were laid by 1859 – but by then Brunel was very ill. As he lay dying he had to order the sale of the property. He died on 15 September 1859.

Isambard's favourite flower was the blue convolvulus or Morning Glory; it is busy, and makes a new flower each day and dies by the evening. After his death a bunch of Morning Glory buds was sent to his London home, in Duke Street, Westminster, each day by train, to be placed under his portrait.

He had worked like the Morning Glory all his life. He set out to create beauty within the constraints – often outside the constraints – of the Great Western that employed him. The London–Bristol line cost three times its estimate, very largely because of his management methods and his concerns for beauty.

The Brunellian concept remains the major strategic London–Bristol corridor. The concept was so strong that it has not been superseded by the mid-twentieth-century motorway, but remains vital to this very day. The choice and design of the great trunk was brilliant, and can be savoured from Brunel's vantage point, watching a high-speed train as it sweeps through the Goring Gap, shoots the Thames on the noble bridge at Gatehampton, and races westwards on imperceptible gradients, running 80 mph (130 km/h) faster than Isambard's original – and then outrageous – dream.

Select bibliography

Bourne, J.C. (1846) *History and Description of the Great Western Railway*, Bogue, London.

Rolt, L.T.C. (1957) *Isambard Kingdom Brunel: A Biography*, Longman, London.

Vaughan, A. (1977) *A Pictorial Record of Great Western Architecture*, Oxford Publishing Company, Oxford.

Vaughan, A. (1991) *Isambard Kingdom Brunel: Engineering Knight Errant*, John Murray, London.

The Brunel Collection at University of Bristol, the library of the Institution of Civil Engineers, British Rail Civil Engineering Department, and GWR contract drawings held at Swindon were consulted in researching this chapter.

Keith Falconer and Barrie Jones

Railway engineering works:
the legacy

Railway engineering works and their associated settlements are very much the poor relations of the railway heritage. Whereas stations, viaducts and bridges have attracted due attention, the buildings of these constructional and servicing elements of the railway system have received scant recognition, and accordingly they have suffered more harshly through neglect and demolition. Cattell's chapter in this volume discusses the historical context, development and conservation of the railway housing associated with the Swindon Works, and this chapter will look at these issues nationally in respect of railway engineering works themselves. It will focus on the surviving legacy as seen from the perspective of emergency recording undertaken by the Royal Commission on the Historical Monuments of England (RCHME), and will thus provide only an introduction, illustrated by case studies, to a subject that warrants consideration in much greater detail

The historical and technological background to the development by railway companies of an independent engineering capacity is discussed in some detail in relation to Swindon in Cattell and Falconer (1995), and need only be summarized here. The pioneering nature of the development of railways in this country meant that most of the early solutions to what were novel problems were necessarily experimental, often individual, and not always successful. Thus it is difficult to generalize as to the pattern of development of railway engineering works in the first two decades after the opening of the Stockton and Darlington Railway, but trends in solutions to common problems can be identified. Paramount amongst those problems was the limited operational range of early locomotives. Whishaw, the noted railway commentator, recommended, even as late as 1840, that engines should not be run for distances of over 30 miles (48 km) without servicing (Whishaw, 1969).

Chronological overview

The first generation of locomotives on public railways had evolved from the engines that ran on the short-haul colliery tramroads of northern England. They were the product of local, general-purpose, engineering workshops, and the locomotive manufacturing industry became established in centres such as Tyneside, Lancashire and Leeds. These private works are not considered here in any detail, and in any case few buildings survive of the earliest phase other than elements of c.1830 date at the Stephensons' works in Forth Street, Newcastle, the buildings comprising the Timothy Hackworth museum at Shildon, and some fragments of the original buildings at the Vulcan Foundry, Newton-le-Willows.

The first main-line railway – the Liverpool & Manchester – was only 30 miles (48 km) long, and initially had engine sheds at both ends of the line, at Edge Hill in Liverpool and Ordsall Lane in Manchester, and with repair workshops nearby. By 1840 it had consolidated all its heavy repair facilities at Liverpool, where the workshop were shared by the Grand Junction Railway. It was, however, the 112 mile (180 km) long London & Birmingham Railway that was to be the model for many of the succeeding railways. Its central depot at

Fig. 6.1 Interior of the boiler shop, Stephenson's Works, Forth Street, Newcastle upon Tyne. Established in 1823, the works expanded in the 1830s and 1840s. Note the cast-iron columns and timber roof structure of this workshop, which is being restored to house the Robert Stephenson Museum. (RCHME)

Fig. 6.2 Workshop, Shildon Works, Stockton & Darlington Railway, now the Timothy Hackworth Museum. Established in the 1820s, the works was taken over by Timothy Hackworth in 1833. (RCHME)

Wolverton opened on a greenfield site in 1839, and certainly influenced the Great Western Railway in the siting of its 'principal engine establishment' at Swindon in 1841. The original Wolverton works survived until recently, albeit in a much altered condition, but have now been demolished for a supermarket development. The other formative site is Derby, where three adjacent works had been built for separate railways by 1840. The surviving buildings at Derby are discussed in some detail below, as are the nineteenth-century buildings of the Swindon Works.

By the early 1840s the rudiments of a national railway system were in place, and many locomotive depots including Bromsgrove, 1840 (demolished c.1965), Brighton, 1840 (demolished c.1965), Cowlairs, Glasgow, 1842 (demolished c.1968), and Miles Platting, Manchester, 1840 (demolished 1966) had developed into sizeable works.

However, the middle of the decade witnessed such an expansion of the railway network as a result of the railway mania that the private locomotive builders could not cope with the demand for new engines, and the larger railway companies had to 'tool up' to manufacture their own locomotives. In many instances, they were quite ready and willing to do so, as they were facing problems through operating such a variety of rolling-stock from different sources; they had become increasingly dissatisfied with the lack of quality control over engines supplied from outside manufacturers. There had been an earlier false start. The Stockton & Darlington Railway had initially flirted with the manufacture of its own locomotives at its Soho Works in Shildon, but the experiment was abandoned by 1832.

The first tentative steps at self-sufficiency were at Edge Hill, where, following the advice of the Grand Junction Railway's Chief Engineer, Joseph

Locke, that a workforce with ten years' experience of repairing and rebuilding engines were well placed to manufacture them, the works embarked on the small-scale manufacture of locomotives in 1841. In March 1843 Locke transferred the GJR work from Edge Hill to a new maintenance works being built on a 3 acre (1.2 ha) site at Crewe – at a junction on the GJR's own line. The Crewe Works officially opened in December 1843, and its location reflected those at Wolverton and Swindon. The Crewe Works was involved from the outset, albeit to a limited extent, in the manufacture of locomotives. *Tamerlane*, which had been started in Liverpool, was completed in October 1843, but it was not until July 1845 that *Columbine*, an entirely Crewe-built engine, was finished. The Old Works at Crewe, as the depot was to be known, were entered from the railway via a handsome masonry arch surmounted by a clock tower, but were disused by the early 1970s and demolished. Many of the other existing works, including Derby, Miles Platting, Swindon and Wolverton, were considerably expanded to take on this new role, but there were also several new works, such as Ashford, 1847 and Stratford, 1847, built specifically to manufacture as well as repair locomotives and rolling-stock. Many of the early buildings survive at Ashford, but the Stratford site has been cleared.

This trend continued throughout the next few decades, with several new works being built to replace existing works on cramped or now inappropriate sites. Thus the Great Northern Railway moved its works from Boston to Doncaster in 1853. In 1856 the Caledonian Railway moved its works from Greenock to Springburn, Glasgow. There, the new St Rollox Works were designed from the outset to build and repair locomotives, carriages and wagons, but now, much reduced in size, operate only as a maintenance depot. In 1858 the GWR expanded the Stafford Road Works, Wolverhampton, to be the

Fig. 6.3 Clock tower of the old works, Crewe, Grand Junction Railway, 1843. Became the principal works of the L&NWR in 1846. Photograph taken in 1973 prior to demolition. (RCHME)

operational base of its standard-gauge Northern Division. The works had been built in 1849 by the Shrewsbury & Birmingham Railway to repair rolling-stock but, from 1859, under the Armstrong brothers, Joseph and George, they additionally manufactured standard-gauge locomotives. The site has now been cleared. The North Eastern Railway moved its locomotive works from Soho, Shildon, to Darlington in 1863, leaving Shildon to concentrate on wagons. Even more drastically, in 1887 the Lancashire & Yorkshire Railway transferred its works from Miles Platting and Bury to a greenfield site at Horwich, where an entire integrated works and settlement were built in the space of a few years. Most of the works buildings survive in changed use, as do the terraces of housing, each named after a famous railway engineer.

New works, especially for the construction of wagons and carriages, continued to be built well into the twentieth century, only to fall victim to the rationalization of the industry under British Rail in the 1960s. York gained a large carriage works in 1884, which operated until 1995 (see below); Temple Mills Wagon Works, London, was built in 1896 and closed in 1965; Lancing Carriage Works opened in 1888 and closed in 1962; Eastleigh Carriage works, built in 1891, closed in 1968. The locomotive works at Eastleigh fared better; built in 1909 it is one of the few works still operating. The most northerly integrated works, that at Inverurie, Aberdeenshire, was opened in 1903, and though it closed in 1969 many of the stone-built shops survived until 1995, when the fine erecting and boiler shop was due to be demolished. Faverdale Carriage Works near Darlington has the distinction of being the shortest-lived works: it opened in 1923 and closed only 39 years later, in 1962.

Four case studies are presented here, the first three dealing with what are probably the most important surviving complexes of railway engineering works buildings – those at Derby, Swindon and Ashford. They will demonstrate the very different approaches of the railway companies to the design of their early works buildings, and will show the richness of the legacy that still, somewhat precariously, survives. They will also highlight the inadequacy of the protection given to the later buildings at these crucial sites, a point that will be underscored by the last case study – York Carriage Works. York is included as representative of the later generations of railway workshops, which constituted the majority of buildings on most sites. These later structures are often quite spectacular in scale, and of considerable interest in construction, but have attracted few champions, and on most closed sites have been swept away.

As mentioned earlier, the problem that faced early locomotive engineers was the maintenance (and frequently repair) of locomotives after each run, varying between 30 miles (48 km) on the intensively worked Liverpool & Manchester Railway and 80 miles (129 km) on the eastern section of the GWR. Such maintenance was undertaken in engine sheds, which varied greatly in shape and arrangement. None of the sheds dating to the 1830s survives, but Whishaw (1842) describes in some detail the engine houses of the London & Birmingham Railway at Camden, London, Wolverton and Birmingham, while Bourne (1839) illustrates that at Camden. These were all rectangular, with turntables to manoeuvre the engines. The layout at Wolverton, being the 'principal station for locomotive engines' on the most prestigious line built to date, should, one might have thought, have greatly influenced the next generation of works.

However, such was the experimental nature of railway development at this time that architects such as Francis Thompson and engineers such as Brunel, while taking cognizance of the locational factors and facilities at Wolverton, came up with their own solutions.

Derby

The history of the Derby locomotive works has its origins in the mid-1830s, when three major railway enterprises were under consideration in the Midlands, based on a network of routes linking Derby, Nottingham, Leeds and Birmingham. The companies engaged in promoting these lines were, respectively, the Midland Counties, North Midland and Birmingham & Derby Junction railways, which all shared the common destination of Derby. As these schemes evolved, several factors encouraged efforts towards a uniting of the companies' resources at Derby, not least of which were the reduced cost of building one combined station and the potential revenue to be gained from through traffic. It was also decided that Derby would be the most suitable location for all three companies' locomotive and rolling-stock maintenance depots. The site chosen was conveniently situated next to the Derby Canal, but the natural ground levels were low and inclined to flooding, so that the ground had to be raised artificially by around 8 ft (2.4 m) to place the passenger station and main works yard above potential flood levels.

The Midland Counties Railway opened in June 1839, the Birmingham & Derby Junction opened the following August, and the first stage of the North Midland Railway in May 1840. The works, begun in the autumn of 1839 and completed in 1840, comprised three quite separate groups of workshops and running sheds. The Midland Counties Railway also had carriage and wagon shops in Leicester until 1842, when work was transferred to Derby. The segregated facilities prevailed for four years until May 1844, when the mutual interests of the companies led finally to their amalgamation to form the Midland Railway. The original workshops of the Midland Counties and North Midland Railways have survived largely intact, and now form a group of unique listed buildings, including the famous North Midland roundhouse, in the centre of a rapidly changing City Challenge Area.

These buildings provide a fascinating insight into the early evolution of railway workshops. The individual character of the overall schemes employed by each railway company, and yet the similarities demonstrated in some of the constructional detail, gives testimony to the lack of design precedents, the extent of specialized building/engineering technology then available, and the wide range of thought on the subject at that time.

The works of the Birmingham & Derby Junction Railway, which was demolished prior to 1881, originally comprised a running and repair shed 150 ft (46 m) long and 48 ft (15 m) wide, which was built by T. & W. Cooper at a cost of £4000. It incorporated a smiths' shop and an office. The shed, which is shown on the site plan of the works in 1844, had a simple rectangular plan, and encompassed three parallel railway lines, which entered the north end of the building, nearest to the passenger station. The tracks were linked by three turntables, arranged in line, a short way to the north.

In contrast, the North Midland Railway facilities were rather more impressive, costing some £62 000 to construct, and including a clock tower and offices, a roundhouse, carriage and engine repair shops and smiths' shops. The workshops were designed by the architect Francis Thompson, whose appointment was made by Robert Stephenson. Thompson designed the buildings around three sides of a low-level rectangular yard, making use of the site's contrasting ground levels to enable this yard, at canal level, to link with extensive basements beneath each of the buildings. In one corner of the yard Thompson designed a 16-sided polygonal running shed, 130 ft (40 m) in diameter, and known as the roundhouse. This stands over a raised basement, with access to the ground floor from the tracks on the level of the upper yard and passenger station. The roundhouse consists of brick outer walls with an internal polygonal colonnade of cast-iron columns, which is concentric with the outer walls and supports a 'ring' of cast-iron beams. The roof structure is principally of wooden construction, with some ironwork in the form of plates and shoe seatings for the timbers. The roundhouse accommodates 16 stable tracks, each one originally capable of standing two engines, although two of the tracks were used for bringing locomotives in and out of the roundhouse, via a central turntable. The access tracks were covered by single-storeyed entrance blocks, each of which has a fine stone and brick portal facing towards the passenger station. The basement has an inspection pit beneath each track, these being used for raking out ash and clinker, and for carrying out minor repairs and servicing. Between the inspection pits the basement has a series of wedge-shaped chambers, used for storage, and which are of fireproof construction.

Across the front of the roundhouse, enclosing one corner of the yard, Thompson built offices, again constructed of brick with sandstone dressings, and including a fine pedimented entrance flanked by rusticated stone pilasters. The office was originally single storeyed, but was raised in height in two subsequent phases to give three floors. Above the entrance to the offices a clock tower was built, and which was also raised as the adjoining office building was heightened. The office basement is of fireproof construction, and probably contained mess rooms, foremen's offices and stores, all of which were accessed solely from the low-level yard.

Adjoining the office and roundhouse, extending along two sides of the yard, were the carriage and engine shops, each of which had a smiths' shop at its extreme end. The engine shop, which was 184 ft (56 m) long and 70 ft (21 m) wide, was destroyed by fire in the 1950s, but was of a form and construction similar to that of the carriage shop. The carriage shop is 191 ft (58 m) long and 70 ft (21 m) wide, and for its time was advanced in its design, built with brick walls and with an internal cast-iron frame. The building was originally of two storeys with a basement store, the basement and ground floors having two rows of cast-iron columns carrying cast-iron beams and timber joists. The first floor was carried in part using trussed composite timber and iron beams. The roof, like that of the roundhouse, was largely of timber construction, with some cast iron used for joints and timber seatings. The carriage shop was particularly well lit, with large cast-iron window frames set beneath segmental gauged brick arches. It originally had a single track entrance from which, it is assumed, the rolling-stock was transferred through the building by means of turntables. In

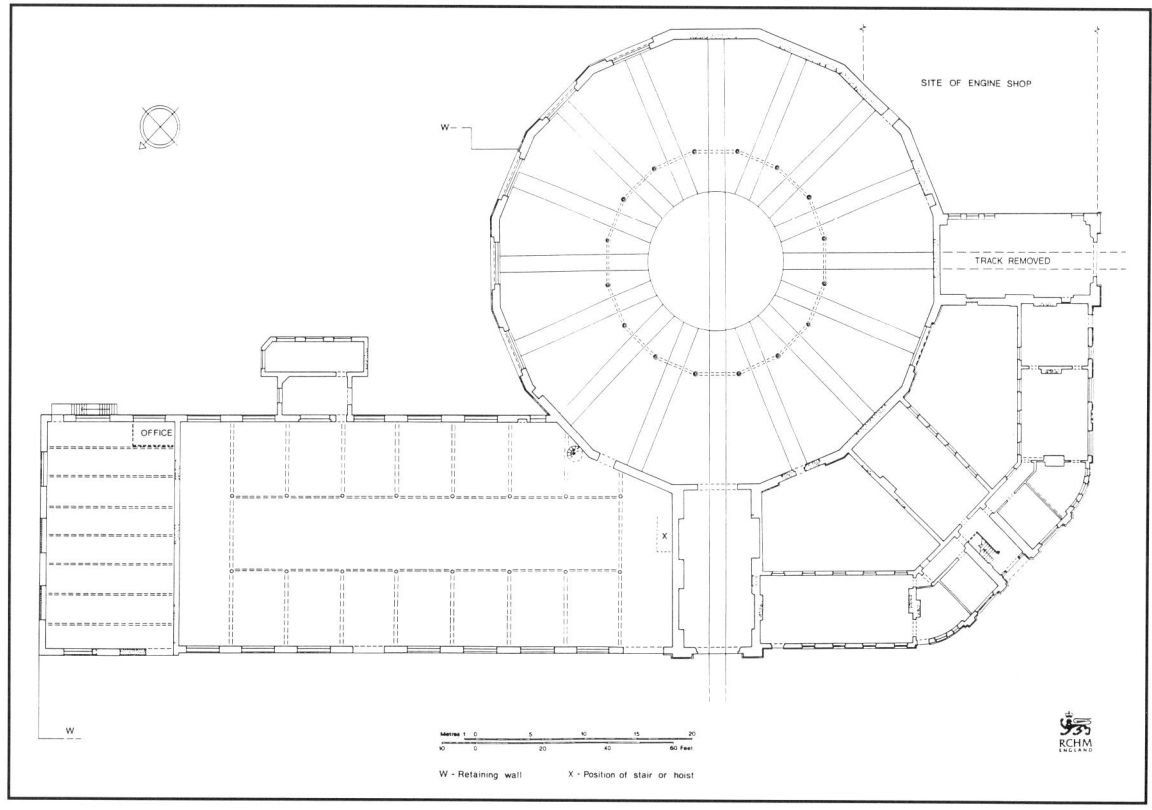

Fig. 6.4 Ground plan of the North Midland Railway roundhouse, workshop and office, Derby, 1839–40. The plan of the carriage shop (left of centre), with a blacksmiths' shop at one end, was originally repeated for the engine shop (top right), which was destroyed by fire in the 1950s. (RCHME)

contrast, the engine shop had a range of eight parallel tracks entering the west side of the building, and which were linked by a line of eight turntables. The third side of the North Midland yard was occupied by a range of buildings that were demolished in the nineteenth century, but which appear to have accommodated forges and smiths' shops. On its fourth side the yard was open to the Derby Canal.

The Midland Counties Railway also had a substantial works, comprising three separate buildings: a running shed, a large maintenance workshop and a blacksmiths' shop. The running shed and workshop were built in line with one-another, with the smiths' shop standing at 90° to them. The Midland Counties Railway buildings were built of brick with gauged brick semicircular arches to the windows and doors. The 134 ft (41 m) long running shop, demolished in recent years, was adjoined by a repair shop 93 ft (28 m) long with a width that expanded from 52 ft (16 m) to 88 ft (27 m). It was single storey, and built using pier-and-panel construction.

The main workshop range comprises a single-storeyed maintenance block and a two-storeyed block containing fitting and turning shops. In its entirety the building is 200 ft (161 m) long and 93 ft (28 m) wide, and incorporated a stationary beam engine for driving the machinery within the building, much of which was situated on the first floor. The single-storeyed maintenance shop has two rows of cast-iron columns supporting the roof, which is principally of

96

timber construction, similar to the type of form found in the North Midland Railway buildings. In the north end there were originally entrances for two railway tracks, each one occupying an aisle of the building, and leaving the third aisle for use as a working area. One of the tracks, in the west aisle, continued through into the two-storeyed part of the building. Here the ground floor is divided by an axial brick wall and two rows of cast-iron columns support trussed beams similar to those used in the North Midland Railway carriage shop. The roof structure is similar to that used over the single-storeyed maintenance shop.

The smiths' shop was originally of a tall single storey, with an L-plan, and is built of brick to match the other Midland Counties buildings. At the time of recording by RCHME, the significance of the Midland Counties workshops and smiths' shop had not been recognized. The buildings were unprotected and were awaiting demolition, but have now been listed Grade II*.

In 1844 the three companies amalgamated to form the Midland Railway, and the disparate works were integrated. On the basis of an 1866 Midland Railway plan it would seem that the layout of the North Midland workshops determined the functions of the various buildings in the combined works. The carriage shop was given over to wagon repairs, as was the Midland Counties running shed.

Fig. 6.5 Interior of the roundhouse, North Midland Works, Derby, 1839–40. cast-iron frame and radiating roof trusses; cast-iron shoe seatings form crucial timber joints. (RCHME)

The latter company's main workshop was used for carriage repairs and painting. Engine repairs and construction centred initially on the North Midland Railway engine shops, although with extensive additional ranges built during the 1850s and 1860s. The original roundhouse was augmented by two other 'round' running sheds, built in 1847 and 1852, and the original roundhouse was soon found to be too small for the railway's larger locomotives, and was used for the repairs to those engines that it could accommodate. In the early 1850s the works built the Midland Railway's first in-house locomotives, and by 1880 had increased in size several-fold, with new buildings including iron and brass foundries, boiler shops, spring smiths, coppersmiths, paint shops and a gas works. In the mid-1870s carriage and wagon manufacturing and repair were transferred from the original works to a new site, Litchurch Lane, Derby, and the works then concentrated solely on locomotive work. In successive reorganizations the original workshops were downgraded in use. The carriage shop was altered to form a minor erecting shop, by removing the central part of the first floor and installing a travelling crane. As for the Midland Counties workshops, these were rapidly converted for use as stores, including the running shed, and the group retained this function for the greater part of their working life. Typically, most of the extensive later buildings that supplanted the original buildings were unprotected, and were cleared in 1995, leaving only the small 1840s core.

Swindon

Brunel had the advantage of seeing both Wolverton and Derby in operation while he was designing the engine houses for the GWR, and his private sketchbooks show that he was open minded as to the configuration of these buildings. Thus he used a wooden and cast-iron framed roundhouse (modelled on Derby) for the temporary shed at Paddington, and sketched several layouts of rectangular engine houses served by turntables for that at Bristol. Brunel was uncertain where to locate his 'principal engine establishment', and initially considered Reading and Didcot but decided on a location further west. In September 1840 his 'locomotive superintendent' Daniel Gooch recommended the junction of the GWR and the Great Western Union Railway at Swindon as being 'by far the best point we have for a Central Engine Station'. Gooch's letter was accompanied by a plan showing a huge roundhouse with radiating engine sheds and workshops, but Brunel's sketchbooks show that he had already several months earlier decided on a novel arrangement for his principal maintenance facility, comprising a long running shed parallel with the railway, with a large engine house at right angles served by a traversing table with ancillary workshops and offices forming an open courtyard. The running shed as built was 490 ft (149 m) long, and its four lines of track could hold 48 engines and tenders, while the engine house to the north was 290 ft by 140 ft (88 m by 43 m) with side stalls for 36 engines. Most of the buildings were of a distinctive pier-and-panel construction, partly for reasons of economy, but also enabling them to be lightly founded on the heavy clay.

Bourne's illustration of the engine house is well known, but little survives of the central buildings other than the western wall of the engine house and two relocated bas-reliefs of a Firefly-class locomotive. The eastern range of offices, stores, workshops and smiths' shops have survived, albeit in an altered state, and the headquarters of the RCHME and the National Monuments Record are housed in the southern part of the range. The northern two-storey range still retains its unique trussed wooden floor girders, designed by Brunel to carry steam-driven machinery over a clear space 210 ft (64 m) long by 45 ft (14 m) wide.

Within four years of opening, the facilities at Swindon were greatly extended to provide a manufacturing capacity for both locomotives and wagons. Further courtyards of pier-and-panel construction were built to the north and west, and the works achieved the extent and appearance depicted in Edward Snell's painting of 1849. The northern courtyard was demolished in the rationalization of the works in the 1960s, but many of the buildings of the western courtyard – including the two-storey machine shop and the Fox & Henderson metal roof trusses of the paint shop and smiths' shops – survive, incorporated in later developments.

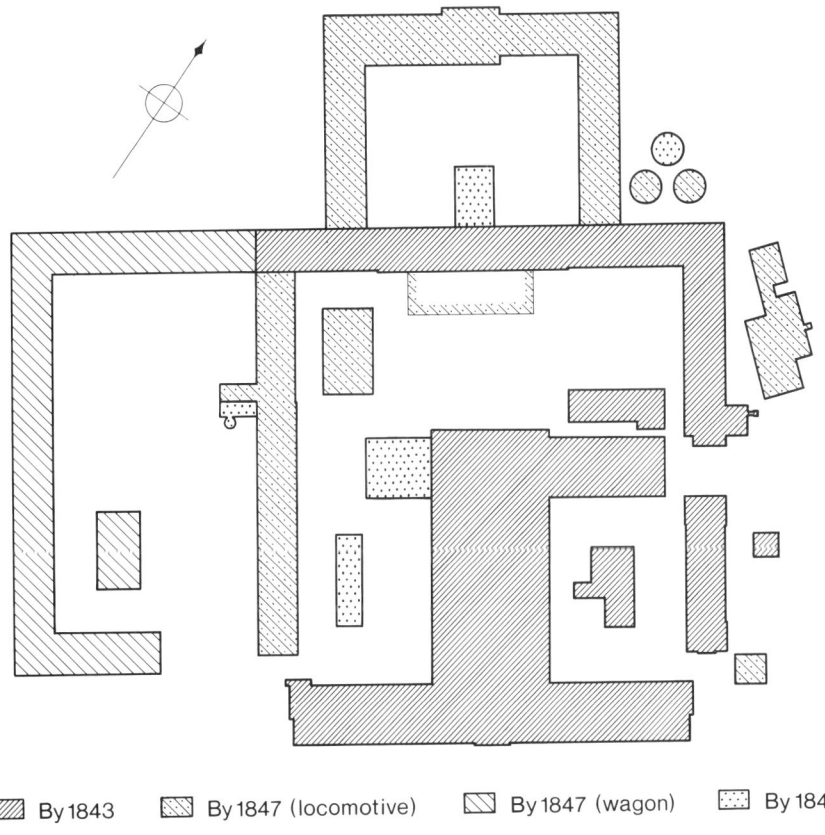

By 1843   By 1847 (locomotive)   By 1847 (wagon)   By 1849

100   0   500 Feet

100   0   100 Metres

Fig. 6.6 Development plan of the early core of GWR Works, Swindon, 1842–49. Designed in 1842 as a maintenance and repair facility; rapid expansion occurred over the next seven years to provide a manufacturing capability for locomotives and wagons. (RCHME)

99

Fig. 6.7 Aerial photograph of the historic core of the GWR Works, Swindon, looking west, taken in 1987. The L-shaped building in the foreground was the general offices of the GWR, and was converted in 1994 to house the headquarters of the RCHME and the National Monuments Record. (RCHME)

The next major expansion was achieved under Joseph Armstrong, Daniel Gooch's successor as Locomotive and Carriage Superintendent, from 1864 onwards. Initially, he consolidated developments on the original site by roofing over the courtyards on either side of the engine house, extending the office block eastwards and infilling the northern courtyard. From 1869 onwards he also built a large carriage works to the south of the main railway line on land that was occupied by the large gardens of houses of senior company officials. Though essentially simple, large covered single-storey workshops framed by tall cast-iron columns, the carriage works was built level with the main line and had a lower level housing a large canteen, workshops and the main subway entrance to the locomotive works. The formidable two-storey high, cliff-like exterior presented to the town was so reminiscent of a prison or fortress that the term 'working inside' was applied to works employees.

The earlier of the roofed courtyards dating from 1865 survives in use as steam locomotive restoration workshops, and hopefully will soon house the proposed railway heritage centre; but the huge eastern No. 19 shop has been demolished, and only a listed wall of 1874 has been retained. The 1874 chain test house, with its original hydraulic testing machinery, is listed Grade II*, and with its adjacent spring shop, which is being used as a go-kart circuit at present, will be restored as part of the commercial rehabilitation of the northern buildings. Churchward House, the former works manager's office, has already been restored as high-class office accommodation. Much of the central portion of the carriage works survives in use as an industrial estate, while the buildings of the western section, which housed the steam-driven sawmills, have been cleared for car parking. The facade to Bristol and London Streets has survived relatively unaltered.

By the early 1870s Armstrong had run out of space within the original site, and he embarked on a most ambitious scheme to build a new integrated locomotive works on an adjoining site, effectively doubling the size of the works. The new buildings were mostly brick built, in contrast to the masonry of the earlier buildings, but he did provide a masonry facade to the foundry, which faced the main line. Much of the 1870s complex survives, and is listed Grade II* in recognition of its technological interest. The 57-bay eastern elevation of the main building machine shops is virtually intact, though partially obscured by minor later accretions. The huge erecting shops behind stretch back to Rodbourne road, where their gable ends and arcaded boundary wall form a *tour de force* in brick. To the north and south, however, they have been demeaned by mean twentieth-century elevations. They were extended northwards in 1879 and to the south by 1886. Their magnificent double-tiered, cast-iron-columned interiors bear witness to these changes, though the southern wall of the original building has been retained within the expansion. The large tender and paint shop to the north has similarly been mistreated, and now retains only its eastern elevation unaltered, but its cast-iron-framed interior still retains some of its overhead cranes. There are plans to convert the main buildings, with relatively little physical disturbance, into a massive factory outlet shopping mall, which would be the largest of its kind in southern England. The ancillary buildings, such as the Hooter House and Pattern Store, would be converted into bars and restaurants, while the foundry building to the south would then house the locomotive restoration workshops displaced by the Railway Heritage Centre.

Most of the later development of the works took place to the west of Rodbourne Road and to the east of the Gloucester line. The famous A shop, which at the time of its construction was claimed to be the largest covered workshop in the world, and almost all the other later buildings, other than the central stores, the steaming shed and the weigh-house and turntable, have been cleared. The weigh-house is being converted into a real ale brewery and its machinery moved to the Heritage Centre, while the turntable is being restored *in situ*. The future of the other buildings is as yet undecided. The works, which once stretched for more than 1½ miles (2.5 km) alongside the main line and occupied an area of 326 acres (130.4 ha), has shrunk to an area of 38 acres (15.4 ha), which approximates to its nineteenth-century extent. Fortunately, almost all the buildings of the historic core are protected, and little further demolition is proposed.

Should all the various heritage and retail schemes come to fruition, the buildings of the works will be opened up to the public in a way quite unthinkable in the days of the GWR. It will be part of a new cultural quarter developing in Swindon focused on the former GWR buildings. This quarter will include the restored railway village, the rehabilitated Milton Road baths and leisure complex, the town museum and art gallery (relocated to the Barracks when the latter is vacated by the move of the GWR Museum to the Railway Heritage Centre across the line), and, hopefully, a restored Mechanics Institute. When seen alongside the National Monuments Record Centre the quarter will become a cultural centre of considerable national importance.

Ashford

The works at Ashford were the creation of the South Eastern Railway, which moved its locomotive repair facilities from New Cross in 1847. While not quite in the same league as Crewe, Derby or Swindon, Ashford nevertheless was of considerable importance, with a workforce of several thousand at its peak in the 1920s and host to a succession of notable engineers such as R.C. Mansell, James Stirling, Harry S. Wainwright, R.E.L. Maunsell and O.V. Bulleid. It also shared several of the features of the larger works. It was built on a greenfield site at a main junction, and from the outset had to provide some company housing. This grew into a self-contained railway settlement of 272 houses complete with company schools, public baths, shops and a public house.

Benefiting from several years' experience at New Cross, and able to observe the major developments at Crewe, Derby, Wolverton and Swindon, the Southern Railway pioneered a somewhat novel working arrangement, which combined elements of Wolverton and Swindon. The integrated locomotive works comprised a single long range, served by a traversing table in a central avenue with an arcaded maintenance and erecting shop and steam-driven machine shops on one side, and associated smiths' shops and boiler shops and tender shops on the other side.

This longitudinal arrangement had the advantage of being easily extended in both directions; and, indeed, in three separate phases it more than trebled its original length of 396 ft (121 m) by 1912. These extensions were carefully designed to match the original buildings, and in 1990, when plans were being drawn up to redevelop the site in association with the construction of the new Ashford International Station, it was thought that no early buildings of significance had survived, and the entire range was dismissed as of twentieth-century date. Fieldwork soon proved that most of the 1847 works, including the beam engine house and water tank in addition to the workshops mentioned above, constituted the central core of the range, and accordingly they were recommended for statutory protection.

Extensive carriage and wagon works were built to the south of the locomotive works in 1850, and over the next half century were greatly extended at the north-west end of the site, which by now was becoming cramped. The next generation of large carriage shops, constructed in 1898 and 1900 and named Klondyke and Kimberley respectively, had therefore to be built on a detached site alongside the Hastings line. The Kimberley sheds were demolished in the 1980s and the Klondyke sheds in the early 1990s. On the main site, part of the carriage and wagon works survives, including the re-roofed shell of the original wagon shops and machine shops, a paint store of c.1860 with a fine cast- and wrought-iron-framed roof, and the interesting, and largely unaltered, north-western complex, which developed in stages between 1860 and 1898, by which time it was equipped with an automatic sprinkler system fed by tanks in a water tower. Most of the early buildings have been listed, but their future is uncertain, pending expansion of the new International Station nearby.

York Carriage Works

In 1880 the North Eastern Railway determined to concentrate carriage production and maintenance on a greenfield site in York, and the first phase of the Holgate Road works was begun in 1880–81. In the 1860s it had removed wagon manufacture and repairs from the original locomotive, wagon and carriage workshops, opened in 1842, on Queen Street near York station.

Fig. 6.8 Exterior of building, varnish and paint shop, NER Carriage Works, York. The workshops, dating from the early 1880s, were extended in the late 1890s and the building shop was rebuilt following a fire in 1944. The complex was run by ABB until its closure early in 1996. (RCHME)

The carriage works was opened in 1884 as a fully integrated facility, with workshops purpose built for the particular processes involved. The workshops include painting and varnishing shops, a sawmill, smiths' shop and machine shops. They are built of brick, with bands of contrasting coloured brick and stone dressings, and have internal frames constructed of cast-iron columns and wrought-iron beams. The works was laid out to facilitate a production flow, and subsequent expansion such as that between 1896 and 1900 involved extending the main workshops *en masse*, in one direction, presumably to minimize disruption to the lines of production.

By 1906 the works catered for the entire production and the majority of the maintenance of carriage stock for the North Eastern Railway, and also a large proportion of the East Coast Joint Stock and Great Northern and North Eastern Joint Stock. By the same year the works occupied an area of over 45 acres (18 ha), and had 13 acres (5 ha) of roofed buildings. The works incorporated a wheel shop, stores, frame shop and carriage-building shop, and in addition specialized shops for woodcarving, cabinet-making, polishing and gas-fitting, the latter, in the early 1900s, being extended to include an area for servicing and repairing electric carriage lighting systems.

Following the Grouping of 1923, the carriage works became the principal carriage works of the LNER, and long after nationalization in 1948 continued its specific role of carriage manufacture and repair. With the works having closed early in 1996 the future of the buildings is uncertain.

Conclusion

The Derby locomotive works originated in 1839–40, Swindon in 1842 and Ashford in 1847. The surviving structures on these sites are therefore of great significance in the history of the railway workshop, and tell us a great deal about contemporary railway practice. Their subsequent evolution is no less interesting or informative, reflecting the expansion of the railway network that caused the great locomotive shortage of the 1840s and 1850s and the separation of locomotive work from carriage and wagon work, with each branch having specialized buildings. Many of the earliest and most significant sites have already been demolished with no attempt at reuse; those that do survive must be treated more sympathetically. Even more threatened are the later buildings, and if only the currently protected buildings are to survive, the engineering works element of the railway heritage will be represented by buildings dating from only the first 50 years of development; the succeeding century will have no testimony. The impressive restoration of several important buildings at Swindon and the exciting plans for all the protected buildings on that site have demonstrated the potential of railway engineering works for successful reuse. The significance of other such sites must now be urgently assessed, and the appropriate protection accorded, so that the preserved buildings of the railway heritage truly represent that heritage in all its ramifications.

Select bibliography

Bourne, J.C. (1839) *Drawings on the London and Birmingham . . . with an Historical and Descriptive account by John Britton, FSA*, Ackerman, London.

Cattell, J. and Falconer, K. (1995) *Swindon: The Legacy of a Railway Town*, HMSO, London.

Larkin, E. and Larkin J. (1988) *The Railway Workshops of Britain 1823–1986*, Macmillan Press, London.

Larkin, E. (1992) *An Illustrated History of British Railways' Workshops*, Oxford Publishing Company, Sparkford.

Radford, J. (1971) *Derby Works and Midland Locomotives*, Ian Allan, London.

Spedding, R. (1988) *Shildon Wagon Works*, Durham County Library, Durham.

Whishaw, F. (1842, repr. 1969) *Railways of Great Britain and Ireland*, David & Charles, Newton Abbot.

John Cattell

Swindon Railway Village

Two years ago, staff from the Swindon and Salisbury Offices of the Royal Commission on the Historical Monuments of England began a project to survey and research the surviving buildings making up the former Great Western Railway Works at Swindon. The project arose in response to moves to redevelop the site for commercial and retail uses, and the need to record the various workshop buildings prior to their conversion and, in some cases, demolition. Also, one of the most architecturally impressive buildings on the site, the former General Office building, has recently been refurbished as the Royal Commission's new head office, and renamed the National Monuments Record Centre to underscore the organization's role as the curator of the national archive on historic buildings and archaeological sites.

Why should an organization like the Royal Commission, with its national remit, devote itself to the detailed study of a single site? There are several reasons. First, Swindon was the principal locomotive (and later carriage and wagon) works for the Great Western Railway, which in its heyday was responsible for a rail network stretching from London to the Midlands and down to Cornwall. 'God's Wonderful Railway' has long been an alluring and romantic subject for rail historians. The grandeur of its buildings and structures, the immense achievements of Isambard Kingdom Brunel as its first engineer, and the company's revolutionary but eventually ill-fated broad-gauge engines, have all contributed to its continuing appeal. The Swindon Works itself, which was opened on 2 January 1843 with a complement of about 180 men, was by the mid-twentieth century providing direct employment for over 14 000 people. By the time the company was nationalized in 1948 the works site had expanded from its original two fields to cover an area of 325 acres (131 ha), stretching for over 1.5 miles (2.4 km) from east to west, and it was claimed that the works were one of the largest in the world.

While initial recording work was focused on the works, it quickly became apparent that the factory buildings could not be considered in isolation from the cottages and welfare buildings erected by the GWR for its employees at Swindon, and it was decided to give equal emphasis to the latter, extending the scope of the project to include an analysis of the company's influence on the wider development of the town. The results of the study were published by the Royal Commission in late 1995. Other authors have dealt with the engineering achievements of the GWR at Swindon, but there has never been a detailed study made of the company's surviving buildings and what they can tell us about the lives of the inhabitants in the nineteenth and early twentieth centuries.

The subject of this chapter, the Swindon Railway Village, consists of 300 cottages and larger dwellings built for the GWR from 1842 to 1866. It is the

Fig. 7.1 Detail of a birds-eye panorama showing Swindon Railway Village, by Edward Snell, 1849. The church, parsonage and school are in the foreground, part of the works to the left, and the station and canal in the distance. (RCHME)

best-preserved early railway estate in the country. Much of the early railway housing in rival settlements such as Wolverton, Derby and Crewe has been demolished in recent years. The Swindon Railway Village, which, as we shall see, came close to suffering a similar fate in the 1960s, survived, and from 1970 was restored and refurbished by Swindon Borough Council to exceptionally high standards.

Works and village

In order to understand how this settlement came to be built in a remote part of rural North Wiltshire, it is necessary to look briefly at the early history of the company and the choice of Swindon as its principal locomotive repair facility. The Act of Parliament for the creation of the Great Western Railway, which was to connect London with Bristol, received Royal Assent in 1835. Its termini were to be located at Paddington and at Temple Meads in Bristol. The main line was to be joined at Swindon by a branch line to Cheltenham built by the Cheltenham & Great Western Union Company. The London–Bristol route was reconnoitred by the GWR's engineer, Isambard Kingdom Brunel. Brunel was conscious that a sizeable locomotive works would be required for the repair of the engines working the line, and his initial preferences for the location of the works were Reading and Didcot. However, it was his young Locomotive Superintendent, Daniel Gooch, who made a well-reasoned case for the choice of Swindon as the site best suited for the new works.

Although Swindon is much closer to Bristol than it is to London, it is also the highest point on the line. It separates the gentle gradient to the east from a series of steep inclines to the west, of which Wootton Bassett and Box were the most severe. Gooch argued that the choice of Swindon was a logical one from the operational viewpoint, because it would be necessary at first to change engines there to cope with the severe gradients to the west. Also, a large passenger station would be required at Swindon to allow passengers to change beween the two lines. Gooch's one reservation was the likely difficulty in obtaining sufficient water for the new establishment. However, the Wilts and Berks and the North Wilts Canals met at a point just to the south-east of Swindon Junction, and he was confident that sufficient water could be obtained from these sources. In the early days of railway freight, coal, coke and other raw materials could be transported to the factory more cheaply by canal than by rail.

Gooch's recommendation was endorsed by Brunel and accepted by the company directors on 6 October 1840, and planning for the new factory and a settlement to house the workforce was begun. The site lay about 1 mile (1.6 km) to the north of the hill-top market town of Swindon, in a marshy and sparsely populated area of the Vale of the White Horse. Writing in 1875, the author and naturalist Richard Jefferies described the site in 1840 as

> the poorest in the neighbourhood; low-lying, shallow soil on an endless depth of stiff clay, worthless for arable purposes, of small value for pasture, covered with furze rushes and rowen.

The local economy was reliant on agriculture, and the majority of the population were rural labourers or tradesmen with no experience of heavy engineering. This meant that the skilled artisans needed to run a factory of this type would have to be imported, with their families, from the heavy industrial areas of Scotland and the north of England, as well as Bristol and the textile-milling areas of Gloucestershire. An analysis of the 1851 census statistics for New Swindon, as the settlement became known, shows that 92% of GWR employees residing in the railway village were from outside Wiltshire. Most of the remaining 8% were employed as general labourers in the factory.

The GWR was conscious that in order to attract men of this calibre to a greenfield site it would have to build a suitable settlement with adequate housing, shops, a market, a school and a church. Brunel, while designing a temporary station and repair works at Wootton Bassett Road just to the west of Swindon in 1840, was also turning his mind to the layout of the new settlement. In late 1840 he sketched two possible designs for it. The one that was adopted by the company consisted of terraces of cottages arranged parallel to the main line to form a grid. In the centre was an area of open ground, while the buildings that bordered it are shown hatched, suggesting that they were to incorporate shops or houses for senior employees. Thus this part of the village seems to have been earmarked by Brunel as the civic and commercial heart of the settlement. An expanded version of this 1840 sketch plan was to be translated into stone and mortar, a process that was largely complete by 1854, although company building work continued in the village on a small scale until the 1870s.

In the provision of different types of accommodation in the village, Brunel drew heavily on the example of Wolverton, an important station and repair establishment on the London & Birmingham Railway, erected on a greenfield site from 1838. By the end of 1841, 165 cottages had been built at Wolverton, along with nine shops, a library, school, market square and a substantial piggery. There were six classes of dwelling, the most numerous being plain terraced cottages made of brick and containing only two rooms. Brunel was also aware of the elegant late-Georgian style terraces designed by Francis Thompson for the North Midland Railway at Derby in about 1840. Thompson had helped Brunel with the design for Swindon Station. The designs by John Cunningham for the housing at the rival new settlement at Crewe are exactly contemporaneous with Brunel's work at Swindon, and were therefore less likely to have influenced him to any great degree.

The GWR was anxious to have the 300 cottages in the village ready for occupation by the time the factory was opened on 2 January 1843. However, as a result of difficulties encountered in the construction of the line and the excavation of the Box Tunnel, the company was forced to spend nearly twice the £3 million raised in 1835, and was therefore unable or unwilling to fund the construction of the cottages. Instead it hit upon the ingenious ploy of persuading a firm of private contractors, J.D. & C. Rigby of Holywell Street, Westminster, to build the cottages at their own expense on GWR land. In return Rigbys would be paid annuities equal to 6% of the cost of building the cottages, to be collected by the company entirely out of rents paid by its employees. The net result of these dealings was that the company would obtain a cottage estate at no expense to itself. As an additional incentive, Rigbys were also given the right to lease the opulent refreshment rooms in the new Swindon Station building they were erecting.

The company agreed to make Swindon Station the only refreshment stop for the 4-hour train journey between London and Bristol, and to stop all trains there for 10 minutes for this purpose. Rigbys were therefore guaranteed a monopoly, and they immediately sublet the business to a Cheltenham hotelier for a considerable sum. The hotelier and subsequent proprietors quickly recouped their initial investments by charging exorbitant prices and offering poor service – so much so, in fact, that in the early days the refreshment rooms became infamous amongst rail travellers.

The cottages

Brunel designed the first block of 44 cottages himself as a model for the later terraces. He staked out the site in March 1842, and construction began shortly afterwards. Rigbys, though, were already involved in the construction of Swindon Station and the works, and seem to have had considerable difficulty in assigning sufficient manpower to the construction of the cottages. Consequently it took them six summer months to complete the first block, and correspondence between Brunel and Rigbys shows the former beginning to despair of having enough cottages ready by the anticipated opening date for the works.

Although he was instructed to keep the cost of each cottage to £100, Brunel went to considerable effort to embellish the facades so that they would present an attractive face to the main railway line across the open field to the north. He designed the facades in a simplified Jacobean style, arranging them in pairs along the terrace.

Swindon stone, a dark-yellow calcareous sandstone obtained from quarries in Swindon, was used for walling, while Bath stone, a limestone from the Box and Corsham areas, was employed for quoins, as well as for window and door surrounds. Nearly all of the buildings in the village were to be built of these types of stone. In 1842 Rigbys had built a temporary tramway to transport large quantities of Swindon stone down to the new settlement from the old town.

Although their exteriors were very elaborate, internally the cottages were very basic. They contained just two heated rooms measuring 17 ft by 11 ft (5.2 m by 3.3 m). In the early years of the settlement it was not uncommon for these cottages to house two families as well as lodgers. Each cottage had its own rear yard containing a privy and dust hole for the disposal of ashes and other household refuse. The privies drained into cesspools located under the narrow alley that ran between the yards of the two terraces making up each block.

Contemporary accounts of the cottages are extremely rare. An important exception is the diary of 1842–9 written by Edward Snell. The diary affords valuable insights into life in the new settlement. Snell arrived in New Swindon shortly after the opening of the works to take up employment as an engine erector. He had been living in relatively comfortable circumstances in Bath, where he had completed his apprenticeship, and was very unimpressed with the new settlement. He felt it resembled a frontier town, and sketched a forlorn-looking family of 'settlers', as he referred to them, making their way through the rain and mud from the station to the company cottages. In the description that accompanied the sketch, Snell wrote of New Swindon:

> a precious place it is at present, not a knocker or scraper in the whole place. Most of the houses very damp and containing only two rooms. Not a cupboard or a shelf . . . and the unfortunate inhabitants obliged to keep the grub in the bedrooms . . .

There were no kitchens, so cooking had to be carried out on the open fires.

The rents for each cottage were high by the standards of the day. They were set at 3s 6d (17½p) per week, which was almost twice that of similar-sized cottages at Wolverton. The high rents encouraged overcrowding, and were a direct result of the GWR's policy of recouping all of the construction costs from their tenants.

The next two blocks of cottages making up the western half of the village and built to the south of the first block were probably designed by Brunel's assistants. They were completed by the end of 1843. Most of the cottages in the two later blocks contained two rooms and were identical in plan to those in the first block. However, 10 cottages at the east end of each block contained four rooms, with those on the first floor being accessed by a stair tower, which projected into the rear yard. These 'double cottages', as they were called by the company were let for seven shillings (35p) per week, and appear to have been used as tenements housing two or more families and lodgers.

The cottages in the western half of the village became progressively plainer in their external appearance as work progressed in a southerly direction. The shortage of available housing was acute, forcing Rigbys and their subcontractors to speed up the construction programme. Rigbys had to bear the costs themselves, and so had every incentive to keep outgoings to the absolute minimum. In contrast to the roughly dressed Swindon stone used for the earlier cottages, the facades of the third block of cottages are made of squared, coursed Swindon stone rubble, and brick was used for dressings in preference to Bath stone. Chimneys are also of brick, and there are no Jacobean motifs or bay windows to help enliven the facades.

At the end of 1843, Rigbys ceased all works for the GWR at Swindon, having completed less than half of the 300 cottages they had agreed to build. The reasons for their withdrawal are unknown, but a dispute over the terms of the 1841 agreement and delays in their reimbursement by the company would appear to be the most likely causes. Their withdrawal cleared the way for other contractors to become involved in the construction programme.

Church, school and shops

In 1843 a committee of GWR directors was established to oversee the construction of a church, parsonage and school on a site immediately to the west of the village. All three buildings were designed by Scott and Moffatt and completed by 1845. Most of the school was demolished in the early 1880s, and the church and the parsonage have both been extended.

No further dwellings were erected in the village until 1845, when Brunel was instructed to prepare plans for a series of new blocks to be erected on each

Fig. 7.2 Two-roomed cottages in Bristol Street, Swindon, forming part of the first block of cottages to be erected in the village in 1842. (RCHME)

Fig. 7.3 Plain cottages on the north side of Taunton Street, Swindon, built in 1843. (RCHME)

Fig. 7.4 A shop block built in 1847 on the east side of Emlyn Square (formerly High Street), Swindon. It is almost identical to three slightly earlier blocks in the square. (RCHME)

Fig. 7.5 Looking east along the alley between the cottages making up the Exeter/ Taunton Street block on the west side of Swindon village. (RCHME)

side of High Street. Four of these blocks were built between 1845 and mid-1847. They possessed two, three-storey shop/residences, each located on the corner of High Street and the adjoining streets. The taller blocks were designed in Brunel's characteristic Jacobean idiom, with gables containing keyed *oeils de boeufs*. They form part of Brunel's original scheme for an avenue of shops and superior houses lining the main route leading from, to the south, the Old Town northwards to the main entrance of the works. This concept of the 'grand avenue' or 'promenade' enclosing the commercial and market area of the new settlement was unrivalled by other railway towns.

The shops were sorely needed, because there were at that time no facilities of this kind in the village, and the inhabitants had to walk up to the Old Town for essential provisions. The eight new shops supplied basic items, such as clothing, groceries, meat and bread. In 1847 the company built a slaughterhouse and a bakery (both demolished by c.1853) at the south-west corner of the village, and two of the shops were used as retail outlets for them. Between the shops, four-roomed houses for more senior employees faced onto the High Street, while along the sides of the new blocks were eight-roomed lodging houses for single men and two five-roomed cottages.

Villas and terraces

From 1845 to 1846 detached villas were built for the works manager and the station superintendent to the north of the east side of the village. These were substantial houses, incorporating two floors and a basement containing service quarters. Brewhouses were contained in the yards at the back of the villas. Both buildings were surrounded by formal gardens, and were demolished to make way for the new carriage works of 1868–76. The villas were the only two houses at New Swindon built specifically for senior works employees. The other, larger houses in the village seem to have been occupied by whoever could afford them. In this respect the village differed from other railway towns such as Crewe, where a more heirarchical approach to the provision of housing for different classes of worker was adopted.

At the same time as the shop blocks and managers' villas were going up, work started on the first terraces on the east side of the village. Houses in London Street were built with gabled window bays to match the appearance of the first block of cottages on the other side of the village. The new houses were also visible from passing trains and from the villas, so their appearance had to impress. These houses contained eight rooms, and were much larger than the earlier cottages. Original plans show that the houses were subdivided into four two-roomed tenements, although by the time of the 1851 census many were occupied as single, large houses by the families of professional men and more senior works employees.

Over the next two years two further blocks of cottages were built to the south of the eight-roomed houses. The new blocks comprised five-roomed cottages with kitchens. These cottages had built-in furniture, such as a shelved pantry and a large dresser in the kitchen. They were occupied by skilled workers and their families along with lodgers, while the smaller, earlier houses on the west side of the village tended to be tenanted by less-skilled workers.

This flurry of building activity in the village from 1845 coincided with the great boom in railway construction throughout the country known as the 'railway mania'. However, by mid-1847 the bubble had burst, and in August of that year the GWR directors ordered a cessation in all building work. Construction work on a fifth shop block adjoining what is now Emlyn Square had only just begun and was halted immediately. Work on a model lodging house designed by Brunel for single men in Emlyn Square was also abandoned. This had been carefully designed in the Jacobean style to blend with the earlier shop blocks making up the 'grand promenade'.

Additional plans for Jacobean-style blocks to screen off the rear yards and alleys on the east and west sides of the village did not progress beyond the drawing-board. A sketch by Brunel for a town hall for the settlement was taken no further. Between 1847 and 1849 the workforce was reduced from 1800 men down to 618. Some of the discharged men were able to obtain casual employment as farm labourers in the surrounding area, while others were reliant on support from their colleagues who remained in work. Those with few savings were forced to seek cheaper private accommodation in New Swindon, thus leaving some of the GWR's cottages tenantless.

The company's economic fortunes began to improve through 1850, but it was not until 1853 that work began on the construction of 50 new cottages in the village. These were built to five different plans in blocks on the west and east sides of the estate and in a terrace at the south-west corner. The two-storey end blocks match the earlier shop blocks in style but have been given a better degree of finish through the use of Bath stone ashlar for exterior walling. The intention was to reduce the housing shortage in the village and to hide the more unsightly rear alleys. The cesspools under the alleys were prone to flooding, owing to inadequacies in their design and poor drainage. This in turn led to constant outbreaks of disease, including cholera in 1849.

In 1854 work was resumed on the model lodging house or 'barracks' as it became known. The completed building is a bigger and more austere-looking structure than that designed by Brunel in 1846–7. Its main facade to Emlyn Square is anchored at each end by massive, buttressed towers. The building was originally U-shaped in plan and contained over 100 sleeping rooms, each provided with a bed, chest of drawers and a chair. Day rooms, a bakery, kitchens and a coffee and eating establishment were also provided for the lodgers. The company's aim was to ease overcrowding in the cottages by providing single men working away from home with a place of their own.

Although it was regarded as a laudable social experiment, the barracks was not a success. Single men preferred to lodge with families rather than being herded together in an institution, and the building became a white elephant almost from the day it was opened in 1855. In 1861 it was converted into a series of two- and three-roomed flats to house the families of Welsh iron-workers who had come to New Swindon in that year to operate the company's new rail mills. However, in 1864 the Welsh moved into a new housing estate they had built for themselves to the south-west of the railway village, and the Barracks became empty again. In 1868–9 it was converted into a Methodist chapel, a process that left the main Emlyn Square facade of the barracks virtually unaltered, and in 1960–2 it was converted, yet again, to form the Great Western Railway Museum.

Recreation and self-improvement
Senior GWR staff, especially Daniel Gooch, took a personal interest in the health and welfare of their workforce at Swindon, and in the patriarchal spirit

114

typical of most railway companies of the day, attempted to provide the men with a range of suitable facilities. A Mechanics' Institution was established in 1844 in one of the factory workshops. The heart of the institution was its library, which was stocked with books, periodicals and newspapers donated by senior staff or paid for out of members' subscriptions. The men could use the library to improve their education and thereby increase their career prospects within the company. The institution also ran a programme of lectures and soirées calculated to educate and entertain the people of New Swindon.

By the early 1850s the space occupied by the institution within the works was required for manufacturing purposes, and it was decided to erect a substantial new building on the area of open ground between the shop blocks in Emlyn Square. The New Swindon Improvement Company was formed to raise funds for the building and to oversee its construction. It was designed by Edward Roberts, a London architect, in a robust Perpendicular Gothic style, which was somewhat at odds with the prevailing Brunellian Jacobean adopted for the rest of the buildings in the village. The building contained a reading-room, washing baths, a members' dining-room and other facilities on the ground floor and a theatre on the first floor. Attached to its southern end was an octagonal covered market containing bays for 36 stalls. The covered market was demolished in 1891 to make way for a large new extension to the institution containing a reading-room and new classrooms for those attending technical education courses there. The building was vacated in 1986 following closure of the works. It is currently in a very poor state of repair, and is very much in need of a new use. It was for many years the focus of New Swindon's cultural life, and its refurbishment would help to revitalize what is now a rather neglected part of Swindon town centre.

In 1868 the company built washing baths for the GWR Medical Fund at the southern end of the village, and Turkish baths were added in 1876. Swimming baths were provided within the works boundary in 1868. In 1871 the armoury of the Company's XI Wiltshire Volunteer Rifle Corps, located to the south of the Mechanics' Institution building, was converted to a cottage hospital to care for the large numbers of men injured in the factory. At about the same time, the cricket ground on the west side of the village, bought by the GWR in 1844 for its workmen and their families, was landscaped and a series of formal gardens created. In 1892 a large brick building containing public swimming baths, a dispensary and later Turkish and washing baths was opened on the south side of the village. These welfare and recreational facilities provided by the company led to a gradual improvement in the standard of living of New Swindon people in the second half of the nineteenth century.

Virtually all available building sites in the village were built on by 1866 following the completion of a terrace of six cottages on the north side of the armoury. The GWR's precarious financial position at that time brought a shift in policy away from the direct funding and construction of cottages for its employees. The population of New Swindon in 1861 was 4167, and the company could not possibly meet the demand for new housing. Instead it attempted to persuade its employees to save enough to be able to afford to buy their own houses, and it actively supported the establishment of building societies for this purpose.

Fig. 7.6 The north end of the disused and partially vandalized Mechanics Institution building in the centre of Swindon village. It was built in 1854–5 and extended in 1891–3. (RCHME)

Conservation

The railway village remained virtually unchanged until 1966, when it was sold by British Rail to Swindon Borough Council. The council came to the view that the cottages were beyond repair, and it applied to demolish and rebuild them. Fortunately, Wiltshire County Council objected to the proposal, and the borough decided to embark on a major refurbishment programme for the whole village. This began in 1969, and was completed by the early 1980s. Work began on the south side of the western half of the village, and involved the demolition and rebuilding of unsightly lean-tos in the rear yards. In the process, considerable effort was expended on reusing original materials and retaining the original character of the rear alleys. The external walls were cleaned, roofs were repaired, and the individual front gardens were replaced by communal lawns and landscaped areas. Internally, in addition to new kitchens provided in the rebuilt lean-tos, new bathrooms were built on the first floor and gas heating units were installed. Alterations to the original internal plans were kept to a minimum as part of the programme. The scheme was regarded as an exemplar of 1970s conservation practice, and it won several awards.

The project did involve some demolition work; 19 cottages built between 1853 and 1866 were demolished to create car parking areas for the residents. The yard walls of these cottages have been retained to indicate their former locations. Nevertheless, the project has ensured the preservation of nearly all of the village. This has been reinforced by the listing of all of the buildings and a regular programme of maintenance carried out by Thamesdown Borough Council.

The village is in many ways the epitome of a mid-nineteenth-century railway company town. It is also standing testimony to the vision of its creator, Isambard Kingdom Brunel, and a reflection of the fluctuating economic fortunes of the Great Western Railway. The overall stylistic and visual unity possessed by the buildings is attributable to Brunel's long involvement with the site, and the consistent use of Swindon and Bath stone. For all of these reasons the village deserves to be better known and valued as an important component in Britain's railway heritage.

Part Three
Conservation

H. John Yates
The conservation context

The study of railways and their history has too often been conducted in isolation, regarding them as a self-contained phenomenon as if they were a spectator sport. This is a pity, as it threatens the quality of that study, and it diminishes the esteem in which the subject itself is held. People involved with the railway heritage must expect jokes about anoraks, but should not despair or retreat into a corner. The subject is too important for that.

Almost all study of the past has started as an amateur activity, and has then been taken up – as has now happened at York – by the academic establishment. For example, the study of 'modern' (i.e. post-Roman) history was typically the pursuit of the country clergy, until nineteenth-century academics reluctantly lifted their eyes from the classics and gave it intellectual respectability.

So this chapter looks at the wider context in which we can identify, protect and display the railway heritage, as an integral part of our understanding of the past through the evidence it has left us. It aims to complement and build on the arguments presented in the chapter by Peter Burman.

Conservation philosophy
The first context to examine is that of conservation philosophy – a field in which transport conservation has until now been curiously old-fashioned and undeveloped. While smaller objects (up to and including locomotives!) can be preserved on the basis of whim or sentiment, the resources involved in keeping large objects, such as buildings or whole sites, need firmer rational justification. A sound intellectual foundation is even more important if private owners are to be constrained by law from doing as they wish with their own property.

As anyone involved on the practical side will confirm, long-term physical conservation of any kind is an unnatural activity; if mineral and vegetable materials were not in steady decay there would be no sedimentary rocks, and the land would be covered in logs. Before moving on to consider the more usual justifications for heritage conservation in cultural terms, we should first acknowledge the ecological considerations, which are likely to become increasingly important. Building materials represent and consume finite resources, which should be allowed to serve out their time. Bricks and cement represent energy consumed; stone is quarried at the expense of the landscape; timber can only grow at its own pace. We should therefore not wilfully waste buildings, regardless of cultural considerations.

Nevertheless, the more usual current justification for conserving our heritage is in cultural terms. Sites and structures are themselves historical documents, carrying messages from the past to us and the future about how we thought, how we lived, and how we built. Most railway buildings can tell us something about all three of these fields, but competition between the three underlies a century and a half of conservation debate.

While the great public conservation battles have been fought over whether to keep or whether to destroy, the relative importance of the design and of the actual fabric has preoccupied the world of conservation since the times of John Ruskin and William Morris. The fabric will carry information about what has happened to the structure during its life, and about how it was built. It may have sustained considerable alterations, which are themselves interesting in terms of economic or technical history, but which may conceal or distort the original design intention. Weathering may also blur the design, so why not right the wrongs of history and 'restore to former glory'? Against this there is the near certainty that a shifting historical perspective will change the relative importance of different elements. For example, in the middle of this century the National Trust preserved and presented its great country houses almost solely as a portrayal of taste, whereas today we are interested in the social and economic stories that these buildings tell. The Trust is changing the emphasis of its presentation accordingly, but much evidence of the service arrangements was lost in the course of earlier restorations. If the fabric is destroyed in the course of 'restoration', future generations will not be able to study and reinterpret it. Another consideration is that future generations are likely to have more sophisticated ways of investigating fabric, and that loss of that material would deprive them of that opportunity. For example, we are now developing techniques to carbon-date some metals, and to look into walls.

The present conservation orthodoxy and best practice is therefore to 'conserve as found'. This is the starting point for English Heritage, and indeed for the whole process of statutory protection, although there are cases where some restoration to an earlier form may be appropriate. Such cases arise when the later work is of very poor quality, where it would not survive repair, or where we can be absolutely confident that the special interest of the building is entirely concentrated in an early phase.

A salutory point is that in the ultimately long term only the design and location can survive, as all fabric will be replaced in the very long run. This process is well under way with some ancient timber and soft stone buildings. It is a recognized paradox in maritime conservation, where the clock of decay runs faster than it does on land: 'restoring' a historic wooden vessel to sailing condition will usually result in a replica in little more than a century. The same happens with vehicles and – over a much longer period – with buildings. However, this does not free us from the responsibility to pass on as much fabric as possible from the tiny proportion of our output selected for conservation, as that fabric carries messages from the past to the present and future.

There is a risk that this fairly recent (and almost exclusively Anglo-Saxon) shift towards archaeological values might be leaving behind public interest and goodwill, without which conservation becomes a narrow and sectarian activity, and without which statutory intervention cannot be justified. A large part of the traditional appeal of old buildings and places is romantic – these were the actual places where great deeds were done, or where mysterious people lived their very different lives. These romantic associations are sustainable only if the structure is at least in part materially authentic, if it is *in situ*, and usually if it bears some resemblance to the associated period. These places and things then become a ticket to time-travel; an extra dimension – the time dimension – is added to the mental maps by which we perceive our surroundings. At the conference that initiated this book a mysterious stone was passed around the delegates. They were then told that they had all held a piece of the Euston Arch (or Propylaeum, to be pedantically correct). That stone tells us a little about the fabric of this totem of the first railway age, nothing about its design, and nothing about its social and economic importance. But it was actually there, and that is itself a stimulus to thought and interest. It is a relic, no more and no less. Yet is it more 'the real thing' than a complete full-sized replica would be? What is the special interest of the Euston Arch? What needs to be perpetuated to maintain that special interest? The fabric or the design? The archaeology or the architecture?

This romantic view can degenerate into personal nostalgia – a dangerously transient companion for conservation, although it has been the driving force behind all too much transport conservation. Most of the preserved railways were set up by people re-creating the scenes of their childhood: thus the earlier ones (such as the Bluebell Railway and the Worth Valley) tend to depict an earlier era than the more recent entrants. There is now a tendency for 'preserved' locomotives to be presented in their 1950s liveries, because that is how they are remembered by their custodians. An earlier generation, as predecessors of the National Railway Museum, concentrated on Edwardian express locomotives, and ruthlessly stripped away all alterations in order to present their original appearance. The idea of 'conserve as found' is still novel in the world of transport conservation, where 'restore to former glory' is the norm. In terms of presentation, the more thorough railway preservationists are now very advanced museum keepers – they display an aspect of the past in its entirety. However, in terms of building conservation philosophy they are often over a century behind the times, practising restoration as if they were the early Victorian clerics scraping the layers of history from their parish churches to reveal a medieval golden age.

Having established the philosophical context, let us now look at how the railway heritage relates to the rest of the built heritage, how it is identified, and how it can be managed.

Railway architecture?

Is there really any such thing as 'railway architecture'? I suggest that there isn't. It is easy to demonstrate that the major railway buildings, usually designed by established practitioners, were simply the result of an application of contemporary taste and technology to the briefs of the railway companies.

Thus the styles, materials and construction techniques of the great stations can also be found in the country houses, town halls, exchanges and commercial buildings of their periods. For St Pancras, look also at Scott's Kelham Hall or Walton Hall; for Euston, see Philip Hardwick's extension to St Bartholomew's Hospital. Even the great iron roofs of the train sheds are not unique to stations, as similar structures were provided for markets and exhibition buildings when the brief called for a large span. Iron construction had been pioneered in the textile industry in the 1790s, and was well-established technology by the 1820s. Nash used it in the Brighton Pavilion; Smirke gave Eastnor Castle an iron roof. Iron and glass construction was also well advanced, as it had been developed for botanical glasshouses.

The smaller early railway buildings are now fairly rare, as their success often led to the construction of larger replacements, but where they do survive they are usually indistinguishable in style from the later canal buildings. A good example is the recently restored Liverpool Road Station at Manchester, original terminus of the Liverpool & Manchester Railway opened in 1830. It could easily be mistaken for a canal office and warehouse. Fortunately it is now restored and interpreted as part of the Museum of Science & Industry in Manchester, along with the remarkable collection of contemporary warehouses. Most such buildings were essays in Georgian rationalism, the style ridiculed within a few years by Pugin but rehabilitated by twentieth-century modernists under the somewhat moralistic label of 'The Functional Tradition'. The buildings that come closest to being 'railway architecture' are those built in the second half of the nineteenth century, often to the standard designs developed by the major companies. This idea of 'corporate image' – pioneered by the canals – is particularly well exemplified by the North Eastern, the Great Western, and the Midland Railway companies. In each case the designs of their stations, signal boxes, goods sheds and footbridges are unmistakable. However, the architectural elements involved are in no case unique to them. They simply draw on the good-quality, commercial vernacular of the day, with elements that one might also find in a model farm, a factory, a pumping station or an estate village. One tends to regard this period and quality of building as belonging to the railways because their own essays in it were so ubiquitous, and because they were publicly accessible.

That is the key to the real importance of railway building in the architecture of this country. For the first time since the arrival of the French monks in the Middle Ages, here was large-scale investment and a consistency of approach superimposed on the local pattern of land ownership and political influence. The Industrial Revolution had been running for at least a century, but in most of Britain the arrival of the railway was its first major visible symbol. It both brought and symbolized a new way of living for ordinary people; it changed their horizons. Railway buildings would be of great historic importance for this

Fig. 8.1 Liverpool Road Station, Manchester, opened in 1830. The more formal entrance was for first-class passengers. These buildings are now preserved as part of the Museum of Science & Industry in Manchester. (M.J. Stratton)

alone, even if they did not also exemplify – as they do – the best of Victorian commercial architecture.

We should also consider the global historical context. This country's greatest influence on the world was undoubtedly the effect of the Industrial Revolution in the nineteenth century. At every other period she has been relatively provincial in cultural and economic terms. The major monuments of our industrial revolution, such as the early trunk railways, are thus particularly important in international terms. Sir Neil's proposal for a Great Western Railway World Heritage Site is wholly justifiable; we pioneered railways, and railways changed the world.

Conservation legislation

World Heritage Sites are the latest and grandest identification for places of cultural importance, but this process of identification and protection has now been going on for over a century. The Victorian pace of change – accelerated by the railways themselves – brought a reaction from those gentle antiquarians and artists, appalled by the mutilation and loss of important prehistoric, Roman and medieval sites. The railways themselves were often the villains, mutilating the castle at Newcastle and strangling it with track, or demolishing the magnificent medieval Paul Pindar's house to widen Liverpool Street station. Statutory protection was proposed, and eventually (after an eight-year parliamentary battle) the first Ancient Monuments Act became law in 1882. For the first time there was legal weight behind Morris's view that important heritage sites were, in effect, common cultural property as well as individual private property.

In the following century the power and scope of heritage protection legislation have been extended, and now it takes three forms relevant to the railway heritage: scheduled ancient monuments, listed historic buildings, and conservation areas.

Ancient monuments of national importance are identified by English Heritage and scheduled by the Heritage Secretary, under the Ancient Monuments and Archaeological Areas Act 1979. Any works (including repairs) require scheduled monument consent from the Heritage Secretary, who is advised by English Heritage. While the railway owned 59 scheduled ancient monuments in 1995, very few are operational railway structures, the more likely historic railway candidates for scheduling being the most important remains of the early horse-drawn mineral tramways. A national survey, known as the Monuments Protection Programme, is now well advanced; it tackles sites on a thematic basis, in order to identify the most important of each type. Scheduled monuments are generally sites and structures without a major practical use.

Listed historic buildings, on the other hand, usually do have a practical use. These 'buildings of special architectural or historic interest' are also generally identified by English Heritage – although anyone can put a building forward for listing – and are listed by the Heritage Secretary under the Planning (Listed Buildings and Conservation Areas) Act 1990. In 1995 there were 1383 railway-owned structures among the half million listed buildings, which represents about 3% of our total building stock.

A wide range of railway buildings have been listed, under criteria that set out in broad terms that the less old a building is, the more special it has to be. Thus one would expect most complete railway structures of the 1840s to be listed, while only the better-quality late-Victorian buildings are chosen, and only the truly outstanding examples of post-war architecture are selected. Surveys for listing are now carried out on a thematic basis akin to that for scheduled monuments. The survey of post-war commercial buildings has resulted in the listing of Coventry Station, a marvellously airy structure by W.R. Headley and Derick Shorten completed in 1962 and rightly listed Grade II*, and the more assertive signal box at Birmingham New Street, by Bicknell & Hamilton and dating to 1964. Manchester Oxford Road, with its timber roof arching up in a manner similar to the form of Sydney Opera House, was designed by the Timber Development Association and built in 1960; it is currently undergoing repairs after being listed Grade II*. The listing criteria are included in the Government's Planning Policy Guidance (PPG) 15, which sets out official policy on how the built heritage is to continue to enrich our lives yet remain economically viable.

It is therefore recognized that listing does not 'stop the clock', but that it identifies the building as culturally special, and brings in a process to assess proposals for it in terms of that special interest. This process is called 'listed building consent', and is normally carried out by the local planning authority. It frequently involves compromise between the ideals of conservation and the ideals of use. A particularly prominent example of such a compromise is the 1970s building at the front of the Grade I listed King's Cross Station. It undoubtedly harms the architectural purity and effect of Cubitt's great train shed, but it is reversible in the longer term, it replaced something far worse in terms of design quality, and it has enabled the building to continue to function.

In cases like this concerning the most important listed buildings (Grade I and II*) English Heritage is consulted, and the agreement of the Secretary of State for the Environment is required. His agreement is also required, and the national amenity societies are consulted, if demolition is proposed.

Fig. 8.2 The booking hall of Coventry Station, viewed from the overbridge. This station, designed by W.R. Headley and D. Shorten, dates to 1962, shortly before the London to Birmingham main line was electrified. It is now listed Grade II*. (M.J. Stratton)

Conservation Areas are defined in the above 1990 Act as 'areas of special architectural or historic interest the character or apperance of which it is desirable to preserve or enhance'. They are designated by local planning authorities. The main effect of designation is that conservation area consent is required from the local authority for demolition of any building within the area. Trees are also protected, and there may be special requirements under an Article 4 Direction concerning external changes to buildings. Although conservation areas were devised to protect historic towns and villages, the legislation has also successfully been applied to other types of historic area where special character is formed by a whole entity as much as by the individual components: many canals and their immediate surroundings have been designated on these grounds. Over 1000 railway buildings are already included in conservation areas as components in good townscapes, but a powerful case can be made for the designation of historic railways as conservation areas.

Some preserved railways are more visitor attraction than heritage site, but others have conserved the formerly commonplace so effectively that they are now 'areas of special architectural or historic character', which fully deserve designation as conservation areas. Their managers would probably regard this as a mixed blessing, as it brings a closer involvement of the planning authority, but it has important benefits. It brings the possibility of Conservation Area Partnership grants, while the demolition controls reduce the desirability of their operational sites to potential asset-strippers. Conservation area designation may also be appropriate for a few particularly intact operational lines, and has been under consideration for the Settle–Carlisle Line.

Sometimes grant-aid can tilt the economic balance towards survival or to achieve a better-quality repair. English Heritage can only offer grants towards repairs of ancient monuments, Grade I and II* historic buildings, and buildings

Fig. 8.3 Signal box at New Street Station, by Bicknell & Hamilton, erected 1965–6 as part of the major reconstruction programme at Birmingham. The box has been listed as an example of 1960s 'Brutalist' concrete architecture. (M. J. Stratton)

Fig. 8.4 King's Cross Station, London, designed by L. Cubitt and built for the Great Northern Railway, 1852, with the 1970s booking hall partly screening the frontage. (English Heritage)

in selected conservation areas where it has a partnership programme with the local authority. Railway examples of such grants include £1 million towards repairs to Ribblehead viaduct, and almost £100 000 to the Severn Valley Railway for repairs to their cast iron Victoria Bridge, built by Sir John Fowler in 1860. The National Heritage Lottery Fund can make even more substantial grants for repair, enhancement or interpretation, but can only assist bodies that do not distribute profits. The Millennium Commission has already offered £4.3 million for reconstruction of the Welsh Highland Railway, but will support only exceptional projects bringing major public benefit. Local authorities can offer grants towards repairs of any historic building or in any conservation area, but the sums available are usually fairly small. Other possible sources of funding include the Railway Heritage Trust, the National Heritage Memorial Fund, the Architectural Heritage Fund, and the European Union. Some heritage projects will also qualify for grants aimed at economic regeneration by national governments and the European Community, but these change too rapidly to set out in a book of this nature.

New pressures, new uses

There can be no doubt that over the next few years we shall face a crisis in railway heritage, and may find ourselves fighting on several fronts and forced into hard decisions on priorities. The whole operational network faces the greatest uncertainties since the Beeching era, while the engineering requirements of high-speed lines to European standards are increasingly difficult to accommodate within existing infrastructure. At the same time, much of that infrastructure is passing its 'best before' date at about the same time – a problem faced by many other Victorian creations, ranging from parish churches to seaside piers.

Fig. 8.5 Victoria Bridge, Severn Valley Railway, by J Fowler, 1862, restored with a major grant from English Heritage.
(Severn Valley Railway)

There is a heritage orthodoxy that the best use for an historic building is its original use. Implicit in this is the feeling that a part of the character of a building comes from the activities in and around it, and from the continuity of those activities – an idea of the 'spirit of place' that perhaps finds more echoes in the East than in Western cultures. Paradoxes abound. For example, an historic church may be less materially altered if it becomes redundant rather than be adapted to modern patterns of worship. To take a hypothetical railway example, would the character of St Pancras Station be better conserved by physically preserving it as a railway museum, or by adapting it to take Eurostar trains?

Meanwhile we see historic buildings of all types being adapted to new uses, yet continuing to tell their stories of the past. Barns and schools converted to houses, warehouses to flats, chapels to shops – the possibilities are limited only by the imagination. Most railway buildings are robustly built and readily adaptable. Probably the most spectacular examples of new uses are the GMEX exhibition hall at Manchester, and the supermarket carpark in the former Bath Green Park Station. GMEX was created by converting the huge, single-span shed of Manchester Central, which had deteriorated severely since the staion closed in 1969. It took a private and public sector joint venture between an assurance company and Greater Manchester Council to fund the £20 million scheme, completed in 1985. The strangest adaptive reuse project must be the residential conversion of an overbridge on a closed line in Worcestershire. Many goods sheds and locomotive depots have found a new life in light industry, while station buildings on closed lines make highly desirable resi-dences. Redundant station buildings and signal boxes on operational lines can be a more intractable problem, as local railway managers are sometimes reluctant and inflexible towards new users, even boarding up newly restored buildings rather than see other parties become involved. This is particularly shortsighted in the case of unstaffed stations, as occupation of the buildings helps deter vandalism elsewhere on the site.

Fig. 8.6 GMEX, Manchester, formerly the Central Station erected 1876–9 to designs by Sir John Fowler. The station closed in 1969, but was reopened as an exhibition centre in 1985. (M.J. Stratton)

We may have to recognize that certain large structures may only be 'preserved' by record, inadequate though that must be by comparison with survival of the structure for future examination. English Heritage has recoiled from the long-term financial implications of preserving a major steelworks as a monument, as the technical problems of preserving large steel or reinforced concrete structures over long periods are very challenging. We must therefore hope and work for a technological breakthrough if such structures are to survive without economic uses.

Where recording is all that is possible it should be done with a recognized methodology, and not the few haphazard photographs and drawings that are all we have of so many lost structures. How much information was saved, for example, from the Chepstow Bridge or the Crumlin Viaduct? Heritage recording is generally the responsibility of the Royal Commissions on Historic Monuments, and of the county sites and monuments records. These bodies have a consistent system of recording to defined levels, depending on the importance of the site and the resources available, and keep records to good archival standards.

While the statutory processes can identify and protect important sites, they are still essentially reactive. The agencies involved are not well equipped for taking initiatives, or even for setting priorities. If the important sites are to survive, a clear strategy is required, which recognizes the options available and deploys them in the most appropriate ways. Beneficial use on an operational railway will usually be first choice; adaptation for new uses will often be acceptable; preservation by record will be the last resort. But the first step must still be to identify what is important, which can be done only by understanding its context.

Steve Pilcher

Changing attitudes to the conservation of England's railway heritage

The railway preservation movement

Railways and steam engines (locomotives) have fascinated people for generations. The sight, sound and smell of a steam engine is a powerful, enduring image. Film makers have capitalized on this in various successful films, including the 1937 *Oh! Mr Porter*, starring Will Hay, the 1952 *Titfield Thunderbolt*, and the 1968 *Railway Children*. More recently, the Revd W. Awdry's *Thomas the Tank Engine* stories have continued to be a resounding success with younger children.

The closure of many railway lines in the 1950s and 1960s prompted the creation of the railway preservation movement. It started in a small way with the reopening of two narrow-gauge railways, the Talyllyn and the Ffestiniog, in Wales in the early 1950s. The first standard-gauge railway to be reopened by volunteers was the Bluebell Railway in Sussex in 1960. The rapid decline in use of steam engines on British Railways over the following decade prompted a surge of interest from railway enthusiasts to save what still remained. Since then, over 60 railways and steam centres have opened or been rebuilt, and the railway preservation movement has been one of this country's post-war success stories. No other country in the world has a railway preservation movement that has saved as much. Some railway preservation organizations are now big businesses, attracting over 100 000 visitors, creating a turnover of over £2 million. Very few have received grant aid or subsidies; all of them have relied on volunteers and donations to get started. Virtually all of them still rely on volunteers to operate their services, but significant numbers of paid staff are also employed.

Most of the successful railway preservation schemes have been born from a locally based desire to save a particular route from closure or a wish to reopen a line. Virtually all the operating preserved railways have shied away from taking on a line with any large-scale architectural features, because funds are usually very tight in the first few years of any railway preservation scheme. Thus only a few of the schemes have involved the preservation of a notable structure such as the Grade II listed Victoria Bridge on the Severn Valley Railway. However, a number of listed signal boxes and a few disused station buildings have on occasion been successfully moved and rebuilt at preserved railways.

It can be argued that the railway preservation movement's main forte is in the restoration of rolling-stock. To most people with an interest in railways it was the steam locomotives and carriages that captured people's enthusiasm and imagination. When British Railways was disposing of steam locomotives *en masse* in the 1960s, it was possible to purchase a modest-sized steam locomotive for under £1000 and a carriage for just a few hundred pounds. Obviously, allowing for inflation, these were considerable sums at the time. However, following the formation of various small societies and the launch of public appeals, no less than 106 former British Railways locomotives had been purchased for preservation when steam locomotives ceased to be used on British Railways in 1968. Subsequently a further 213 steam locomotives have been purchased from a scrapyard at Barry, South Wales, where the owner, Dai Woodham, decided to set aside the collection that he had purchased and concentrate on other work. As a result, just over 70 of these once-derelict steam locomotives have now been restored to full working order. Without them, a number of railway preservation projects would not have had any locomotives to haul their trains. This activity has enabled certain engineering skills, such as boiler repair, pattern-making and large-scale machining, to carry on, and younger people have been able to learn old skills.

Although the National Railway Museum in York has an impressive collection of rolling-stock, there were and are major gaps. The voluntary preservation movement has a key role in ensuring that the physical record is a comprehensive one. The first steam locomotive to be recorded officially as achieving 100 mph (160 km/h), 4472 *Flying Scotsman*, was purchased by Alan Pegler in 1963 to save it from being scrapped. The last main-line express passenger locomotive to be built, and to a unique design, 71000 *Duke of Gloucester*, also had to be saved by preservationists.

The railway preservation movement covers broad interests. Following the demise of some of the earliest classes of diesels there has been a growing interest in the preservation of both diesel and electric locomotives. Today there are now more ex-British Railways diesel locomotives preserved than there are steam engines! In some ways this is surprising, as they require quite skilled maintenance; however, the main components were often quite robust.

Railways are a means of transport, and cannot be fully appreciated in a static 'museum' form. The preservation movement is able to re-create the atmosphere and character of the working railway, which no railway museum can hope to achieve. There is minimal grant assistance for preserved railways, and they need to attract significant numbers of volunteers to man them and a high volume of visitors in order to be commercially viable. Many preserved railways try hard to re-create an 'authentic atmosphere', but their efforts are often thwarted by the compromises that are required to provide modern facilities for

their visitors and workshops for their rolling-stock. In addition, there are difficulties in finding, restoring and operating vintage rolling-stock that is appropriate to the area and a chosen era. These factors have to be borne in mind when looking at a preserved railway and judging whether they do faithfully recreate the image of pre-Beeching steam operation. That said, the railway preservation movement is conscious of the need for historical authenticity, and various annual award schemes are operated to encourage high standards of restoration for rolling-stock and buildings.

Preserved railways are run on the basis of people working together as a team, often in arduous conditions. Successful preserved railways are able to become a positive focus for their community and create a useful leisure/social facility as well as a working historical document. Their popularity is self-evident by their visitor numbers, and they will continue to be successful as long as they are able to attract workers, visitors and capital resources.

Steam locomotive depots

Steam locomotives, by the standards of the late twentieth century, are relatively simple but robust machines. In order to be kept in good running order they required labour-intensive maintenance and servicing procedures to be undertaken. The scarcity of skilled labour in the 1950s and 1960s, the general rise in wages, combined with cheaper diesel fuel and electricity, led to the end of steam as the main form of locomotive power on British Railways in 1968.

The term 'locomotive depot' applies to the complex of buildings that steam locomotives visited for routine servicing and storage when awaiting their next turn of duty. Locomotive depots varied greatly in their size and the facilities provided. To some extent this was a function of the number of locomotives based there, but also the different railway companies had different designs for the structures and facilities. The principal building was the engine shed, which provided a covered facility under which minor routine running repairs could be undertaken. In addition there would usually be some form of coaling facility, a water tower that supplied water cranes that filled the locomotive's water tank (also possibly a water-softening plant), ash disposal facilities and associated pits, offices, machine shop and, at larger depots, sometimes a dormitory for locomotive crews who needed to stay overnight after a long run from their home depot.

The engine shed was usually the building of most architectural interest. It could vary from a small structure to house just one locomotive at the end of a branch line, through to a major 'roundhouse' (where locomotives were stabled in a circular building with tracks that radiated off from a central turntable), or a multiple-tracked straight-through shed that could house anything up to 50 engines. In rural locations a small shed could often be found built of timber, or stone if it was available cheaply. Larger structures would be built from brick with either wooden or steel-framed roofs. Concrete structures were pioneered by the London & South Western Railway just after the First World War. From the 1920s onwards some of the larger sheds (notably on the Southern Railway and the London Midland Scottish Railway) were built with reinforced concrete frames, with a steel-framed roof, usually clad in a lightweight material such as sheets of corrugated asbestos. In the 1930s, a number of lighter constructions were erected, steel frames having solid infill at lower level and clad in asbestos sheets higher up.

All depots would have some form of coaling facility. The most basic would be a simple wooden platform, coal being shovelled by hand onto the tender. Larger depots would have a coal stage. These were usually wooden, brick or steel-framed covered structures, from where coal was shovelled out of coal wagons into smaller trucks, which were then tipped into the loco's bunker. There is a good survivor at Didcot in Oxfordshire, where the brick-built coal stage provides a base for a large water tank. By the 1930s some of the railway companies were building fully mechanized coaling plants, where wagonloads of coal were unloaded into a large bunker. Engines were then coaled up very quickly from the bunker. These structures were built from reinforced concrete. One survives at the preserved locomotive depot at Carnforth, Lancashire and is listed Grade II*. The Great Western Railway and subsequently the Western Region of British Railways never installed such mechanized coaling plants, even up to the end of steam in the 1960s. This was partly because of the nature of the Welsh coal used in the area, which was prone to break down into small lumps and dust in such coaling plants. Also, this could reflect the lack of investment that has so bedevilled the railway industry in Britain.

Steam engines generated great mounds of ash. This was collected in an ashpan under the boiler; it could not be allowed to fall onto the track because of the risk of starting a fire on top of the wooden sleepers (rail ties). At the end

*Fig. 9.2 GWR 38XX class
2-8-0 3822 by the coaling
facility at Didcot.
(M. Frackiewicz)*

of each working day, when a locomotive returned to its depot, its fire would need to be cleaned out to remove clinker, and its ashpan emptied into a pit. The ash and clinker would then need to be removed from the pit (mostly by hand) and disposed of. This was a dirty and very unpopular labour-intensive task. In the 1930s some concrete mechanized ash disposal plants were built, often complementing the form of contemporary coaling plants. Ash would be lifted out of the pit by the use of mechanical grabs, lifted into a bunker, and then dropped into wagons to be taken away. Only one survives, again at Carnforth; it is listed Grade II.

All depots had some form of water tank to supply locos when they arrived or departed from the depot. They were usually constructed from cast-iron plates and mounted on a brick plinth or a steel or concrete frame. Good examples survive at the former Kentish Town shed in London and at Sheffield Park on the Bluebell Railway in Sussex.

The change from steam to diesel and electric traction was achieved in about 10 years. Diesel and electric locomotives have very different repair and maintenance requirements from those of steam engines. Technically they are much more complex, and they need to be maintained under much cleaner conditions than prevailed at steam locomotive depots in the last years of steam. The engine sheds had often been neglected and allowed to become dusty, ill-lit places. New cleaner major maintenance depots were often constructed, with all the new machinery required to undertake diesel/electric engine servicing. Thus the old King's Cross shed was closed and a new depot opened at Finsbury Park in North London when the East Coast main line changed to diesel traction. This depot has itself been cleared following electrification of the services to Scotland. Occasionally a number of old steam sheds continued in use as depots for diesels, such as at the Barrow Hill roundhouse, near Staveley, in Derbyshire, and the small engine sheds at St Blazey in Cornwall. The former steam engine sheds at Hither Green in South London were still in use until 1995 to house diesel locomotives.

Diesel and electric engines can be used much more intensively, and do not need the constant attention to fuelling, oiling-up and ash disposal of the steam engine. Therefore a much smaller number of locomotives are required to undertake the same duties. Dieselization and electrification therefore eliminated the need for large numbers of engine sheds. Some of the sites of big depots were in prime locations, and were quickly redeveloped when they closed (for example, Nine Elms in South London, which is now the site of the New Covent Garden Market). Very occasionally they survived with some other use, such as at Kentish Town in North London, where a large London-based construction company uses the old sheds to service and maintain its road vehicles. The most important such survivor must be the former London & Birmingham Railway roundhouse at Camden, which was built in 1846 and is the oldest surviving railway locomotive engine shed in the country, if not the world. It closed in 1860, as it was incapable of housing the increased size of locomotives operating into Euston. It became used as a goods shed and warehouse, and from the early 1960s until 1983 it was used as a theatre. It is now empty, but may have a future as a home for the historic drawings collection of the Royal Institute of British Architects.

The National Railway Museum at York was until 1992 housed in what was then a unique surviving engine shed – one with two internal turntables. It was a post-war brick-built structure with a concrete beam roof structure. The steel reinforcement within the concrete beams was rusting, and the beams were becoming potentially hazardous to visitors. Inevitably the roof required replacement, and – quite controversially – it was replaced with a modern lightweight steel structure, which resembles an aircraft hangar. In addition, one of the two turntables was removed and sold in order to allow more usable space to be created for housing exhibits. There was quite an outcry at the time. The building was without question of historical interest because of the presence of the two turntables, and it has now been transformed totally out of recognition. However, it is fair to say that when it was adapted in the early 1970s for use as the railway museum it lost its character as a locomotive shed. The presence of all the spotless railway rolling-stock and exhibition displays had already totally transformed the nature and character of the whole building.

What survives today?

There are around 12 former steam engine sheds in use still by British Rail as locomotive running sheds. It is estimated that 13 are still used by British Rail for other purposes. The numbers are still on the decline; in 1995 British Rail demolished most of what survived at Hither Green.

Very few engine sheds have been listed. The most notable listed examples are the Camden Roundhouse – the oldest survivor – and Carnforth, which still has its concrete mechanical coaling and ash plant, and as such is unique. The combined coal and water tower at Didcot should be considered for listing. Likewise the preserved engine shed at Swanage should be listed as the best example of the very few surviving typical country station engine sheds.

Fig. 9.3 Coaling plant with 150 ton capacity and capable of loading four locomotives in 10 minutes, erected at Carnforth locomotive depot from 1939. Now part of Steamtown Railway Centre. (M. Stratton)

The railway preservation movement has managed to retain three former locomotive depots and open them to the public as attractions in their own right. These are at Didcot in Oxfordshire, the home of the Great Western Society, who have the country's most comprehensive collection of Great Western Railway locomotives and rolling-stock; at Carnforth in Lancashire, which provides a base for privately owned locomotives to be restored and maintained for use on the main line; and the former Southport Depot near Blackpool, which has become a home for a mixed collection of railway locomotives and vehicles. In addition a few of the preserved operating railway lines have (mainly by chance) restored routes that happened to host a modest former locomotive depot. The largest such preserved facility is the former Buckley Wells work-shop and shed on the East Lancashire Railway at Bury. The most attractive must be the already mentioned London & South Western Railway single-road shed, with table and coaling platform, at Swanage in Dorset, home of the Swanage Railway Society. In addition there is a society who are trying to purchase and restore the Barrow Hill depot, which is one of the few remaining steam locomotive roundhouses. It has been listed Grade II.

The three leading contenders for the most authentic preservation of a working steam depot are in my opinion the Didcot and Carnforth depots and the small shed at Swanage. They are very different in their architecture and size. I think it would be fair to say that in all these cases the owners regard the sites as a home base to operate and maintain their fleets of locomotives. Because the

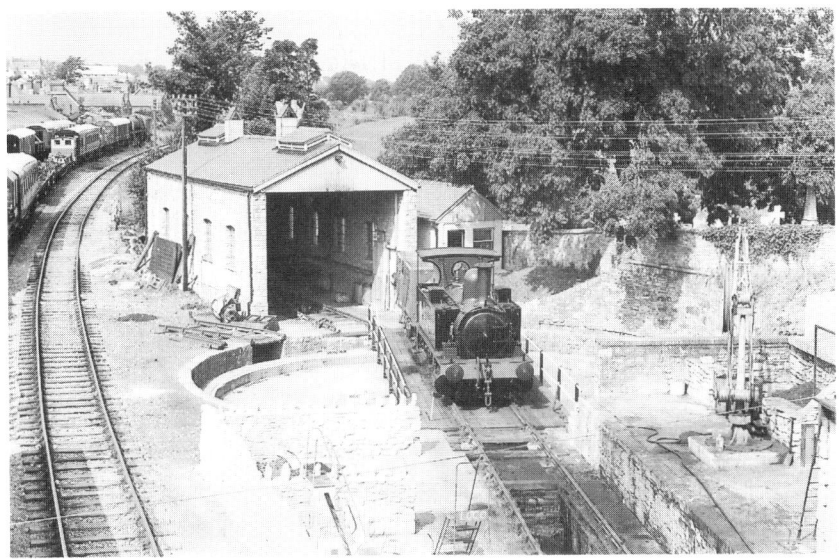

Fig. 9.4 LSWR B4 locomotive Normandy *on the turntable in front of the preserved shed at Swanage, Dorset.*
(M. Frackiewicz)

sites were obviously designed for this purpose, there has been little need to alter the facilities. At Didcot, further buildings have been constructed to provide covered accommodation for their large collection and undertake overhauls. These structures have been constructed quite discreetly behind the original buildings, in materials that echo those originally used. Buildings to house facilities for visitors have been built discreetly to one side. On a day when the locomotives are in steam it is therefore possible to absorb the full atmosphere of a steam locomotive running shed with locomotives being lit up both in and outside the shed, being watered from the water cranes, and then moving across to the coaling stage. At Carnforth the 1944 concrete sheds and facilities have been altered very little, and the facilities at Swanage also largely retain their original form.

This article would be incomplete without mentioning that in eastern Europe there are a few pockets of commercially operated steam still in operation at the very end of the twentieth century. In the former East Germany there are a number of steam-hauled narrow-gauge lines with proper steam locomotive depots. Perhaps the most impressive venue is the Wolsztyn depot in north-west Poland, which is the last place in all Europe where everyday local services are operated by standard-gauge steam locomotives. It is possible to both ride on the trains and visit the depot and see how the locomotives are maintained and operated. It has a very different atmosphere from the two main preserved depots in England, where keen volunteers maintain the locomotives and sites with true enthusiasm. At Wolsztyn, men are required to turn out at all hours and in all weathers to undertake the arduous and dirty tasks of maintaining and operating steam locomotives. Needless to say one's enthusiasm, in 1996, for lighting up a steam locomotive at 3 o'clock in the morning and oiling in inaccessible spots can wane when it is primarily a way of earning a living. The locomotives are all over 40 years old and have to be maintained to withstand the rigours of everyday use. There is always a locomotive in steam, day and night, and some activity on the shed, servicing the locomotives. About half the locomotives based at the depot are part of the preserved national collection. The Poles have decided that it is appropriate that they be kept in working order and used regularly by the state railway. The other locomotives represent the few survivors of classes of locomotives that were in everyday use in Poland until quite recently, and are kept working for as long as is economically feasible.

Outside Europe there are a few other countries that still use steam regularly. There are small pockets of steam in Pakistan, India and Zimbabwe. Cuba has a major network of narrow-gauge steam-powered railways running from the sugar cane fields. But the one major stronghold of steam is China, where steam locomotives are still being built in small numbers.

Select bibliography

Fiennes, G.F. (1967) *I Tried to Run a Railway*, Ian Allan, London.

Hardy, R. (1989) *Beeching: Champion of the Railway?*, Ian Allan, Shepperton.

Hamilton, K. and Potter, S. (1985) *Losing Track*, Routledge & Kegan Paul, London.

Signal Box Study Group (1986) *The Signal Box: a Pictorial History*, Oxford Publishing Company, Poole.

Warren, A. (1983) *Rescued from Barry*, David & Charles, Newton Abbot.

Leslie Soane

The Railway Heritage Trust
and its achievements

The theme of this chapter concerns the built environment of the railways –
designed and constructed by engineers and architects whose works often remain
in operational use some 170 years after completion. To ensure an understanding
of terms, by dictionary definition architecture is 'the art or science of building,
one of the fine arts', whereas an engineer is 'one who designs and constructs
public works, such as roads, railways, bridges etc . . .' and also one who does
public works 'requiring little skill'. Brunel and Stephenson were engineers
whose skills made significant contributions, along with eminent architects and
contractors of the day, to the enormously rich and diverse built heritage in the
United Kingdom vested in the railways.

The opening, in 1825, of the first public railway between Stockton and
Darlington, linking coalfields in the north east of England around Darlington
with the port of Stockton-on-Tees some 25 miles (40 km) away, was to be the
start of a railway building era that swept the country – and the world. The final
seal on railway development occurred in 1829, when Robert Stephenson's
locomotive *Rocket* won the Rainhill trials and opened the way for passengers to
travel between Liverpool and Manchester at new levels of speed and comfort.
Over the following 50 years the network of railways spread throughout the
country as investors built lines in a highly competitive rivalry, often duplicating
routes and facilities, which benefited passengers, but where freight traffic in
remote areas was unlikely to be profitable. In addition to the basic facilities of
track and signalling required for railway operation, some 9000 stations, 1000
tunnels, and 60 000 bridges were constructed, and an enormous range of
ancillary buildings was needed – warehouses, rolling-stock building and
maintenance sheds, signal boxes, coaling plants, water towers, offices, and even
hotels.

The first railway stations were generally in keeping with the local architecture, and would not have looked out of place in the high street of any small country town. Modest in size, using local materials and styles, they were plainly adaptations of existing building types, with speed and economy of construction being a major consideration in their design. There were a few notable exceptions, where neo-classical, Gothic or even Moorish-style buildings were intended either to reassure nervous passengers or to impress prospective investors. The fame and prestige, not to mention fees and salaries, associated with this work attracted the leading architects, engineers and contractors, resulting in the good design and construction of buildings and structures that have stood the test of time – 170 years in some instances – and are now our rich and varied railway heritage. The range of buildings and structures so built was inherited by British Railways (BR), established in 1948 when the former private railways were merged into one.

Thus variations of the country estate 'gatekeeper's lodge' or 'Cottage Orné' style served for small stations, frequently adopting the design of buildings used on the large estates through which the railway passed, such as the Duke of Bedford's estate at Woburn Abbey. Larger stations were first cousins of the toll-road coaching inns, and early locomotive sheds were seen as 'stables for the Iron Horse'. The second half of the nineteenth century and the early years of the twentieth was a period of tremendous traffic growth for the railways, and by 1914 they had reached a pre-eminent position. During this time their power and prestige were expressed in the many ambitious buildings and structures that were needed to handle the ever-increasing business. The decline in railways since then is reflected in the reduction in bridges from 60 000 to 52 000 and in stations from 9000 to today's 2550. Many of the former are on closed lines but still owned by BR. This railway heritage is vast, reflecting the all-embracing influence of the railways on Victorian and Edwardian society. I have already referred to the various types of railway building in BR's portfolio, but in addition they acquired several historical oddities through land purchase. These include such items as a fourteenth-century refectory pulpit in Shrewsbury, a medieval bridge at Ware, several sections of both the Antonine and Hadrian Roman Walls, an Anglo-Saxon cemetery west of Ramsgate Station, a Georgian mansion near Watford, and the site of a Roman governor's palace at Cannon Street in London.

Formation of the Railway Heritage Trust
In the 1950s and 1960s – the Beeching era – many of the lines and routes that had not already died a commercial death were axed, and old buildings were seen as an embarrassment when trying to present a modern railway image. Demolition of the old was often seen as the means of creating a 'new look' railway, and many grandiose stations were cleared away to be replaced by smaller ones designed for present-day usage, and clearly indicating that horse and steam power were relics of the past. After the Second World War, the poor condition and demolition of many fine buildings, such as country houses, town halls, theatres and railway stations, generated an interest in conservation. This was reflected by government action in creating lists of buildings of architectural

or historic interest, in scheduling Ancient Monuments, and in creating Conservation Areas and Areas of Special Scientific Interest. The grade of listing given to a building – ranging from the highest Grade I, to Grade II* as next most important, and finally to Grade II – is used as a guide for prioritizing the award of grants by the Railway Heritage Trust. In Scotland, the equivalent gradings are Category A and B. The rising public interest in conservation and pressure by government to complete the 'listing' survey, which had dragged on for 20 years, led to a massive increase in BR's buildings being so designated. In 1985 the total was 630, and this has now risen to 1256 – a 100% increase in 10 years. BR, publicly criticized for the poor maintenance of its listed buildings, caused an outcry when the 1838 Doric Arch at Euston – the gateway to the Midlands via the London & Birmingham Railway – was demolished to make way for the new Euston Station. To counter this adverse publicity, BR offered to set up an independent trust whose aims were:

> to conserve and enhance Britain's railway heritage and to encourage the widest public enjoyment of it; in pursuit of this aim to secure for the public benefit the preservation, restoration, improvement, enhancement and maintenance of buildings, features and objects of historical and industrial interest built for or used by the railways throughout the United Kingdom.

Thus the Railway Heritage Trust was born in 1984. Although funded by BR, the Trust is independent, and is registered as a company limited by guarantee with a board of four: the chairman, Sir William McAlpine, and three directors, Christopher Jonas, Marcus Binney and Leslie Soane (executive). The Trust is not of charitable status, as the only beneficiary from its work was deemed to be BR. It is a non-profit-making organization, owning no assets, and is thus exempt from corporation tax. To advise and assist the Trust's board, a panel of advisors was appointed, drawn from all parts of the country, whose members had an interest in the work of the Trust and were experts in their field, such as architects, journalists, academics, politicians, historians and archaeologists. They are the eyes, ears and sounding-boards for railway heritage issues, and are encouraged to alert the Trust to any building or structure observed in the course of their travels to be in need of attention. This has enabled us to advise BR of such reports and encourage action by offering grants.

BR offered to fund the Trust in its first year with £1 million to be used, as decided by the Trust, for the conservation of BR's ancient monuments and listed buildings that were still in operational use. The non-operational portfolio of BR's Property Board also contained many historic buildings, and a further £200 000 was offered to the Trust to be used on these assets. A significant role for the Trust due to its independent role was to act as a catalyst between BR and other interested parties in attracting extra funding to schemes in partnerships to the mutual benefit of all concerned. The most successful projects have usually been as the result of a funding package involving several different organizations, where the cost to any one party would have been unacceptable. In 10 years, the Trust has provided grants of £12.6 million for over 500 schemes and has attracted funding of £12.4 million from other parties. The Trust's budget has been increased each year by index-linking, but remains on an annual basis, and for 1994/95 it received £1.8 million.

From 1 April 1994, Railtrack became responsible for the operational property formerly held by BR, leaving the latter with the non-operational elements. Railtrack agreed to continue funding the Trust with £1.5 million, and BR now provides £300 000 for its non-operational buildings and structures. Among parties who provide support are local authorities, whose communities frequently identify with 'their' station and are prepared to assist with station garden schemes or even with maintaining and cleaning the fabric. To gain such interest is a good means of overcoming the vandalism and graffiti that so often despoil the environment. A number of organizations are prepared to assist in such work, on a voluntary basis, and a competitive spirit can be engendered this way. As previously indicated, railway buildings are often of outstanding design, workmanship and grandeur, and can be the most dominant structure in a town or village. When restored, they give a sense of civic pride and are a tourist attraction. Instead of BR's view of disused structures and buildings as dilapi-dated eyesores, managers and staff now envisage new uses and life for them – again with revenue benefit potential.

The Trust's role as a catalyst and pump-primer in the sale or lease of disused viaducts has enabled the BR Property Board to dispose of several such major properties by setting up a local trust or other responsible organization to take over future maintenance. The resulting restoration is beneficial to the local environment, and footpaths and cycleways can be established, or other uses found.

How the Trust functions

Railtrack's (and BR's) first priority is to provide and run a safe railway. Because of insufficient railway funding over many years, the maintenance of many buildings has not achieved the high standards required in aesthetic terms, especially for historic buildings. When proposals for renewal or maintenance of listed buildings are formulated by Railtrack in annual programmes, the detailed plans and estimates are discussed with the Trust for grant-eligibility. Advice and suggestions are made concerning the design, choice and use of material, and other information appropriate to obtaining planning approval and/or listed building consent. From the Trust's experience of dealing with English Heritage, Historic Scotland and Cadw, a good working relationship and understanding of the requirements of these bodies has evolved, which often reduces the timescale of planning procedures. The Trust's Advisory Panel includes members from these three national heritage organizations. Many local authorities now seek the Trust's comments on railway schemes, because of our wide experience in this field and our independent role. As a guide to scheme sponsors, we offer grants of up to 40% of eligible repairs, and this can attract other parties to join in the funding of projects that may otherwise not be authorized as planned. To suit budgets and to complete the schemes to an acceptable standard, it is often preferable to programme work over two fiscal years, making the reduced annual expenditure level more manageable.

Each year, requests for Trust grants far exceed our budget, and a prioritized list is produced based on the building's listed status, maintenance priority for repairs, funding by others, and the sponsor's assessed ability to spend the estimated funding in the given timescale. Some experience and judgement is essential to achieve the best results from balancing large versus small projects for grants. The effect of funding a clock renovation for £600 is sometimes more satisfying than grant-aiding a major roof repair with £60 000.

Progress to date

Over the past 10 years, a wide variety of projects has been supported by the Trust – over 500 in total – ranging from major station restorations, through medium and small, to items associated with railways: clocks, water tanks, ornamental railings, crests, war memorials and weather-vanes. These schemes are best illustrated by some examples.

Aylesford Station

A Grade II listed building, this station on the Medway Valley line in Kent was opened in 1856. It was originally built with Kentish ragstone and Caen stone dressings. The brick chimneys were removed in the late 1960s, and by 1986 serious deterioration had set in. A full restoration scheme was agreed and completed in October 1988 at a cost of £231 000, of which the Trust contributed £75 000. The restoration of the decayed Caen stone provided many problems, with over 40 trial mixes of cast stone being tried until one of a suitable colour and texture was found. The badly decayed stone was either replaced or repaired and the remainder cleaned and restored to its original condition; the roof cladding was removed and renewed with weathered Kent peg tiles and a chemical damp-proof course injected to prevent rising damp from penetrating the building. The most delicate repair was the removal of the windows, which had rusted into the frames and damaged the surrounding stonework. These were removed, cleaned, repainted, reglazed and rehung. The six chimneys, removed 20 years previously, were also carefully rebuilt to complete the full restoration of the building.

Bridgwater Station

The Bristol & Exeter Railway was opened in 1841, with Bridgwater one of the 11 intermediate stations. The single-storey buildings were designed by Brunel, and are in stuccoed brickwork, with platform canopies and an enclosed footbridge. An early photograph suggests that the front elevation of the main building on the down, westbound, side originally had a canopy supported on square columns. In 1876, the Bristol & Exeter amalgamated with the Great Western Railway.

The buildings and footbridge were altered in 1892; the present platform canopies date from this time, as does the unusual forecourt canopy, with curved corrugated iron roofing and traceried cast-iron brackets. Although an adjacent parcels office was relatively recently demolished, the station and footbridge, listed Grade II, form a particularly attractive group. The balusters of the footbridge are cast iron, fabricated by the same firm in Bridgwater that was responsible for casting the pipes laid in the track for Brunel's ingenious but ill-fated atmospheric propulsion system for the South Devon Railway.

Fig. 10.1 Aylesford Station, Kent, South Eastern Railway, 1856, after restoration, 1989. (Railway Heritage Trust)

Strongly supported by Sedgemoor District Council and the Trust, restoration was put in hand and completed in 1994–5. The buildings and platform canopies are re-roofed, internal alterations have been effected to restore the ticket hall, a new ticket office has been provided, the stuccoed chimneys have been re-instated to the 1892 appearance, and passenger and staff accommodation has been brought up to modern standards. The 1892 drawings suggest that much of Brunel's 1841 design survived till then. The restored station, not as well known as it deserves, represents both further recognition of the great engineer's work and an elegant contribution to the town of Bridgwater.

Bristol: Cheltenham Road bridge

The Temple Meads–Severn Beach branch passes through the northern districts of central Bristol and, just west of Montpelier Station, crosses Cheltenham Road on an arched cast-iron bridge, with stone abutments. The balustrades and the spandrel panels of the five arches have attractive raised decorative patterns. The bridge appears to have been manufactured by Smedley Bros, Belper, Derby, in 1873. The bridge was in a poor condition, with vegetation on the abutments; a number of advertisements were displayed on the parapets and abutments. The Trust agreed to support refurbishment of the bridge, provided all the advertisements were removed. Following the removal of advertisements, repair and cleaning of the stone abutments, with clearance of vegetation, the bridge has now been repainted in a striking blue-and-white colour scheme, funded by Regional Railways and the Trust. Bristol Civic Society awarded the refurbished bridge an Environmental Award in the autumn of 1993.

Bristol Temple Meads Station

This station area contains the largest complex of listed Grade I railway buildings in the UK. I.K. Brunel's original 1840 Great Western station, with its attractive boardroom and offices abutting the train shed, was the first building to receive a Trust grant (£110 000), for the restoration of the facade in early 1985. Since then the Brunel and Digby-Wyatt train sheds have had extensive roof, glazing and wall repairs effected, all with grants. The essential work to waterproof these buildings and ensure functioning drainage has been completed, and has enabled use to be made of otherwise derelict property. The space is to gain an imaginative new use, with the future Museum of the Empire refurbishing the interiors with an opening planned for 1996. When the Bristol & Exeter and the Great Western Railways were linked, a joint station was designed by Sir Matthew Digby-Wyatt – Brunel's architect colleague – and was completed in 1878.

By 1990, a major restoration of the roof was required. The main framework of the roof consists of 26 wrought iron barrel-shaped arches, with a span of 125 ft (38 m) and a height of 55 ft (17 m) above platform level and arranged to curve along its 500 ft (150 m) length. The problem of providing access for the repair work, while the station remained fully operational, was resolved by erecting scaffolding suspended from the roof trusses covering four bays at a time. As each bay was completed its scaffolding was dismantled and moved to the next work area. The scope of the work consisted of timber and ironwork repairs/renewal, reglazing, painting and resheeting the outercovering. Extra work was required to eradicate dry rot caused by water seepage through defective lead valley gutters. A Trust grant of £100 000 was provided.

In addition, the former Midland offices, adjacent to the Digby-Wyatt shed (Grade I listed), had deteriorated badly, and have also been renovated, with stonework and chimney stacks needing treatment. The HQ offices of the Bristol & Exeter Railway front onto the GWR's train shed. Brunel, who designed the attractive building, was its engineer. A full renovation has now brought this Grade II* building back to good condition. The above improvements have helped to restore this station's complex of historic buildings, but there is still a huge programme of essential maintenance ahead.

Bury St Edmunds Station

As with many large projects and their funding, this station has been planned for restoration in stages, with the first two completed. Designed by the architect Frederick Barnes, this Grade II listed building was completed in 1847 as an imposing two-level station for the Ipswich & Bury Railway. It was originally a terminus, with an overall roof framed by twin towers, and adapted as a through station in 1854. The roof was replaced in 1893 by Great Eastern Railway canopies. Because of deterioration, the station was placed on Suffolk County

Fig. 10.2 Restored roof and end screen, Bristol Temple Meads Station, by M. Digby Wyatt, 1865–78. (Railway Heritage Trust)

Fig. 10.3 Restoration work in progress, Bury St Edmunds Station, Ipswich & Bury Railway, by F. Barnes, 1846. (Railway Heritage Trust)

Council's 'Buildings at Risk' register. The first stage was the former station-master's house, which is located in the down-side building, at a total cost of £200 000, including a Railway Heritage Trust grant of £50 000. On completion the house was used as a restaurant/bar at street level.

The second stage was the structural restoration of the two domed towers and the station entrance facade, stabilization of the track-level building over the main entrance, and repair and re-cladding of the entrance canopy. Also included in the works was the cleaning and repair of brickwork and stonework with the characteristic tuck pointing carefully replaced or repaired.

Durham Station

Dating from 1857 and listed Grade II, the attractive Tudor-style building and the very fine North Eastern Railway canopy on the down platform had long been of interest to the Trust. The deteriorating condition of the down platform canopy was of particular concern, and at a visit in September 1992 the Trust agreed to contribute to the restoration, in two phases, of the whole structure; both Durham County Council and the European Regional Development Fund joined InterCity and the Trust in meeting the £250 000 cost. The first phase, which also included refurbishment of part of the platform building and provision of a new canopy on the forecourt side, was completed in time for the 900th anniversary celebrations of Durham's beautiful Norman cathedral.

The second phase consisted of further work to the down platform building, with grants for the restoration of the stone chimneys, for production of cast-iron bollards to an original North Eastern Railway design discovered on the site, and for completion of internal restoration of the passenger lounge. Authenticity of the chimney design came from consulting the original drawings, which happily had survived. Having supported restoration of the down platform canopy and building with five grants, the Trust looks forward to the restoration of the main station building on the up platform.

Hellifield Station

Since the Trust's first days of operation in 1985, this station and the challenge it represents have been of concern. Hellifield defines the railways' heritage in its starkest light: a large layout based on operational needs long abandoned; extensive premises dating from 1880 but provided for uses now virtually ceased; severe decay, posing some threat to the surviving railway activity; minimal public use; a remote rural location; listed status, located in a conservation area, adjacent to a National Park and recognized as a building at risk; inability of marketing to attract new users – in short, a 'particularly intractable example' was the BR Property Board's own candid description.

Reprieve of the Settle–Carlisle line in 1989 changed the circumstances, and had the recession and the then undefined proposals for privatization of the railways not intervened, restoration associated with development of the whole station site could well have taken place. It cannot have been an easy decision for Regional Railways North East to authorize and put in hand the restoration of the Midland Railway station building and platform canopies. Listed building consent was obtained in January 1994 for a scheme, the details of which were approved by English Heritage and the Trust. When completed later in the year, it made available a marketable building, re-roofed and soundly repaired, surrounded by the restored cast-iron glazed canopies, long recognized as the leading feature of the station.

The Trust led the funding partnership with a grant offer spread over 1993/94 and 1994/95; English Heritage matched this, and contributions have also been made by the Rural Development Commission, Craven District Council, the Settle & Carlisle Railway Trust, and the BR Group Partnership Fund. Fees and supervision costs were met by Regional Railways and Railtrack. A second stage will follow, comprising improvements to the operational part of the station and the subway.

Leaderfoot Viaduct

In 1992, restoration started on this elegant 19-span viaduct, listed Category A, $1\frac{1}{2}$ miles (2.4 km) east of Melrose, Borders Region. When it is completed, public access will be provided over the viaduct, overlooking the two nearby highway bridges spanning the River Tweed: the older a masonry arch bridge closed to traffic, the newer a steel box girder bridge carrying the A68 trunk road. The viaduct was built in 1865, and carried a single line of railway between Duns and St Boswells until closure in 1965.

The work includes repairs to piers by replacing defective masonry and brickwork, to brick barrel arches and voussoirs, and pressure injection of grout to the arches. Repairs were carried out to masonry spandrel walls and, underwater, to one of the cutwaters. Costs have been shared between Historic Scotland, BR Property Board and the Trust. It is planned to open the viaduct for public use in 1996.

Kilsby Tunnel main airshaft

One of the epics of engineering history in railway construction, Kilsby Tunnel between Bletchley and Rugby was designed and constructed during 1834–38 under the supervision of Robert Stephenson. The tunnel is 1 mile 682 yards (2.2 km) long, 28 ft (8.5 m) high and 25 ft (7.6 m) wide. To allay public fears of smoke suffocation at this early development stage of rail travel, 10 ventilation shafts of 8 ft 6 in (2.6 m) diameter were constructed in the tunnel roof and a further two large shafts of 60 ft (18.3 m) diameter were also provided, one 120 ft (37 m) deep and the other 90 ft (27 m). The larger shafts were built in random blue and red bricks with castellated parapets, and rise 50 ft

Fig. 10.4 Restored platform buildings, Hellifield Station, Midland Railway, 1880; brackets showing the Wyvern symbol. Photographed in 1994.
(Railway Heritage Trust)

Fig. 10.5 Detail of repairs
to stone and brickwork from
scaffolding, Leaderfoot
Viaduct, Berwickshire
Railway, 1865. Photograph
taken in 1994.
(Railway Heritage Trust)

(15 m) high above ground level. The tunnel portals and ventilation shafts are
Grade II listed structures. On the night of 25 January 1990, storm-force winds
caused severe damage to the castellated parapets and other sections of the
southern large ventilation shaft. Scaffolding of the entire shaft, 50 ft (15 m)
high and 200 ft (60 m) circumference, was immediately erected and the
damaged brickwork made safe.

The Trust was pleased to award a grant to repairs of the north main
ventilation shaft, listed Grade II*. Repairs and repointing were carried out to the
inner skin, by steeplejacks working from cantilevered scaffolding inside the top
of the shaft. The electrified railway was protected by raked protective decking
supported by scaffold towers. The external skin, built quite separately, was
repaired, with the upper 3 ft (0.9 m) of the castellations being taken down and
rebuilt in mixed red and blue bricks, to match the existing appearance. Coping
and corbel stones have been carefully reused; the two skins have been pinned,
and the void between grouted. Between 7% and 10% of the brickwork below the
corbelled and castellated upper ring of the shaft was also refaced, removing
some earlier blue brick repairs.

London Marylebone Station: porte-cochère

Melcombe Place separates the station from the nearby hotel, and the Great
Central Railway's elegant glazed porte-cochère links the two premises; the
Dorset Square Conservation Area includes Melcombe Place. The restoration
project attracted funding not only from the Trust, but also from English
Heritage, the City of Westminster and from Hazama Corporation (UK) Ltd, the
hotel owners.

Fig. 10.6 Restored porte-cochère with new zinc cladding, Marylebone Station, London, Great Central, by H.W. Braddock and D. & F. Fox, 1899. (Railway Heritage Trust)

Evidence of some structural movement, serious corrosion to column heads and decay of timber glazing bars was examined and radical restoration proposals agreed. The roof structure was stripped, dismantled and removed from site, for systematic repair. Following re-erection on the columns, the roof was reglazed in aluminium-framed laminated glazing, and the attractive cast-iron decorative details refitted. Two particular features are of note. The original construction included a large number of decorative zinc pressings, which were repaired or replaced. There were glazed end screens too, in 1899, long since removed; these have been replaced with the help of surviving evidence on the structure and from a photograph of 1902.

The whole structure was repainted in agreed colours, and now beautifully complements its two neighbouring buildings.

Newcastle Station clocks

In 1993/94, the Trust was pleased to assist with the repair of the three portico clocks. Because of safety requirements, external maintenance was discontinued some years ago, so that the west- and north-facing clocks were no longer in working order. The east-facing clock was dismantled at the time of the Metro's construction, but unfortunately never replaced. InterCity East Coast arranged for the missing clock to be provided and for the two surviving clocks to be repaired; access and movements now conform to current safety requirements.

Each cast-iron case weighs over 2 tonnes, without glazing or movement. Some 90% of existing material from the surviving clocks was reused, with existing components used as patterns for those new items needed. The cases were assembled in the specialist's works, transported to site and lifted into position by crane. Maintenance access has been provided through the parapet wall into the rear of each clock. Three new clock mechanisms were also provided, together with internal lighting and new translucent panels to the decorative cast-iron faces.

Neither Dobson's florid but unexecuted design nor Prosser's plainer and eventually completed portico included clocks, which were a later addition by the North Eastern Railway. These familiar features of the city are now all back in position and in working order.

Wemyss Bay Station

A ceremony at this station on 25 March 1994 celebrated the conclusion of one of the most satisfying conservation projects with which the Trust has been associated. Wemyss Bay Station, listed Category A, was rebuilt in 1903 for the Caledonian Railway to a design by James Miller and Donald Mathieson. A showpiece of railway operations of the day, its efficiency as an interchange for passengers between trains and Clyde coast steamers is more than matched by the charm and elegance of the architecture, which combines a clock tower and buildings, half-timbered and harled with sandstone plinths and dressings, a glazed concourse around the semicircular ticket office, long curving glazed canopies along the platforms, and a glazed roofed ramp down to the pier: it is one of Scotland's, indeed Britain's, finest stations.

In times very different from those in which the Edwardian crowds thronged the station, a jointly funded project has achieved a high standard of restoration to the whole of the original railway station. Led by ScotRail, the partnership included the European Regional Development Fund, Historic Scotland, Strathclyde Passenger Transport Executive, Inverclyde District Council and the Trust.

All parties approved the scope of the restoration, and Historic Scotland the specification. Roofs of the buildings have been repaired and re-tiled or re-slated as required; all the roof glazing has been replaced in patent glazing; all gutters and downpipes have been renewed or repaired; the seaward and landward side screen walls have been restored; structural, stonework and other repairs have been effected; new lighting has been installed; and the station has been painted in a colour scheme said to relate to that originally used in 1903.

The future

The task ahead can best be illustrated by the progress to date. In the 10 years of the Trust's existence, over 500 conservation schemes have been carried out involving only 28% of Railtrack's and BR's total of 1256 listed buildings and structures. Against the background of the continuing ageing of the assets and the increasing number of listed buildings, there should be no diminution of determination to maintain, or even increase, the rate of progress achieved so far. Government plans to privatize BR should also determine how and by whom the future of the railway heritage is to be safeguarded; a decision is awaited. The lottery-financed National Heritage Memorial Fund is intended to benefit five activities, one of which is heritage. Buildings in public sector ownership are eligible for grants for heritage-related conservation work, but those in private ownership are precluded. With Railtrack proposed for privatization during this Parliament, it seems that Railtrack will not benefit from lottery funding unless a wider view is taken of the 'eligibility' definition, as most railway heritage property is in Railtrack's ownership now. The residual non-operational property is the BR Property Board's, but the Government's aim is to privatize this organization in due course, which means that the railway heritage as shown in this presentation will, regrettably, miss out on the lottery funding, which could lead to a decline from the achievements of recent years.

John Hume

The railway heritage and Historic Scotland

The involvement of Historic Scotland in the country's railway heritage is no different in principle from that in any other part of the built heritage. It is, for the most part, governed by the 1972 Town and Country Planning (Scotland) Act, though parts of other Acts also apply. To provide guidance to local authorities, and through them to owners and lessees of buildings, Historic Scotland publishes a Memorandum of Guidance, which spells out the legislation and provides a commentary on recommended practice in the conservation of listed buildings and of conservation areas. The legislation, as with the comparable Acts for England and Wales, provides for protection by listing and the designation of conservation areas, for control of change by listed building and conservation area consent, and for the award of grants for building repair.

All these functions are, so far as central government is concerned, carried out in Scotland by the Heritage Policy Group of Historic Scotland. The functions can be divided roughly into identification, protection and assistance (IPA or India Pale Ale is our mnemonic). Historic Scotland is in the business of identifying, through listing, and categorizing into three categories (not grades) buildings of 'special architectural or historic importance'. The criteria for listing and categorization are contained in our Memorandum of Guidance on Listed Buildings and Conservation Areas, copies of which are available from Historic Scotland. After this stage, there may well follow protection in the form of applications for listed building consent. This consent process is about management of change, not about prevention of change. Listed buildings were built by people for people, and as circumstances change so buildings may very well have to be adapted. The consent process ensures that in changing buildings the character of the structure is understood and respected. We have about 42 000 listed buildings in Scotland, and receive over 2000 applications for consent, all but a handful of which are cleared. Our inspectors are often able to secure a better (and more cost-effective) solution to new uses than the initial proposal.

Scotland's heritage

Scotland's railway heritage is a distinguished one. Though not in the vanguard of the development of railways prior to the nineteenth century, the country's achievements in railway engineering during the Victorian period can rank with any other. Because of the deeply indented coastline and largely mountainous landmass there were particular problems in railway construction, resolved by building viaducts and constructing earthworks on a large scale. The necessity for economy of construction in the more sparsely populated areas of the country led to the use of innovative techniques in viaduct construction. With good freestone available, many structures were made of stone, and Scotland's pioneering role in high-class structural steel production led, in the late nineteenth and early twentieth centuries, to the widespread use of steel in both station and bridge building, as exemplified in the Forth Bridge. A further factor influencing the character of the country's railway heritage was the intense competition between its pre-grouping railway companies, resulting in the cut and thrust of competitive line-building and the erection of grand stations. Had it not been for such competition we would not have had Wemyss Bay Station, the Forth and Tay Bridges, and Glasgow Central Station in its present form.

Protection priorities and problems

So far as protection is concerned, railway structures have featured in listing proposals at least since the early 1960s. As a result of re-surveys initiated in the early 1980s, many railway stations and viaducts, and some bridges, have been added to the lists. Growing public interest in railway heritage led to the thematic study of railway stations and viaducts in the mid-1980s. The overview provided from this study prompted further revision of the lists. The stimulus to the viaducts study was the establishment of the Scottish Viaducts Committee in 1985, and the realization that prioritization was essential if limited finance was to be most effectively channelled. This strategy of concentrating resources is still valid and in use. The station study followed, and the re-categorization of stations that resulted from it has given Historic Scotland and others confidence in deciding on priorities for funding, though there is no 'Scottish Stations Committee' as a coordinator of effort. Both these surveys built on industrial archaeology field surveys conducted at Strathclyde University from the 1960s by John Hume and others.

The problems faced in the conservation of the railway heritage in Scotland differ little in kind from those affecting other aspects of the built heritage. They do, however, differ in extent. The scale and hostile environment of the Forth and Tay bridges pose problems that have recently had a good airing. Less obviously, the massive overall roofs of Edinburgh Waverley, Glasgow Central, Perth and Aberdeen stations, and on a smaller scale the roofs of Stirling and Wemyss Bay stations, are expensive and difficult to repair, and a drain on scarce resources. Only by dint of a good deal of ingenuity was a funding package put in place for Wemyss Bay's repair. The challenge of finding new

156

uses for disused viaducts has eased since the concept of long-distance footpaths and cycleways became fashionable, though there are still some problem cases. A recurrent problem is the reuse of lineside structures, where safety considerations and the natural caution of the railway authorities have made it difficult to reuse some buildings. The island platform station building, such as on the West Highland Railway, is a particular problem, where uses such as restaurants and bars are difficult to accommodate safely.

If an owner cannot find a viable use for a building we expect it to be passed on to someone who can. If no one can find a use for a building it may be preserved for its own sake, as a monument, or it faces demolition, if every other approach fails.

Against this background, let us look first in general terms at some examples of listed railway structures, why they are protected (or not), and how Historic Scotland has been able to help to secure their reuse or preservation. Listing is carried out for reasons of 'special architectural or historic importance', and age is an important consideration. So too, obviously, is straight architectural merit, but technical interest is also taken into account. A few examples will illustrate these points. Ladybank Station, 1847, is both early in date and 'architectural' in that it shows general architectural principles applied to a railway building. Dunkeld and Birnam, 1856, is rather later, and in a different architectural style, but listed for similar reasons. The overall roof at Queen Street Station, Glasgow, 1878, is one of an important group of arched-roof railway stations, and of interest for structural–historical as well as architectural reasons. On another historical plane it is of value as a witness to the effect of inter-railway rivalry in Glasgow in the late 1870s. Dalmeny, 1890, on the Forth Bridge connecting lines, is a good example of the wooden station buildings erected in large numbers throughout Scotland in the 1880s and 1890s, while Bridge of Orchy, 1894, is one of the distinctive 'Swiss chalet' stations on the West Highland, an interesting, architecturally sophisticated solution to providing accommodation similar to the more representative Dalmeny. Dunrobin, 1902, is a one-off: a rare example of a private station, and a most attractive piece of 'Highland rustic' building. Inverurie, rebuilt 1902, has recently been listed primarily on account of its very fine wood-panelled interiors. Both Glasgow Central (extended 1899–1906) and Stirling (rebuilt in 1912) stations are impressive and sophisticated structures designed to handle large amounts of passenger traffic. They represent the apogee of railway station design in Scotland, and a partnership between James Miller, a Stirling architect, and Donald Mathieson, the Caledonian Railway's innovative Chief Civic Engineer.

Turning to viaducts, the Avon Viaduct at Linlithgow, 1842, is one of the early group of viaducts by John Miller on the Edinburgh and Glasgow line. The same engineer designed the viaducts on what became the Glasgow and South Western's line from Kilmarnock to Carlisle. All the viaducts on this line have been listed, including Hurlford, a typical example, and the internationally important Ballochmyle (both 1850). Miller has good claim to be considered the greatest designer of masonry viaducts. The Findhorn Viaduct, Forres, lacks the obvious appeal of the masonry arch, but is an early wrought-iron structure, dating to 1855. Shankend, 1860, is a magnificent complement to the Border

Fig. 11.1 Ladybank Station, 1847, showing its 'villa' style and modest canopies, typical of early station buildings. (J.R. Hume)

hills in scale and proportion. The Forth Bridge, 1890, needs no justification or comment, and the Culloden Moor Viaduct, apart from its visual merits, is significant as the longest masonry viaduct in Scotland, and as one of the last to be completed (1890). Two viaducts are included to illustrate specific problems: the Ness Viaduct at Inverness (1865) was de-listed after it collapsed during a

Fig. 11.2 The arched overall roof and ornate glazed end screen, Queen Street Station, Glasgow, rebuilt by J. Carswell for the North British Railway, 1878. (J.R. Hume)

Fig. 11.3 Dalmeny Station, dating to 1890 and a fine example of a late nineteenth-century wooden station building. (J.R. Hume)

Fig. 11.4 Avon Viaduct, Linlithgow, by J. Miller, 1842. One of a series of viaducts on the Edinburgh to Glasgow route. (J.R. Hume)

serious flood, while Big Water of Fleet, though undeniably a major landscape feature, was de-listed because of the extensive and inappropriate repairs and strengthening of what was clearly a poorly built structure.

The conservation and conversion of stations has been a phenomenon characteristic of the last 10 years or so, compensating in a measure for the de-manning, vandalization, and sometimes demolition of many of Scotland's

Fig. 11.5 Forth Bridge, viewed from South Queensferry. The bridge, completed in 1890, is a pioneering example of the use of steel for a major engineering structure. (J.R. Hume)

stations. Wemyss Bay, 1903, and Dumbarton Central, c.1900, are both examples of large high-profile stations on a scale now in excess of modern requirements. Their status as A-listed buildings has been an encouragement to their extensive repair. The repair of Wemyss Bay was assisted by a grant from Historic Scotland. Historic Scotland was also able to help the Scottish Railway Preservation Society with the repair costs associated with the movement of the 1842 train shed at Haymarket Station, Edinburgh, to Bo'ness. At Brechin the former Caledonian Railway Station, 1848 and 1895, has been acquired by a preservation group for repair and restoration. Strathpeffer Station, 1885, built in elaborate style for a spa town, was closed in 1947 and lay empty for many years. It has now been converted into craft and retail units. A more unusual case is Taynuilt, where the wooden station of 1879 was threatened with demolition before listing. It is now a micro-brewery with an associated public house. Finally, at Melrose the grand station built for tourist traffic to the Scott country by the North British Railway in 1850 was refurbished as a visitor complex by an Edinburgh architect, after a long period of disuse. Historic Scotland grant-aided this scheme.

Historic Scotland has been represented on the Scottish Viaducts Committee since its formation in 1985, and carried out a reassessment of all disused viaducts in Scotland to enable priorities for conservation to be determined. This exercise has not been fully worked through, but has assisted in making the best use of available funds. Where there is a use of a viaduct as part of a footpath or cycleway it is easier to secure preservation. Gryffe Viaduct at Bridge of Weir, 1869, is now part of a cycleway created by Sustrans, and Ballindalloch Viaduct, 1865, an impressive wrought-iron structure, is a link in the Speyside Way, a long-distance footpath. Leaderfoot Viaduct, whose repair has been

Fig. 11.6 Strathpeffer Station, terminus of a short branch off the Highland Railway's Kyle of Lochalsh line, 1885. Restored as craft and retail units. (J.R. Hume)

grant-aided by Historic Scotland, is about to be taken into care by that body. There are many residual problems with viaducts. Inappropriate though well-intentioned stonecleaning at Kilmarnock Viaduct has damaged the structure, and will cause problems in the longer term. Long-disused viaducts are now developing serious defects, and the early mass concrete viaducts at Giffenmill and Lugton, 1903, face demolition. In even worse condition is the Kilmarnock and Troon railway viaduct at Laigh Milton Mill, 1811, disused since 1847, where a repair scheme (grant-aided by Historic Scotland) will, it is hoped, stabilize this structure, which appears to be the oldest railway viaduct in the world. Still awaiting repair is Uddingston Viaduct, 1847, the only surviving early cast-iron viaduct in Scotland, and one of those identified as priorities in the early days of the Viaducts Committee. Larkhall, 1905, one of the last, and the tallest, viaduct in Scotland, has twice been saved from demolition because of its listed status, but awaits conservation.

Active projects at the moment, apart from the stabilization of Laigh Milton Mill Viaduct, include the conversion of Clydebank Riverside Station, 1896, into flats; the adaptation of Cupar Station, 1847, into housing; and the possible relocation of the former signal and telegraph workshops at Ladybank, c.1850, to Markinch as part of a railway preservation scheme. Historic Scotland has had an input in the Clydebank scheme through listed building consent procedures, and will be similarly involved in the others in due course.

Examples

Some case studies will serve to flesh out this summary.

Camps Viaduct, West Lothian

This was the first railway structure to be the subject of a grant-supported repairs scheme. It was built in 1885 by the North British Railway as part of a mineral railway serving the shale-oil works at Pumpherston. It is a tall nine-arch structure spanning the gorge of the River Almond, and is a late example of a masonry viaduct. The scheme of repairs was estimated to cost about £275 000, of which Historic Scotland put up £60 000. The other funders were British Rail Property Board, the Railway Heritage Trust, the Countryside Commission for Scotland, the Scottish Development Agency, and Lothian Regional Council. On completion of repairs the viaduct was handed over to West Lothian District Council, who will maintain it as a feature of their popular Almondell Country Park.

Glenesk Viaduct, Midlothian

This was the second scheme to qualify for a Historic Scotland grant. It was built for the Edinburgh and Dalkeith Railway, opened in 1831 as the first public railway in the east of Scotland. This line was originally horse-worked, but was taken over by the North British Railway and converted to locomotive haulage in the late 1840s. The bridge – for it has only one span – was repaired between 1991 and 1993, as part of a footpath and cycleway. The project cost was about £250 000, of which £110 000 came from Historic Scotland. The other funders were British Rail Property Board, the Railway Heritage Trust, the Countryside

161

Fig. 11.7 North Water Viaduct, Angus and Kincardine & Deeside, Montrose and Bervie Railway, 1861–5. Major repairs part-funded by Historic Scotland as a prelude to passing into local authority ownership. (J.R. Hume)

Commission for Scotland, Lothian and Edinburgh Enterprise, Scottish Widows, and the European Regional Development Fund. The viaduct is now owned by the Edinburgh Green Belt Trust, who are responsible for its maintenance.

North Water Viaduct, Angus and Kincardine & Deeside

This spectacular viaduct was built between 1861 and 1865 by the Montrose and Bervie Railway, engineers Blyth & Blyth. The future of the viaduct was in considerable doubt until the local authorities agreed to assume ownership once repairs had been completed, with a view to creating a countryside walk. This project has involved masonry repairs, underwater works, and fitting handrails. It is still in progress. The cost is about £200 000, of which £65 000 came from Historic Scotland. Scottish Natural Heritage has supported the project on condition that some stonework gaps were retained to provide a home for a breeding colony of Daubentonís bats.

Leaderfoot Viaduct

This viaduct, near St Boswells, has been under threat of demolition more than once since the line closed in the late 1960s. It was built for the Berwickshire Railway, and completed in 1865; 19 arches span the River Tweed. Construction was with a soft type of brick. Maintenance over the years had seen hard engineering brick used for repairs. This mismatch of materials exacerbated damage.

The local authorities became interested in the future of the viaduct, but did not feel able to take over ownership. Discussions also took place with the National Trust for Scotland. Agreement was eventually reached that the viaduct would be taken into state care by Historic Scotland once it had been comprehensively repaired. A scheme was put together for which Historic Scotland, British Rail Property Board and the Railway Heritage Trust each contributed one third of repair costs, which totalled nearly £750 000.

Wemyss Bay Station

Historic Scotland has funded a major repair scheme at Wemyss Bay, in Inverclyde. This remarkable station was built, with a steamer pier, in 1903–4 by

Fig. 11.8 Leaderfoot Viaduct, near St Boswells, Berwickshire Railway, 1865. Taken into care by Historic Scotland, and the subject of major repairs to its decaying brickwork. (J.R. Hume)

163

the Caledonian Railway. In its heyday it was a bustling destination for holiday traffic, but usage has declined substantially. Such a large-scale structure cannot be justified from an operational viewpoint, and in the early 1990s it seemed as though the serpentine canopies would have to be drastically cut back.

However, a partnership of ScotRail, the Railway Heritage Trust, Strathclyde Transport Executive, Historic Scotland, ERDF and Inverclyde District Council was able to fund a repairs scheme costing some £1.8 million. The station was recommissioned in March 1994, having been returned to a traditional painting scheme. Floral baskets are being maintained by local heritage interests.

Wemyss Bay demonstrates the importance of a collaborative approach, with agencies chipping in what they could. There is now a need to make fuller use of the station. The local enterprise company is looking at diversification options, while others are promoting the creation of a youth hostel in coaches facing a redundant platform.

Conclusion

From this brief and selective account it will be seen that Historic Scotland has been and will be deeply involved in the conservation of Scotland's railway heritage. Through listing, listed building consent, grant-aid, and both formal and informal liaison with the railway authorities and other interested parties, Historic Scotland will continue to seek the best possible future for historic railway structures. We attach great importance to the railway heritage, which includes some of Britain's finest stations and viaducts, and see it as something of lasting value for both residents and visitors.

Richard Threlfall
The challenge of legislation:
heritage policy and the
Railways Act 1993

Railway heritage: it undoubtedly means rather different things to different people. My academic training was in modern history, so when I was first told I was to take on responsibility for railway heritage, I had rather hopeful visions of frequent visits to the major steam preservation societies. My images were of beautifully polished steam locomotives and Queen Victoria's royal carriages. I carried these images with me to the first of many discussions with Mr Andrew Dow, then Head of the National Railway Museum, where he immediately brought me back to earth. 'Teaspoons', he intoned; 'teaspoons . . . paintings . . . clocks'. These are, of course, as much of interest to the National Railway Museum as are locomotives. We have a tendency, most of us think, to view heritage in terms of large, attractive packages – buildings, for instance. And most of this book concentrates on architecture. But this paper will explore a different aspect of railway heritage: that which is concerned with artefacts and records.

Railway heritage in the Railways Act 1993
Section 125 of the Railways Act 1993 is optimistically entitled 'Railway heritage'. Within section 125, you might therefore suppose, may be found the solution to the first problem posed by the consultation held at York, namely 'to define and establish the nature of the railway heritage'. Alas not. No mention is to be found in section 125 of buildings or viaducts: no guidance on preservation or restoration. In fact in all of its terribly lucid 154 sections and 14 schedules the Railways Act 1993 makes no mention of historic railway properties at all. And nor need it, for such matters are already well covered by the legislation governing listed buildings.

This chapter is concerned with what happens to historic railway artefacts and records when British Rail or new publicly owned railway companies such as

Railtrack wish to dispose of them. But before ploughing into what the new legislation does, or is supposed to do, it is worth explaining why we decided to replace the existing system, and what we were hoping to achieve.

The need for new legislation

Disposals of artefacts and records are currently subject to the provisions of section 144 of the Transport Act 1968. Interpreting this particular piece of legislative drafting has proved something of a legal nightmare. I have already been offered four different interpretations of it. This is no fault of the original drafting, I should add, although the Campaign for Plain English may take a different view. It is rather due to the fact that the institutions referred to in section 144 have changed over time. Section 144 requires that any artefact or record being disposed of by British Rail is first offered to the Secretary of State for Education and Science. Of course, the DES no longer exists. Worse, we presume that the reason for offering them to the DES was because in 1968 the Science Museum was actually part of the DES. So, in practice, items offered to the Secretary of State were accepted on behalf of the Science Museum. It was not until 1975, as a direct result of the Transport Act 1968, that the National Railway Museum was created at York. Thereafter, so far as I understand, items have been offered directly to the NRM, and the Secretaries of State, 'one and indivisible', have been removed from the picture. So in 1992, when we first began examining the 1968 heritage provisions, we found that the legislation bore little resemblance to what was happening on the ground. Over a number of years a wide gulf has emerged between what the 1968 legislation requires and what is actually being done.

There is, however, a further problem with the relationship between the National Railway Museum and British Rail, and one that is perhaps best illustrated by returning to the subject of teaspoons. Andrew Dow was always concerned at the possibility of historic items of potential interest to the museum, such as teaspoons and paintings, being given away as presents, perhaps to a long-serving railway worker on his retirement. A similar concern is the danger of items of potential interest simply never being brought to the attention of the museum, and being inadvertently thrown away or sold. Such problems are symptomatic of the informal relationship between the museum and British Rail. The National Railway Museum has relied for many years on the rather unsatisfactory system of a network of contacts. Items are not offered systematically to the museum, because there is no coordinating body, even within British Rail, to oversee disposals.

Reviewing the policy

Our starting point was therefore that the existing legislation was obsolete, confusing, and ineffective. Fortunately we had an opportunity to replace it using the Railways Bill then under construction. But we needed to be clear about what we wanted to achieve. So the next step was to review the policy.

We did not in fact change any fundamental aspect of departmental policy on railway heritage. The broad policy remains: to recognize the historical importance of collections of railway heritage artefacts and records, particularly those of the National Railway Museum, the Public Record Office and the Scottish

Record Office, and to aim to secure the status of the present collections while encouraging the acquisition of new items.

However, we did feel that there was a need for a coordinating body to oversee disposals from the railway system. The Railways Act was designed to facilitate the restructuring of the railway network into a number of separate companies, a restructuring that is already well under way. The splitting-up of the unitary British Rail could only make more difficult the problem of identifying and claiming items of interest. We also wanted to avoid placing decisions back on the shoulders of a Secretary of State, as in the 1968 Act, partly because it is extremely impractical and also because the expertise in railway heritage resides outside government, in the museums and in the railway community. We wanted to provide a proper focus for this expertise, so we decided to provide for the creation of a new committee.

We also decided that in creating this committee we should recognize the interests of transport museums other than the NRM, while ensuring that the importance of the museum at York, as the *national* railway museum, was not undermined. It is our policy that the vast majority of artefacts should continue to go to the National Railway Museum, but that items of, for example, particular local interest might be offered to a local museum.

Fig. 12.1 The Great Hall of the National Railway Museum, first built as a locomotive depot in the 1950s, re-roofed 1991–2, and with a re-erected North Eastern Railway footbridge of 1891.
(National Railway Museum)

Section 125: heritage provisions of the Act

The Railways Bill became law on 5 November 1993. Section 125 of the Act gives effect to the policy I have just described. It is, however, largely an enabling piece of legislation, which is why I have been speaking of the 1968 provisions in the present tense. Section 125 enables a piece of secondary legislation to be laid before Parliament, and it is this secondary legislation, to be known as the Railway Heritage Scheme Order, that will actually replace the 1968 provisions. However, section 125 does lay down a framework from which the secondary legislation may not deviate.

The main effect of section 125 is to provide that a committee should be created to oversee disposals by 'publicly owned railway companies, the Board, and wholly owned subsidiaries of the Board'. I will return later to why the legislation does not cover assets that, through the mechanism of the Railways Act, will transfer into private ownership.

Section 125 also sets out the powers of this committee. It may 'designate' items that 'in the opinion of the committee are of sufficient interest to warrant preservation'. I should stress that the opinion of the committee in this respect is not open to challenge or restriction. It may designate anything as worthy of preservation, from the Forth Bridge to a plastic buffet-car cup. The process of 'designation' consists of notifying the owner of the item of its designation. Once the owner has received such a notification he may not dispose of the item except in accordance with a direction by the committee.

So the second power of the committee is to issue directions instructing the owner as to how he should dispose of the item. When to dispose of something is a matter for the owner, but once he has decided that the item is no longer of use to him, he must follow the directions given by the committee. These directions can specify to which collecting institutions the item should be offered, in what order, and on what terms, including the cost (if any) that the collecting institution should pay. The legislation would have indicated that no payment was required, but this would apparently have created a liability on the collecting institution to pay VAT on the full value of the item acquired. Payment of a nominal sum, say £1, renders the institutions liable for VAT only on that pound – not a problem that existed in 1968!

A major advance of section 125 over the provisions of the 1968 Act is that the committee now identifies the items that it considers of interest in advance of their disposal, and owners are put under the obligation to ensure that the item is offered to the museums specified. This should reduce the time and effort that the National Railway Museum currently expends in keeping track of interesting items – waiting in the wings, powerless to register an official claim.

The Railway Heritage Committee

The new committee will be known as the Railway Heritage Committee, and will be set up by the Railway Heritage Order. Public consultations on the final draft of this order have just been concluded, and that final draft was itself a product of extensive discussions with the National Railway Museum and other parties. The order is itself constrained by the terms of section 125, which dictate, for instance, that the chairman and members of the committee will be appointed by British Rail and approved by the Secretary of State. However, the order will also add substance to the Act in a number of important respects.

First, the order will require that the National Railway Museum, the Public Record Office and the Scottish Record Office are represented on the Committee. It will also require that publicly owned railway companies, the Board and its subsidiaries are represented by a total of at least two members. Although the appointments are a matter for the Boards, we can expect, I think, that a representative of the three new rolling-stock companies, which have inherited such a large and important proportion of British Rail's assets, will be appointed.

Second, the order will require that the committee keeps records not only of its meetings, but also of all its designations and directions. I think it is very important that the committee is seen to act openly and fairly. The records of its designations should also, over time, provide a valuable catalogue of the most important possessions of the railway industry.

Finally, the order will specify that the cost of the committee and its secretarial support will be met by British Rail. These provisions will, I hope, lead to the creation of a committee that will be immediately able to take an active and effective role in transferring items of historic value to collecting institutions.

The challenge of legislation: two examples

All this paints a seamless picture of the new railway heritage provisions. I think it only fair, however, and also much more interesting, to share with you a couple of examples of the difficulties that were faced in putting together this new legislation. Our lawyers can confirm that heritage raised unexpected complexities during drafting, quite out of proportion to the place that it now occupies in the Act.

Take items that are transferred to the private sector, for instance. I promised to return to this subject and explain why it is not covered by the Act. When the detailed instructions for section 125 were being prepared, ministers embraced the idea that items of historic interest, currently owned by British Rail, should be transferred to the private sector on the basis that they would eventually be offered free to a collecting institution such as the National Railway Museum. However, this grand plan was tripped up by the discovery, during the Commons stages of the Bill, that it would have been contrary to the European Convention on Human Rights (ECHR). No matter that the direction would be set in Statute; the ECHR states that no person may be deprived of their lawful property without due compensation, which apparently means that even if an artefact was bought on the understanding that it might at some future date be claimed by a museum, it would still be necessary to offer the market value of the artefact in compensation. This raised two difficulties. First, it introduced financial burdens that the collecting institutions could not reasonably be required to meet. Second, it raised the possibility of challenge by aggrieved owners, which implied that a provision for agreeing compensation and an appeals procedure would have to be included. Given these considerable obstacles, it was decided that the issue could more easily be dealt with by an administrative scheme than by legislation.

A rather different type of difficulty was that of introducing proper flexibility into the legislation. We were naturally very anxious to avoid repeating the experience of the 1968 Act provisions – which, as I discussed earlier, were undermined by changes to institutions. There has been a trend away from using real names in legislation for precisely this reason, but it does make it more difficult to specify to whom the legislation applies.

The first problem was how to deal with Railtrack, which is known through-out the Railways Act simply as 'the network operator', and how to ensure that the Act covered new public companies not yet created. It seems simple enough in retrospect, but reaching the formulation 'any publicly owned railway company' took considerable thought. Had we used instead the term 'licensed railway operator', the rolling-stock companies would not have been covered.

There was then the issue of staffing the committee. Here we were deter-mined to specify those institutions, such as the National Railway Museum, that were to be represented. Yet we wanted to avoid using the title 'National Railway Museum' in the Act. Were the NRM to change its name, the legislation would have to be amended, which would require formal debates in both Houses. Parliament's time is too valuable to be spent on such mechanical tasks. The solution was to place all the details of the committee into secondary legislation. This gives the NRM a statutory place on the committee, but if its name changes, the order can be altered by negative resolution – that is, without debate. By making the legislation flexible in these and other respects, we hope that it will be able to adapt to meet the changing structure of the railway industry.

Next steps: policy into practice

This chapter has presented not just an explanation of the new railway heritage legislation, but also a brief insight into the sort of issues and problems that can be posed for government by the creation of any new legislation. My involve-ment with the heritage legislation was often exciting, sometimes wearing, but always a challenge.

It is worth concluding by giving some indication of the work that remains. The final version of the Railway Heritage Scheme Order was placed before Parliament, made on 1 August 1994, and came into force on 1 September 1994. The list of members embraces a wide range of interests, from the National Railway Museum, British Railways Board, Railtrack and Porterbrook Leasing to the Public Record Office and Scottish Record Office. Five experts, embrac-ing archives, railway history and preservation and museums, have been appointed in a personal capacity.

The committee is now fully up and running, meeting, at present, every two months. A Records Working Group, an Artefacts Working Group and a Scottish Working Group have been established – the last two including co-opted members from outside the main committee. Specific sets of criteria have been agreed against which proposals for designation and/or direction must be measured. These criteria target items that are extremely rare; that are illustrative of a type of activity that merits preservation; that represent an important technical, operational or social aspect of the railway; or that relate to important changes, events or persons.

Fig. 12.2 Class 08616 shunter at Birmingham. The last locomotive to be rebuilt at Swindon Works in June 1986, and being considered by the Railway Heritage Committee as worthy of earmarking for preservation. (GWR Museum, Swindon)

One issue recently considered is the fate of the last locomotive to be rebuilt at Swindon Works: diesel shunter 08616, which emerged in June 1986. The 08s comprise the most numerous class of diesel locomotive, and none has hitherto been scheduled for display in a major museum. The shunter has now been formally designated, with a view to its ultimate return to Swindon in the relocated and expanded railway museum. A collection of early structural drawings by Brunel and a silver-gilt Victorian presentation centrepiece illustrating Brunel, Locke and George Stephenson are among the other items already designated. Future deliberations will be aided by databases of historic locomotives, carriages and wagons, held by preservation organizations or still running on the national network.

The committee has already concluded that formal designation is by no means always the most appropriate way forward. If there is no discernible risk, for instance, it may be better simply to come to a suitable arrangement with an owning body. To take another example, even if there was an element of risk, to designate just one of a class of locomotive or rolling-stock could lead to problems were it to be involved in an accident. Here a formal undertaking might provide a better way forward for all parties concerned.

The committee has been given sufficient powers to be able to act effectively on a wide range of issues. A Railway Heritage Bill is currently in Parliament – a measure that would extend the remit of the committee to include the emerging privatized railway. The Bill has received support from all sides, most notably from the Department of Transport, and clearly represents the next and a major step forward.

Part Four
London's Stations

Nick Derbyshire

The Liverpool Street Station story

Construction and extension

The original terminus of the Great Eastern railway had been at Shoreditch, later renamed Bishopsgate, rather as parts of Paddington are known as Kensington. The name change, however, could not disguise the inconvenient location of the terminus, and the Great Eastern decided to extend the railway into the City of London.

The site eventually chosen was alongside Broad Street Station of the North London Railway, which had been built at high level on the end of the North London's railway viaduct from the north. The viaduct solution to crossing existing streets was an old-established and sensible way of building a new urban railway, the Greenwich Railway being an early example. However, the Great Eastern decided to build the new railway in a cutting below the existing streets. This seemingly odd decision meant not only steep gradients to the original line above Shoreditch, but also the attendant difficulties of access to a station below street level. The fact that Broad Street was above street level meant that any connection between the two would be difficult, to say the least.

It seems that the decision was prompted by the wish to link up with the existing Metropolitan Railway running east–west below street level in front of the new station. For many years a link existed between platforms 1 and 2 of Liverpool Street and the Metropolitan, but it was not used to any great extent, and was closed in 1907. Apart from this rather basic misjudgement, the rest of the 1875 station was planned in an exemplary manner. The engineer to the Great Eastern Railway, Edward Wilson, is credited with the design, but the Fairburn Engineering Company of Manchester, which supplied the ironwork for the train shed, may also have had a strong design input.

The station was planned to cater for two distinct types of passenger, long distance and short distance, and as the former naturally required long trains and

175

the latter short trains the platforms and concourse were designed in an L shape, with the short leg at the north end and the long leg running south to Liverpool Street. The angle between the two legs became the access to both, and an L-shaped station office building divided the access area from the platforms. The long leg was not, however, placed adjacent to Broad Street Station but towards Bishopsgate. This was the other misjudgement, as we shall see.

Because of the curving tunnel linking up with the Metropolitan Railway, and because it was thought desirable to separate arriving from departing suburban passengers, the suburban entrance and ticket office were set at street level, and the top of the tunnel provided access from the street. Departing passengers walked along a balcony and down stairs to the suburban platforms. Arriving suburban passengers walked below the balcony and then followed either a ramp to the street or subway access at the same level to the Metropolitan. Long-distance passengers, mostly arriving by cab, followed ramps up and down to the main-line ticket office, which was set at platform level alongside the main departure platform. This followed precisely the pattern set by all the other terminal stations in London. The usual arrangement was a departure platform with ticket office adjacent and porte-cochère beyond. Parallel with this, and usually separated by a number of carriage sidings, was the arrival platform, alongside which was the cab rank. Most terminal stations have now departed from this arrangement, largely because of the need to convert the carriage sidings into additional platforms and the introduction of barriers to check tickets. King's Cross is a good example of this change. Paddington, however, is still used precisely as originally designed, albeit with additional platforms in place of the carriage sidings.

At Liverpool Street the tracks and carriage sidings were extended southwards underneath the adjacent hotel so that coal and laundry could be delivered directly. The platforms were covered by a glazed roof with wrought-iron structure consisting of two aisles and two naves separated by a double line of columns down the centre. A transept was formed over the suburban concourse and crossed the main-line tracks and platforms. The eastern nave and adjacent aisle were extended southwards, one side being supported by the office building. The aisle was modified at the south end to allow for the arriving passengers' cab ramp to the street. Where the nave roof met the Great Eastern Hotel, the facade of the hotel responded with a huge semicircular pediment, rather like an indoor version of the facade of Fenchurch Street Station.

The roof is both lofty and wide; the original Brunel roof at Paddington would virtually sit under it. The south-eastern side of Victoria Station is equivalent in size to the two main naves minus the aisles. Its structural form – cantilever spandrel brackets and suspended trusses – is unusual, and does not fall into any of the usual train-shed roof categories: crescent truss, high-level tied truss, low-level tied truss, or arch without tie.

The roof, although without any overtly Gothic details – the column capitals were classical, in fact – gives an overall impression of neo-Gothic style. This is assisted by the flowing character of the cast-iron spandrels supporting the roof principal trusses and the brick pointed-arched windows of the flanking walls. The twin nave-and-aisle plan and the diagonal views of clustered columns reinforce this impression.

The L-shaped office building, later to be known as 50 Liverpool Street, was more obviously neo-Gothic, and included a clock tower over the suburban ticket office. The Great Eastern Railway was short of money, and Wilson was continually required to reduce the cost of the building. The result was a somewhat pattern-book and rather flat and repetitive facade. However, great care was taken to design the frontage so that it could receive the aisles of the southward-extended portion of the train shed adjacent to the main-line departure platform. This was to prove most valuable in the design of the new concourse.

The separation of suburban and main-line passengers and of in and out routes at the main entrance to the station was obviously somewhat confusing, and an early engraving shows the Portland stone gate piers covered in signs to try to reduce the confusion.

It quickly became apparent that the 1875 station was not large enough to handle the growing suburban traffic of the Great Eastern, and that expansion was necessary. As we have seen, the 1875 station had been designed with the long leg of its L shape towards Bishopsgate. This was the only direction in

Fig. 13.1 Internal view of the original shed at Liverpool Street, London, showing Gothic effect given by the curved ties and the connecting footbridge.

177

which expansion was possible, as the station was hard up against Broad Street Station on the other side. Not only that, but the suburban platforms could not be extended southwards because of the location of the railways' offices and forecourt. Any expansion towards Bishopsgate would therefore be divided from the existing suburban platforms by the main-line departure and arrival plat-forms.

This was exactly the result when the 1894 station was added. For almost the next 100 years Liverpool Street Station was really two stations divided by what became platforms 9 and 10: not a unique situation – Victoria is two stations side by side, as is London Bridge – but Liverpool Street is probably the only one all built by the same railway company. Attempts were made to ameliorate the situation; a bridge was built adjacent to the hotel over platforms 9 and 10, and eventually the tracks under the hotel were filled in, a short linking platform end was built and the platforms shortened. The east wall of the western train shed was opened out with arches for much of its length; a pedestrian tunnel was driven beneath the cab road ramp; and, most spectacularly, the balcony facing the original suburban platforms was extended eastwards as a bridge over platforms 9 and 10, which, following a somewhat tortuous route, arrived at street level in Bishopsgate having traversed the 1894 concourse *en route*.

The architect for the 1894 station was W.N. Ashbee, who was head of the Great Eastern Railway's architectural department from 1883 to 1916. He was also the architect of Felixstowe, Colchester, Norwich Thorpe and Wolferton stations. The style was neo-Tudor, and the quality of the brickwork and the detailing was of a much higher standard than that of Wilson's work. The roof over the platforms was not as attractive, however, and was of fairly straightfor-ward pitched glazed trusses on columns slightly reminiscent of those at Paddington. There was much carving of stone and brickwork, and the office building, named Harwich House and built adjacent to the new concourse, had attractively carved brick panels, depicting cherubs carrying out typical railway jobs. The new concourse had its own cab ramp between the extended hotel and Harwich House. The style of the extended hotel and Harwich House had become more florid and Flemish, and tourelles, turrets and steep gables made their appearance.

The old problem of Liverpool Street Station's lack of visibility from the street remained unsolved, and in Bishopsgate the only indication of the new 1894 station's existence was an attractive blank screen wall and another office building, Hamilton House, running parallel with the street. The new platforms were built neither to the length of the original main line nor to that of the original suburban ones, so the operating of the station became even less flexible, with three sets of platforms all taking trains of different lengths.

Thus the station remained for the next 90 years. Early this century two art nouveau tearooms were built at high level adjacent to the balconies, one over the 1875 suburban concourse and one over the 1894. These were delightful places to enjoy a pot of tea while watching the activity on the platforms below. The clock tower was damaged in the Second World War, and lost its pyramid roof. Hamilton House was partly destroyed along Bishopsgate. The 1950s saw the removal of the acanthus leaves from the column capitals. In the 1960s a mezzanine floor was inserted into the main-line ticket office.

Broad Street and Liverpool Street: redevelopment and refurbishment

In the 1970s the difficulties and inadequacies of Liverpool Street for passengers and staff alike, together with the deterioration of the fabric of the 1875 train shed after 100 years of steam and weather, led to British Rail's trying to find a way of rebuilding the station. By this time Broad Street Station was only a shadow of its former self, and the adjacent goods yard was closed. It was thought that the development of the Broad Street site could pay for a new Liverpool Street Station.

The first development plans were revealed in 1975. The architects appointed by the British Rail Property Board were Fitzroy Robinson and Partners. I, then employed as an architect by British Rail, first became involved in the project after a public inquiry and while Fitzroy Robinson were employed as an architect by British Rail, working on a revised version of their original proposals. My role was to carry out the detailed design of the station facilities within the context of the overall development plan.

The public inquiry had resulted in approval to demolish the listed 50 Liverpool Street office building but not to demolish the listed western train shed, although the southern nave could be altered. Once it was clear that the eastern train shed north of the transept was to remain, British Rail decided to carry out major repairs to this part of the roof.

The original roof had been designed to carry ridge-and-furrow glazing running vertically between cast purlins and gutters, rather similar in form to the original Crystal Palace. Relatively early in the station's life the ridge-and-furrow glazing was replaced by more conventional flat patent glazing and the cast gutters became redundant. They were left in place, however, and by the 1970s were putting an unnecessary load on the main structure. The main repair work to the roof involved the replacement of the patent glazing by plastic sheeting. New lattice trusses were stooled onto the old structure to carry the plastic. To the casual eye these were not momentous changes, but in comparison with the remaining southern nave, which was not altered at this time, the result was a coarsening and simplifying of the original.

Even more unfortunate was the replacement of the original fretted end screens with a corrugated metal-sheeted version. Some glass-reinforced plastic replica filigree was added to the new roof structure to try to retain some of the spirit of the original. The main structure of lattice trusses carried on cantilevered cast-iron spandrels was not altered, however. All these alterations were subject to listed building approval, which was obtained.

The Fitzroy Robinson proposal was designed to put as much office building at the south end of the site as possible with its front door on Liverpool Street. It was considered necessary to stay as close to the City as possible, and the north end of the site was regarded as suitable for light industrial use only.

The apparent need to place the offices on the south end of the site immediately conflicted with the need to provide an architectural solution to the new station concourse. Because the southern nave of the western train shed was to be retained, albeit altered, the retention of the Great Eastern Hotel was also assumed. The hotel was not listed but has never been threatened with demolition, although the first Fitzroy Robinson scheme removed the western half of the hotel. The result was a new concourse partly covered by an office development over its western half.

Fitzroy Robinson developed an aesthetic of cascading glazed cubes, which were used to give emphasis to the various entrances to the station. The Bishopsgate entrance was then developed into a roof structure to the eastern concourse that approximately followed the rise and fall of the western train shed. The junction of this new cubic roof, both with the existing shed and with the Great Eastern Hotel, was extremely difficult to handle, and there was a certain relief when this particular scheme was unsuccessful in finding a financier. While this had been happening, Stuart Lipton, then Managing Director of Greycoat City Properties, had been developing an office building known as No. 1 Finsbury Avenue on an adjacent site. The architect for this was Peter Foggo of Arup Associates, and there had been some dialogue between Arups and Fitzroys over a joint square where the two schemes met.

Up to this time it had always been assumed that the minimum size for a new Liverpool Street Station was 22 platforms spread right across the site, including the sites of both Broad Street and Liverpool Street Stations. At this critical moment for the future of Liverpool Street Station, Stuart Lipton, having now formed Rosehaugh Stanhope Developments with Godfrey Bradman, proposed an entirely new development plan to the British Rail Property Board. But to enable the development to get off the ground as quickly as possible and to reduce the overall cost of the new station to British Rail, a smaller station was proposed of only 18 platforms, which did not need to extend into the adjacent Broad Street site. At the same time it was decided not to widen the approach tracks from six to eight, but to allow this to be done at some future date.

Peter Foggo produced a new plan for the Broad Street site that involved the creation of two new squares linked to each other and to a new mall at the level of the new station concourse. Because of the natural fall in the land from Bishopsgate to Eldon Street the mall arrived at Eldon Street almost at existing street level and made a wholly new entrance to the station. The other effect of Peter Foggo's plan was to remove the focus of the development from Liverpool Street itself, pushing it into the new squares to the north, and increasing the land values there.

All these events helped the resolution of the design of the station itself. The development was now physically separate, and no longer covered part of the concourse. The entrances to the station and development could also be kept separate.

Reordering a Victorian terminus

My task was to redesign the station with the simple concourse and equal-length platforms that were British Rail's objectives, while relating properly to its immediate surroundings and respecting the historic and aesthetic requirements of the existing structure.

An overall master plan for the station had already been put together. This indicated a new east–west concourse with ticket office and trading adjacent. A taxi area was placed between the station and the development at concourse level with road access via a ramp from the north. Above this, at street level, was a bus station. The platforms were extended to a common barrier line adjacent

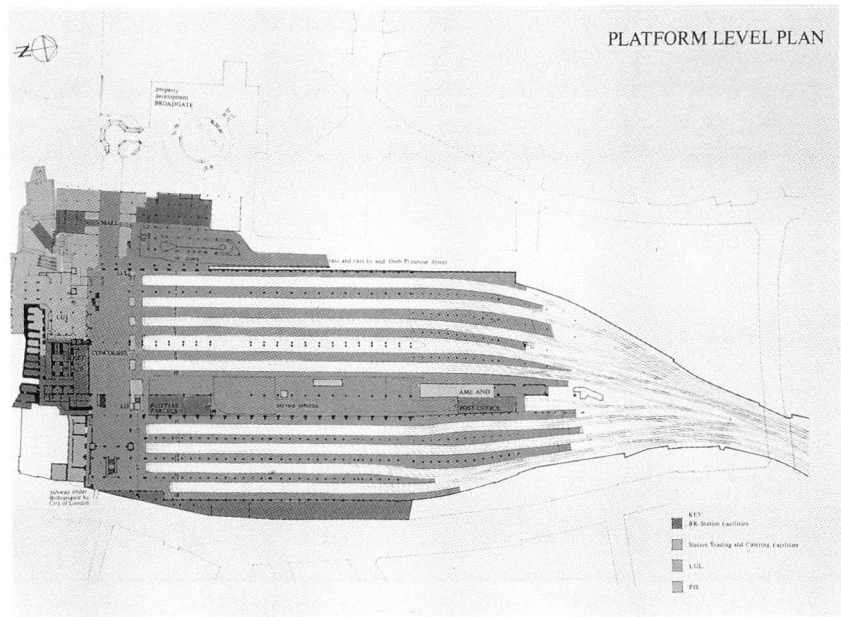

PLATFORM LEVEL PLAN

Fig. 13.2 Plan for reorganizing the platform layout at Liverpool Street, by N. Derbyshire Associates. (N. Derbyshire Associates)

to the new concourse, and the former taxi exit ramp and roadway became a service area for use by delivery traffic.

In the early days of the previous scheme there had been some talk of extending the existing train shed to fill in the gap in the existing L shape and to cover the concourse. My starting point in trying to find a suitable language for the new station was to look at ways in which the language of the existing buildings, both of the western train shed and of the Great Eastern Hotel, could speak to the future. Initially I ignored 50 Liverpool Street, as I assumed that any solution to the new concourse would require its demolition.

I had noticed that the proposed width of the new concourse was approximately the same as that of the existing transept, 27 m, equivalent to three aisle bays. I had also observed that the Great Eastern Hotel exhibited a series of towers, a particularly prominent example being on the corner adjacent to 50 Liverpool Street. This L-shaped building also acted as a buttress to the existing train shed. The roof had virtually no other lateral stability. I started to put these notions together. If a tower could be provided in line with the western train shed's west wall and another on the line of the columns separating nave from aisle, then not only would these possibly buttress the roof but, if properly designed, they could help to tie in the station and the hotel.

The towers needed linking visually, and I first introduced a building between them. An axonometric was produced of this, and served to illustrate the possibilities of the towers, but it also revealed the major problem of the blank end west wall of the Great Eastern Hotel, once 50 Liverpool Street had been demolished.

At about this time another influential figure played a part; Simon Jenkins, then an external member of the BR Board with special responsibilities for the environment, took an interest in the fate of 50 Liverpool Street and the station as a whole. He asked me to find ways of retaining as much of 50 Liverpool Street as possible. The majority of the building would obviously have to go, as the new concourse and extended platforms required its removal. However, the part south of the new concourse perhaps could remain, or at least be rebuilt in replica as it would be over the proposed location of the London Transport ticket hall. The mid-Victorian architect of 50 Liverpool Street had followed the contemporary practice of expressing the different activities within. The southern end of the building, which contained the main offices of the Great Eastern Railway, was virtually a separate building from the remainder. It required only a north elevation to complete it. The east elevation butted onto the Great Eastern Hotel.

Conservation, replication and new design

Taking this as my cue, I developed several alternative proposals for the Liverpool Street entrance. The preferred solution then formed the basis of the eventual architectural resolution of the entrance. In fact, for various structural and staffing reasons, the building that you now see is a replica faithfully copied from the original. There is, however, one significant change. The ground floor of 50 Liverpool Street was then intended to be used as a ticket office at concourse level below. The small windows and single door would not be appropriate for what is in effect a shop. I therefore designed an arcaded ground floor derived from the original door surround. I suspect that few people would be able to tell that this was not part of Wilson's original design.

The space formed by 50 Liverpool Street and the towers marking the station entrance was then enclosed by replicas of the Portland stone piers that had been placed there in 1875. One of these still remained as an example. No drawings of the railings existed, and a gate that remained near Bishopsgate and included the Great Eastern Railway roundel was used as a pattern instead.

The extension of the existing train shed now had to be designed so as to meet with what became known as the south pavilion of 50 Liverpool Street. There was a gap between the new three-bay-wide roof over the concourse and the new north elevation of 50 Liverpool Street. As soon as I remembered that the original aisles had been designed by Wilson to mate with the 50 Liverpool Street elevation along Platform 9, the solution was obvious. I had just designed a new north elevation to 50 Liverpool Street on the original pattern. If two 'aisles' were used to bridge the gap they must match with the new north elevation. This was the solution adopted.

The Bishopsgate entrance to the station was more difficult. By this time the development boom was under way, and the City of London changed its policy regarding new office buildings, with the possible impact of Canary Wharf assisting this. This change of policy was the death-knell of the 1894 extension. This part of the station had never been listed, and plans were quickly prepared to demolish the eastern train shed and build a vast office development over the tracks. The architects appointed for this were Skidmore, Owings and Merrill (SOM), a large American firm based in Chicago.

I developed a proposal whereby a slightly narrowed transept end wall flanked by two more towers could be placed closer to Bishopsgate. The flank walls of this extended concourse would match the existing train shed west and east elevations. This proposal would also provide a means of covering the awkward gap where the hotel service yard divided the hotel into two.

SOM had placed an openwork turret on the southeast corner of their building, and this would dwarf any station tower placed adjacent. Also, it seemed wrong to position the station entrance too close to the pavement. This had been a fault of the 1894 station, and a square similar to that at the Liverpool Street entrance was the answer.

The only other obvious position for the east elevation and the towers was directly between two gables on the hotel north elevation. This looked right, and also minimized the overshadowing of the hotel's windows by the adjacent tower. This position meant that part at least of the adjoining rafted-over platforms would be flanked by the maximum volume of the concourse. The actual stairs and escalators, however, needed to be as close to Bishopsgate as possible, otherwise passengers from the eastern platforms would be doubling back to get to the street.

Several studies of glass roofs to cover the escalators and stairs were undertaken until the eventual form emerged. This was itself influenced by separate design work being carried out for high-level trading units within the extended shed. So far, the design effort had been concentrated on making sense of and finding a language for the historic structures that remained. The intention was not, however, to build a replica of a Victorian station. The trains that would be using the station would be brand new and electric. The expectations of the passengers would be of a twenty-first-century method of transport. Network SouthEast, the prime user of the station, regarded itself in the Ford Sierra market, not a vintage car club. The information systems, the public address, the ticket machines, signing, lighting, would all be of the latest design. How could an extended Victorian aesthetic be reconciled with these modern elements?

I had been fascinated by this issue for some time, and most recently had faced it at Newcastle Central Station, where I had designed a new travel centre to sit within the historic train shed. I designed this as a modern building, but attempted to capture the boldness and vigour of the original. This seemed to offer a way forward at Liverpool Street. If the Victorian forms were replicated as accurately as possible then the other visually more ephemeral elements within could be designed in a contemporary manner.

Because Liverpool Street Station platforms are below street level, a system of balconies and walkways can be designed to enable pedestrian cross-movement without dropping down to concourse level. Initially, the only walkway was over the barrier line intended to service the indicator boards, at that time placed at right angles to the two naves

Trading kiosks had always formed part of the barrier line at concourse level, but even with these and the other areas of potential trading around the concourse British Rail faced a substantial drop in its trading income for the future. The only possible area for expansion of the trading was at high level along the new walkways, the most obvious being the service walkway running across the barrier line. I developed several proposals for this using glazed tunnel-vaulted structures, modelled on an existing glazed building in Copenhagen Central Railway Station. The original entrances to the Paris Métro had always seemed entirely appropriate to their function of advertising an underground railway and providing shelter. These formed the initial inspiration for both the high-level trading units and the entrance from Bishopsgate. The balcony railings were to be of glass so that the shops and people would be visible from the concourse below. The glass spans between the stanchions and in turn supports the handrail. The developed system has also been used for staircase handrails, footbridge structure and television monitor brackets.

At the same time the design of the western train shed extension was being developed. A complete nave bay and adjacent aisle was erected as a prototype for the new extended roof, on some derelict railway land at Stratford in East London. This demonstrated convincingly to all who saw it the quality of what we proposed, even down to the appearance of the original rivets, in this case represented by domed bolt heads.

One fascinating development was the design of a new arch between the nave columns. The original building has two versions of this: a very delicate one was used for all examples except for those immediately adjacent to the crossing of the southern nave and the transept, where a crude and heavy version was used for

Fig. 13.3 New concourse and first-floor shops at Liverpool Street, by N. Derbyshire Associates. (N. Derbyshire Associates)

extra strength. The original delicate arch was no longer possible under current codes of safety. We did not wish to use the clumsy crossing version, and thus the new arch was developed. This was test-erected at Stratford and accepted.

Fig. 13.4 New and restored roof at Liverpool Street. (N. Derbyshire Associates)

Liverpool Street Station now therefore exhibits three different versions of this arch to the cognoscenti; the casual observer would not be aware of this subtlety. However, a future Nikolaus Pevsner, if discerning enough, will be able to read the history of the station rather as a cathedral may be understood.

The old stations and office buildings were full of delightful details, some of which I have already mentioned. It was obviously necessary and important to find appropriate places for the war memorials, but I also wanted to find ways of including other elements. We decided to store all those items that seemed worthwhile for future incorporation in the scheme. In fact, most of them were in such an eroded state that they were not used directly, but accurate copies were made. The carved brick lunettes have been reused, however, as has the lettering 'Great Eastern Railway' saved from the gable of Harwich House and re-erected above the war memorial.

Liverpool Street Station has become a huge popular success, meeting with almost universal approval from passengers and staff. The station serves as a shopping centre in its own right, and has become, together with Broadgate, a significant new place to go in London. Some romantics perhaps regret the loss of the byways and oddities of the original stations, but more may be pleased that an historic Victorian building is capable of adaptation and change to make it still suitable for its original function in the last years of the twentieth century.

Robert Thorne

Major termini: *problems of conservation and urban design*

Our national obsession with railways makes it easy to believe that the conservation of railway buildings and structures is a special activity with its own methods and approach. In some respects this is true, partly because of factors to do with common ownership and also because a working railway imposes particular requirements on the way buildings are conserved and used. However, the decline of the railways, plus the fragmentation in their ownership and operation, makes the idea of a common approach to a uniform set of problems seem less and less realistic. But, more importantly, it is not obvious that all buildings and structures connected with the railways have a major ingredient in common. A typical wayside station may have a clearer kinship with the domestic villa architecture of its time than it has with other railway buildings, and a railway workshop may be best understood as simply another kind of factory building. As regards both history and present-day conservation problems, the railway element can easily be overstated.

Historical perspective
However, no one would deny that there are many building types and structures that are to be found on railways and nowhere else: signal boxes, turntables and engine sheds come immediately to mind. At the head of any list of special railway buildings, pride of place goes to the major railway termini, which still dominate our principal cities. From the 1830s onwards it was recognized that terminus stations presented particular problems in design, layout and operation. In large part this was because of their function, but related to that it was also recognized that they played a major symbolic role within the railway system. Not for nothing was Euston Station dominated by its Doric portico, far grander than the sheds behind, announcing to the world that henceforth London was directly linked to the industrial heartlands of the Midlands and the North. No

subsequent terminus, in London or elsewhere, had quite such a self-conscious symbol as its entrance, but architectural pretension remained a major consideration in the design of such stations. The reconciliation of the architectural contribution with the engineering of the train shed and other railway works seemed to contemporaries to be one of the most important architectural problems of the time, and commentators each had their favourite example of an ideal solution. Where those stations survive, from the father of them all at Manchester Liverpool Road to turn-of-the-century examples such as Glasgow Central, they are rightly regarded as major architectural expressions of their time.

However, the special status accorded to railway termini should not blind us to the fact that most of them are highly problematic buildings, particularly in the way that they relate to the cities they serve. First and foremost there is a strong case for saying that many of the familiar examples would benefit from not being termini at all. In many cities, above all London, railway companies were prevented from carrying their lines through or under the city. In part this was because of the opposition of public authorities and powerful urban landlords, but just as much it was because in the early railway age there was not the technology for running trains in deep tunnels beneath the built-up area. Railway companies, exhausted by the problems and expense of building their lines through the inner suburbs, were content to stop on the periphery and go no further. In London the official cordon to railway encroachment defined by a Royal Commission in 1846 systematized the limit to their activities that the companies were already coming to accept. The eventual result was the line-up of stations along the boundary of the Euston and Marylebone Roads to the north and the Thames to the south, with only one rather awkward link between them. In similar fashion, railways reached but did not penetrate the centres of provincial cities such as Glasgow and Manchester.

The great railway termini are so familiar to us that we forget how inconvenient they are. Except for people destined for the nearby area they mean a change of transport for passengers: to underground, bus or taxi. They concentrate people at points on the edge of the city, rather than allowing them to disperse easily to where they want to go. The Victorians did their best to alleviate the effects of this break in journey, both by designing the termini so that people could come and go freely and by linking the stations with other forms of transport. They also made a virtue of necessity by making the business of arrival and departure a significant and often memorable event. However, for passengers of every kind, especially daily commuters, the need to change to another form of transport at the terminus has always been a cause of frustration and delay.

Many present-day termini also carry the legacy of two other problems. One is the duplication of facilities, the enduring result of inter-company competition and the failure of the Private Bill process to restrain the absurd results of railway rivalries. Though some of the results of duplication have been weeded out, for instance by the elimination of Broad Street Station in London and the closure of Manchester Central, many other examples still continue to exist as a constraint on railway operations and the amenity of travellers.

Another even more important legacy relates to the crude and insensitive way in which railways were inserted into the urban fabric. The social costs of railway building were gradually acknowledged by contemporaries, thanks to campaigning journalism and the requirement from 1853 that companies file a return of the numbers of population displaced by their projects. Those who felt that railway demolitions had a beneficial sanitary effect were eventually outnumbered by those who realized that such demolitions helped create worse slums elsewhere. However, the physical impact of railway building involved much more than just the clearing of slum properties. Railway construction shaped the city just as forcibly as the decisions made by urban landlords and their developers or the regulations imposed by municipalities. The presence of the railways – not just stations, but approach lines, goods yards and other facilities – dictated the character of an area, because of the amount of land they used, the traffic they generated, and the associated noise and smell. Above all, where there were viaducts and cuttings involved, the railway created permanent barriers across the city: there was thenceforth a right and wrong side of the tracks, both socially and in the whole way the city functioned. In a small number of celebrated cases (at Lewes, Nottingham and elsewhere) the impact of the railway on the urban fabric was debated, largely because ancient monuments were threatened, and in an equally select group of cases the arrival of the railway occasioned a new street layout. However, by and large what is most astonishing is how little attention was given to the consequences of these major developments. Certainly there was little attempt to assess what today would be called environmental impact, or to suggest that the urban fabric might take priority over the necessities of railway engineering.

To preface a discussion of the conservation of railway termini by a description of the problems associated with their construction and operation may seem unduly defeatist. The intention is not to question their architectural or historical importance, but to provide a realistic context for considering their conservation. The way in which conservation policies and attitudes have developed since the Second World War has encouraged an emphasis on individual buildings and individual building features, often at the expense of wider issues. More often than not the long-term future of a building is best secured not by an obsession with detail but by an appraisal of the broader circumstances affecting it. If those circumstances are disadvantageous to the building no amount of attention to detail will help it; conversely, if the circumstances can be improved then the details can much more easily be got right. Where the big railway termini are concerned, it can be argued that many of them have suffered from awkward circumstances from the start, and conservationists should be willing to acknowledge that fact. This means being prepared to welcome changes that improve the way the stations work, particularly from the passengers' point of view. Keeping a station in efficient use is the best form of conservation. Equally, it means resisting proposals that display the same kind of crudity as many early railway projects, particularly in their impact on the urban fabric. Termini can be made to work well, and most of them have sufficient flexibility to allow the right kinds of improvement to be made.

In Britain, if not Europe, London is pre-eminent as a city of terminal stations, and displays examples of all their good and bad aspects. Given the size of the West End and the City by the time the railway arrived, it was inconceivable that lines would be built across the centre. Instead the central area was eventually encircled by 15 stations, ranging from the hesitant pioneer at London Bridge, opened in 1836, via the great main-line stations of the mid-Victorian period to the unassuming terminus provided by the Great Central at Marylebone in 1899. Of these 15, two have now gone: Holborn Viaduct has been superseded by a stop on the Thameslink service, and Broad Street, once nearly top of the league in the number of commuters it handled, has disappeared beneath the tide of offices flowing northwards from the City. Others have been transformed, as at Victoria, Charing Cross, Cannon Street and Fenchurch Street, in particular by the building of air-rights structures above the platforms. So far the greatest transformation of all, and generally considered the most successful, has been the redevelopment of Liverpool Street Station in 1985–91, which has turned one of the most awkward and bizarre of termini into a model of convenience and efficiency. It is the dream of those responsible for stations that are yet unaltered to apply the magic of Liverpool Street elsewhere.

This contribution is primarily concerned with three London stations that so far have been very little changed in the present century: Paddington, St Pancras and King's Cross. All are now the subject of major proposals, which will, if carried out as planned, have a dramatic effect on their appearance and the way they are used. With the example of Liverpool Street as a precedent it is tacitly assumed that a similar transformation is acceptable, acknowledging the past but accepting late twentieth-century commercial and operational demands. The key question for conservationists is, how should they respond to these proposals for three Grade 1 stations?

Paddington Station

The present station at Paddington was built in 1851–4 to replace a station slightly further to the west. Like almost all termini its siting and layout were designed with railway operations primarily in mind, and the relation of the station to its urban context was very much an afterthought. From the purely railway point of view it has worked very well, and the claims that were made for the flexibility of the three-bay train shed have proved fully justified. The one significant alteration, the addition of a fourth shed in 1909–16, came about because of increased traffic rather than any defect in the original plan. However, from the point of view of arriving and departing passengers, Paddington can be most frustrating. Although it was on the urban fringe at the time of its construction, almost no opportunity was taken to give it a proper street approach. It was given a frontage on a minor street, and was arranged, following the convention of the time, with separate arrival and departure sides. Because the station is in a cutting, the approaches ramp down from the surrounding streets, with the effect on the departure side of creating a restricted, unattractive area unbecoming to a station of such importance. With the building of the Underground (which the Great Western Railway welcomed as a means of remedying the relative isolation of Paddington), connections to the station for

passengers were hardly improved. Paddington was ultimately served by three Underground lines, in a confusing arrangement with mean and inadequate approaches to all three.

Two major new railway proposals affecting Paddington offer the chance to correct some of the deficiencies that the station has always suffered from. The Heathrow Link, now under construction, will provide a high-speed connection between Paddington and Heathrow, and is predicted in the first instance to attract 18 900 passengers per day. Meanwhile, CrossRail, which is yet to be sanctioned, will link the lines into Paddington to a tunnelled route across London towards Liverpool Street and the eastern suburbs. Indeed CrossRail represents the first large-scale attempt to deliver suburban travellers directly to where they want to go in central London, eliminating the need to change at an existing terminus.

With the design of these two new lines a chance appeared to do what Brunel never fully attempted: to relate Paddington to a proper urban place, and by doing so to make the station a greater pleasure and more convenient to use. What initially happened was a proposal to run CrossRail beneath the centre of the train shed. Our practice (Alan Baxter & Associates) pointed out that this was unwise in engineering terms because of the risk to the train shed, and because the tunnels would conflict with the piled 1930s extension to the Great Western Hotel. It made much more sense to construct the tunnels beneath Eastbourne Terrace, the long road that runs parallel to the sunken station approach road, and to take the opportunity to drop the road to the same level as

Fig. 14.1 Paddington Station, London, by I.K. Brunel and M. Digby Wyatt, 1854. Photograph of 1880s, showing the offices along the main departure platform. (Westminster City Archives)

Fig. 14.2 Eastbourne Terrace frontage of Paddington Station, from GWR Magazine, April 1907. (Westminster City Archives)

the station entrance. Then a proper station square could be created, which would ease the handling of station traffic and give Paddington the kind of street frontage it has never previously possessed.

So far what has happened is that the alignment of the CrossRail tunnels has indeed been moved to beneath Eastbourne Terrace, but the idea of a new station square has been disregarded. Conservationists are content because the new alignment removes a possible threat to the original station, yet that misses the equally crucial issue of how to make the station work more effectively. At the same time it is planned for the Heathrow Express trains to arrive at the narrowest platforms in the centre of the station, where arriving jet-lagged passengers can cause the maximum congestion as they search for their way to a taxi or the Underground. The conservationist response is to worry about how the overhead electric wiring for the new trains is to be fixed, not what the overall effect of this traffic on the station will be. It would have made much more sense to run the Heathrow trains into one of the platforms adjacent to the taxi roads, out of the way of regular passengers heading for their familiar platforms.

King's Cross and St Pancras Stations

The case of King's Cross and St Pancras presents the same kind of problem in a more complex form. These two rival stations, standing alongside each other but at totally different levels, are one of the great sights of London. They are also, if the Underground station beneath them is included, one of the most congested transport interchanges in the country. Yet the fact that such an overloaded interchange exists has been used not as an argument for diverting trains and people elsewhere but as a justification for adding yet more railway facilities. Since 1987, King's Cross–St Pancras has been put forward as the

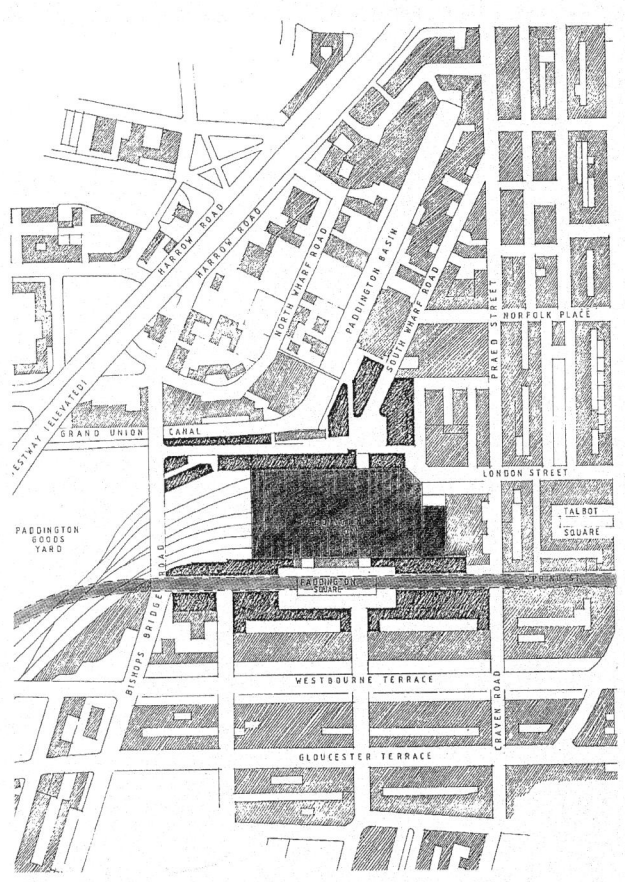

Fig. 14.3 Proposal by Alan Baxter & Associates for the integration of CrossRail with Paddington Station through the creation of a new square on the Eastbourne Terrace frontage.
(Alan Baxter & Associates)

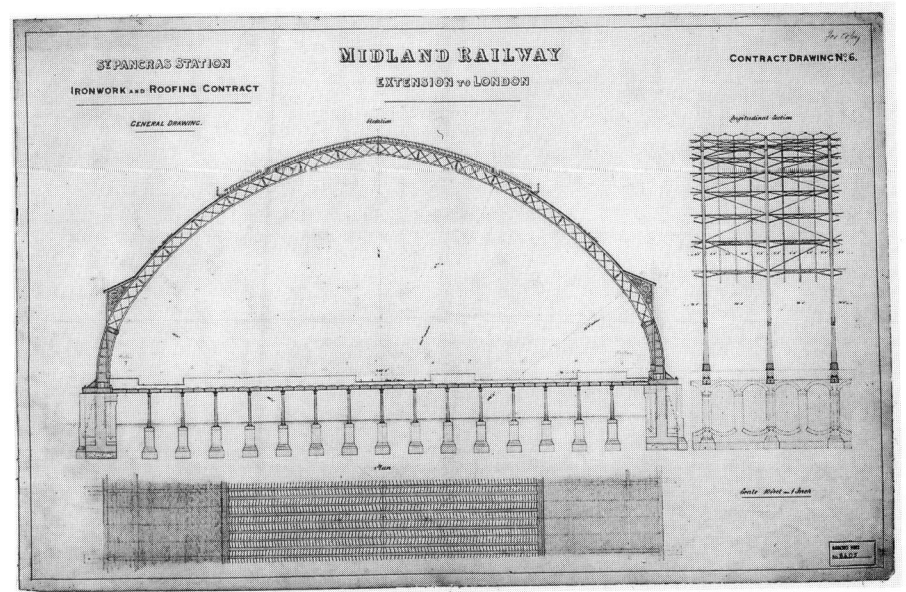

Fig. 14.4 Contract drawing of W.H. Barlow's train shed at St Pancras Station, London, drawn c.1864.
(British Railways Board)

ultimate destination of Channel Tunnel Rail Link services on the grounds that there is nowhere else in London where such good connections can be made to other places. The impact of these services on the people and fabric of the area has always been, as with nineteenth-century railway building, a second consideration.

There have been two versions of this proposed CTRL terminus. The first was for a new station beneath the existing King's Cross, approached in tunnel from the south-east. This would have involved significant demolitions in a densely built-up area near the station, plus the immense difficulty of constructing a new facility beneath the present station. Because of the engineering issues and costs involved, and the dependence of the new railway infrastructure on the development of the railway lands behind King's Cross, this proposal was eventually dropped. In its place, as announced in 1993, is the current proposal to use St Pancras as the new international terminus, with an approach route in tunnel beneath Islington and then across the old King's Cross goods yard. Although it has the virtue of exploiting a major station that is at present underused, this alternative seems to have a list of potential drawbacks almost as long as the original King's Cross low-level idea. It involves extensions to St Pancras that will totally transform its architectural character, and the approach lines will

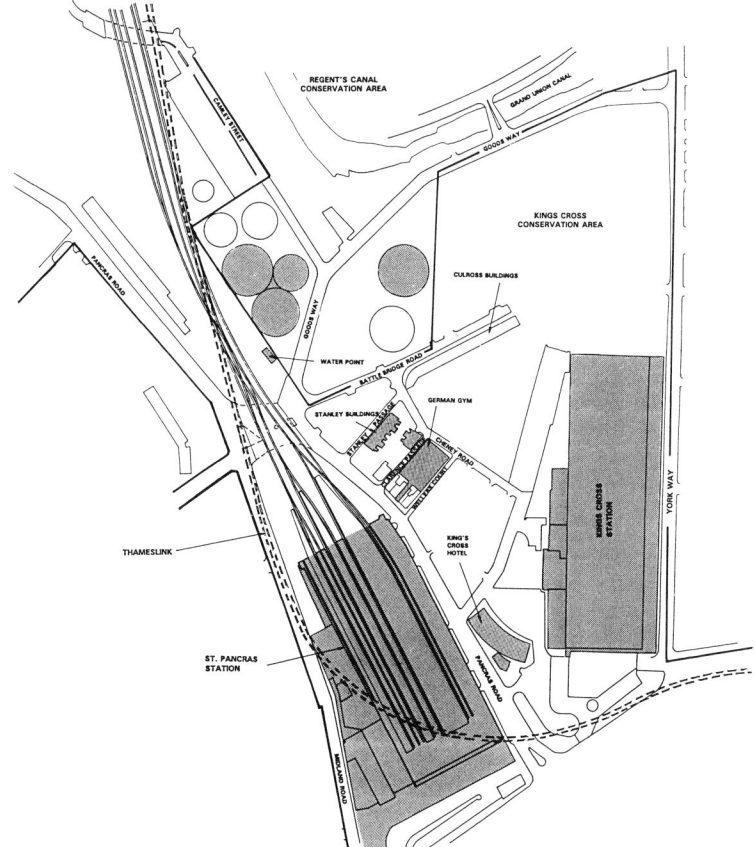

Fig. 14.5 Plan of King's Cross and St Pancras Stations, showing the listed buildings and structures in the area.
(Alan Baxter & Associates)

divide the goods yard with as much ruthlessness as any nineteenth-century engineering project.

The debate about the CTRL at St Pancras is still in progress, and it would be unwise of any historian to judge its outcome at this stage. However, what has happened so far clearly illustrates the continuing problem of our terminal stations. They have been inherited along with the legacy of the peculiar circumstances of their creation. With the exception of the CrossRail proposal there is little sign of that legacy being rethought, or of the fundamental drawbacks of the terminus idea being addressed. Instead most new proposals for such stations have the effect of compounding those drawbacks. They have been devised with as little thought for the urban fabric around the stations as was given when they were first built. There is still an enduring assumption that the railway engineering solution that is proposed must be right, and that all else should be subservient to it.

Conservationists for their part have failed to address the bigger issues of what should happen to these stations. In the case of St Pancras, for instance, there now exists a so-called Heritage Agreement itemizing every detail of how the station fabric should be treated if the CTRL project there is carried out. Yet this does not of course address the fundamental question of how so many passengers will be handled, or whether it is right to expand the traffic

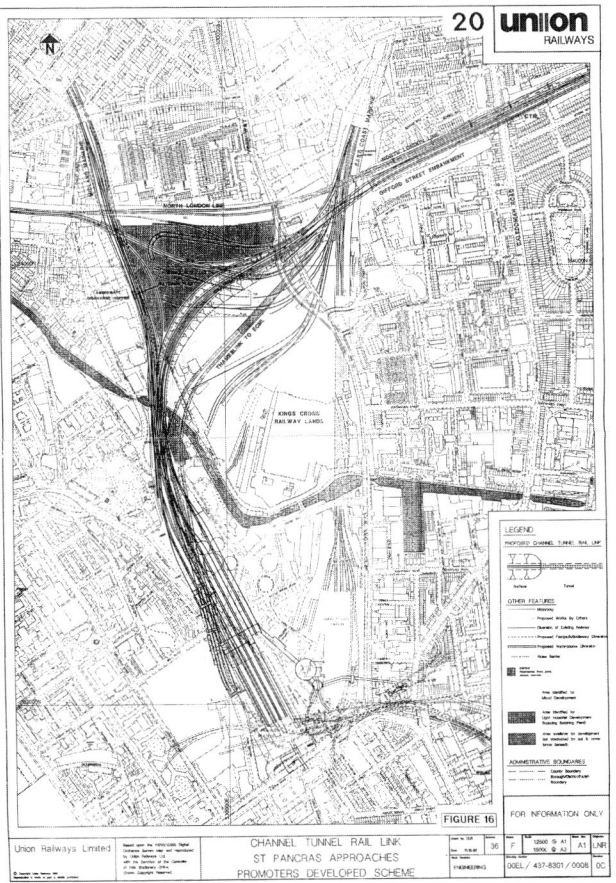

Fig. 14.6 Proposed railway works in the King's Cross–St Pancras area for the Channel Tunnel Link, 1995. (Union Railways)

195

terminating at an already crowded location. The details are important, but the proper time to consider them is when the larger questions have been settled. Railway termini demand an appraisal that takes full account of their past, including the recognition that we cannot simply carry on regarding them as they have been regarded before.

David Lawrence

Underground architecture

A glance at the London tube map will show a network of lines and the many stations that make up the present Underground system, developed since 1863 both to improve access in the metropolis and to encourage the generation of additional revenue through feeding the central area with traffic from the growing suburbs. Architects of Underground stations are faced with the particular problem that when planning subsurface facilities the spaces are generally dictated by engineering constraints, and their role has really been confined to specialized interior design. Of course, for surface structures there is a much wider scope for creativity, and the development of this reflects the changing styles in architectural practice and the railway companies' aspirations to a public image. As the Underground was effectively invisible to the public, and could only advertise its presence through the stations as shop-fronts of the organization their appearance was a critical factor in the attraction of custom.

Cut-and-cover stations

The need for what is now referred to as a house style or corporate image was recognized at an early stage and reflected in the architectural design. For the first line opened by the Metropolitan Railway in 1863 between Paddington and Farringdon, stations were designed by one of the great Victorian engineers, John Fowler, with his assistant Thomas Marr Johnson. With few precedents in this field, architects initially responded to new needs by adapting past styles, and their work was overshadowed by the great achievements of the engineers in constructing the line. One periodical remarked:

> The stations are less remarkable externally, and in architectural details, than they are for their disposition of plan, and the clever construction of some of them. (*Builder*, 1863, p. 23)

Baker Street and Euston Square had inclined shafts through which the smoke could escape and light be admitted. Those at Baker Street were restored with concealed lighting in 1983 to suggest the original appearance. Fowler and Johnson supervised the Metropolitan's extension to Gloucester Road, and the first sections of the District Railway. These surface buildings had simpler detailing, with high windows and iron-and-glass entrance canopies. To avoid the ventilation problems of the original line, platforms were located in cuttings under semi-elliptical overall roofs.

The Metropolitan and District completed in stages, and with some disagreement, what is now the Circle Line, constructing variously styled stations, most now demolished. An extensive programme of works depleted funds, and the District's stations designed by John Wolfe-Barry for the extensions to Putney and Hounslow of 1879–83 were almost devoid of decoration, characterized only by set-out architraves around the doors and windows, and chimneys at the building corners. Putney Bridge remains as an example from this period.

The Tube and corporate styles

The first clear attempt at defining a 'house' style came with the opening in late 1890 of the City & South London Railway, both London's original standard-gauge deep-level tube and the first railway to use electric traction in the capital. T. Phillips Figgis, a prolific architect working in various classical and Arts and Crafts influenced styles, carried out the small red brick and stone stations, made distinctive by their lead-covered domes housing some of the lift gear. Interiors were tiled for durability, and tunnel platforms gas-lit. Ten years later Figgis and S.R.J. Smith, architect to Sir Henry Tate, designed stations for the C&SLR's northern and southern extensions, with Smith's work at Bank partly occupying the former crypt of Hawksmoor's St Mary Woolnoth church.

The success of the City & South London prompted a number of other projects, the first to be completed being the Central London Railway in 1900,

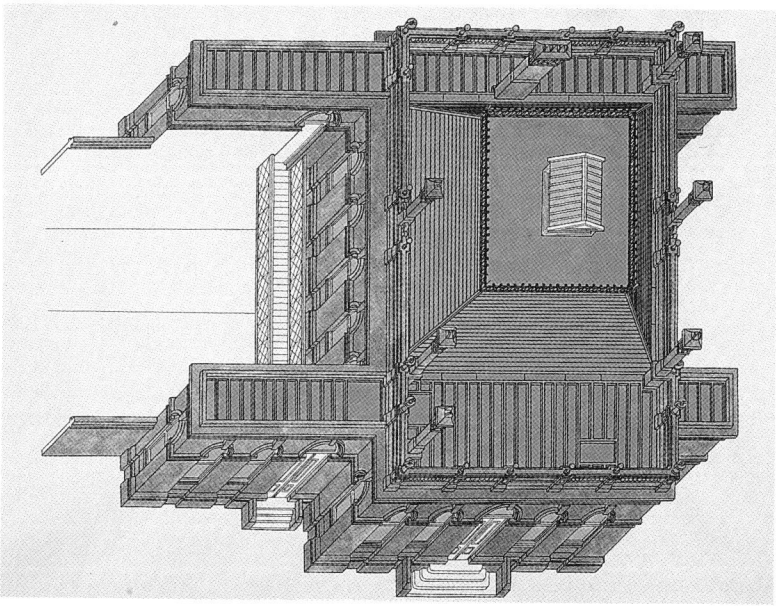

Fig. 15.1 Axonometric illustration of the original District Railway station at Charing Cross (now Embankment), built in the Italianate style characteristic of the late 1860s.
(D. Lawrence)

with a line running west to east from Shepherd's Bush to the City's financial district. Harry Bell Measures designed the stations. It is significant that Measures worked frequently with terracotta, as he was able to put this material to effective use by designing a modular form of building, which could be fabricated from factory-made blocks as a 'kit of parts', and thus providing a series of readily identifiable structures all sharing a common appearance and at reasonable cost. Platform tunnels were again lined with plain glazed tiles, but lit electrically from the start. Shepherds Bush, Holland Park and Oxford Circus are surviving examples of Measures' stations.

A rapid increase in tube railway construction ensued, and in London this was mainly carried out by the Electric Railways of London Ltd. It became known as the Underground group, an American-backed organization formed by dynamic financier Charles Tyson Yerkes, which built, equipped and operated three deep-level railway ventures now comprising parts of the Bakerloo, Piccadilly and Northern Lines. A single architectural style was chosen for stations, promoting a confident and progressive image and advertising the still-novel electric tube. By the time work was completed in 1906–7, architect Leslie W. Green had designed more than 40 stations and other structures. The considerable effort required took its toll on Green's already weakened health, and he died just a year later at the age of 33.

Green took up Measures' practice of using moulded glazed terracotta, hard-wearing and unashamedly advertising the stations through the use of an 'ox-blood'-coloured glaze. Facades were in modular form comprising a series of arches, claimed by Christian Barman in his book *An Introduction to Railway Architecture* to derive from Lewis Isaac's Holborn Viaduct of 1873. It is perhaps no coincidence that Isaacs had a senior position with both the District Railway and Piccadilly tube. While maintaining a standard pattern, each facade was tailored to the site, and the proportion, arrangement and treatment of elements varied. Detailing was mainly in the heavy classical style of the period,

Fig. 15.2 Modular construction in glazed terracotta after the style of L.W. Green for Kilburn Park Station, Bakerloo Line, 1915. (D. Lawrence)

with a minor art nouveau influence suggested by the exterior lettering, cartouches and wrought-iron grilles. Lifts connected with the platforms. Wherever possible, separate landings and passageways were provided at each level so that passengers entered the cars on one side and left them from the other, moving forwards in each case to clear the lift for passengers travelling in the opposite direction. For the platforms many different-coloured tiling patterns were developed to aid passenger recognition.

Following electrification, District Railway staff architect Harry W. Ford rebuilt several stations, including Barons Court, Earls Court and Hammersmith of 1905–6, in which the influence of Leslie Green's style may be seen. Ford went on to reconstruct other District stations on a freelance basis during 1912–15, combining classical detailing with faience or Portland stone. His Fulham Broadway and Temple stations are still in use. Stanley Heaps became architect in succession to Ford, and carried on Green's general style.

From 1915 new tube stations were equipped with escalators, these moving stairways being safer than lifts and permitting a continuous flow of traffic, which increased the passenger usage of stations. After the turn of the century the Metropolitan Railway had begun to capitalize on its street frontages by rebuilding stations below ground, George Sherrin carrying out schemes at High Street and South Kensington, Gloucester Road and Victoria during 1908–9, and his son Frank completing works at King's Cross and Liverpool Street in the years up to 1913. As traffic increased, better facilities became desirable, and the Metropolitan Railway decided that Baker Street would be the location of its centralized headquarters and a 'flagship' station, marking the start of a comprehensive modernization scheme to promote the company's new 'electric' image through clean and improved stations comparable to those of the Underground group. Charles W. Clark, architect to the Metropolitan from 1911 to 1933, supervised the works, most of which were carried out after the First World War. Clark's idiom was typified by an off-white faience cladding, described by the Metropolitan, who favoured the grand manner, as 'neo-grec'. At outlying stations Clark used a domestic revival style. By the late 1920s Clark's work appeared somewhat conservative alongside that of the rapidly advancing Underground group, which promptly retired him with a life pension when it took over the Metropolitan in 1933.

Stations on the Northern Line Edgware extension (1922–3) were designed by Stanley Heaps in a neo-Georgian fashion, with colonnaded entrances and tiled pyramidal roofs. Heaps stated that the idiom was chosen with consideration for the suburban surroundings, mindful of the fact that the public would become aware of this surface line without the use of

> buildings that blatantly advertised the railway. . . sufficiently dignified to command respect, and sufficiently pleasing to promote affection. (Heaps, 1927, p. 36)

Although perhaps conservative in appearance, these stations had the innovation of a combined ticket hall and concourse, which was based on American practice and would be a central feature in the Underground stations of the 1930s.

Pick and Holden

Frank Pick came to the Underground as Publicity Officer and played an increasingly influential role in the undertaking; he was passionately interested in the relationship between art and industry, and met the architect Charles Holden in 1915 through the Design and Industries Association. With increased development of the Underground in mind, Pick saw that a new and appropriate architecture, one that was both functional and attractive, was required to bring order to the system. As an Underground publication of 1926 put it:

> What is a station? An inviting doorway in an architectural setting that cannot be missed by the casual pedestrian. (Underground, 1926, p. 20)

The stations must advertise that they were points where fast and comfortable trains were waiting to whisk the traveller to town, creating the feeling that the city was but a short journey away, and telescoping distances in the traveller's mind. This was particularly important in the face of competition from road transport, and Pick balanced the increase of custom, and so profits and dividends, with a vision of improving the convenience and comfort of the travelling public.

A special relationship between Pick, the 'benevolent dictator', and Holden facilitated the rapid development of plans. Holden was given a more or less free hand, Pick often approving projects from a small sketch, which Holden was able to infuse with the spirit of the design. On the basis of a small commission at Westminster station, Pick retained Charles Holden to reconstruct and provide new stations on the Northern Line works completed in 1924, and the Morden extension opened in 1926. These latter structures were designed to a common pattern, adapted to suit the various road intersections, and Holden used exterior floodlighting as a publicity feature by night. In the *Architectural Review* P. Morton Shand described the stations as 'prophetic beacons of the new age' (*Architectural Review*, 1929, p. 218).

At Bank station the subsurface concourse had proved satisfactory, and it was decided to rebuild the overtaxed Piccadilly Circus on similar lines. An underground concourse of this size had not previously been possible, and the

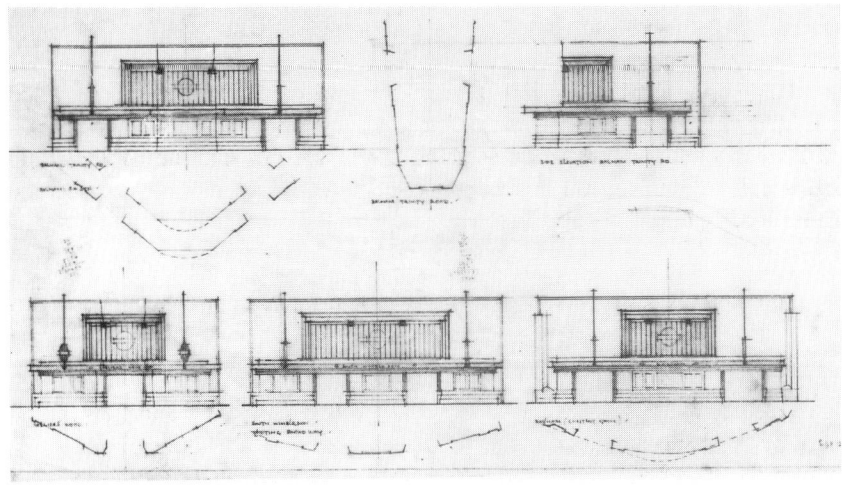

Fig. 15.3 Elevations of intermediate stations on the Northern Line Morden extension by C. Holden, 1926, and showing the adaptation of facade angles for different corner sites. (D. Lawrence)

architects took full advantage of the latest developments in artificial lighting and ventilation to ensure that conditions were satisfactory. By treating the hall as an ambulatory through which travellers and pedestrians alike would pass, it would be of commercial and decorative value, and give additional illumination (without cost to the railway company), to line the hall with showcases. Steen Eiler Rasmussen described Piccadilly Circus station thus:

> In the morning it is like a turbine grinding out human beings on all sides. In the evening it sucks them in again, through the circle and down the escalators to the rushing trains. (Rasmussen, 1934)

With an ambitious expansion programme in hand, a new headquarters building was required. For the first time, Holden was given complete control over planning, and designed a structure of cruciform shape to permit the centralization of lifts and services, and enable the most natural light to reach every office. Named after its postal address – 55 Broadway – the St James's Park block was completed in 1929. Holden had an enduring interest in the use of sculpture, and for 55 Broadway employed Jacob Epstein and six other sculptors including the young Henry Moore. Epstein's work again received criticism when it was unveiled to the public, and caused some controversy within the management of the Underground group. Much correspondence was reported throughout the world's press, and 'Night' was tarred and feathered in protest.

Ealing Common and Hounslow West of 1931 are the last of Holden's Portland stone-faced buildings, with polygonal ticket halls expressed as double-height towers flanked by low side wings. Decorative schemes for the halls were from the hand of Basil Ionides, a leading interior designer of the day. The 'New Works Programme 1930' was prepared for extensions at each end of the Piccadilly Line to areas of speculative housing development in Middlesex. Again, Pick and Holden worked on a suitable building style for the updated and new facilities, and travelled to Europe to take in developments there. They saw several aspects of expressionist and functionalist architecture as interpreted in various countries of Northern Europe, and formulated their own ideas with inspiration from works such as those of W.M. Dudok, municipal architect of Hilversum, Netherlands. It is worth noting that the activities of committed public authorities in the Netherlands have often been held up as a worthy example to English railway builders seeking good design. Dudok and his contemporaries were themselves influenced by the work of the American Frank Lloyd Wright, who would also have been known to Holden.

Fundamental to this architecture was the efficiency of plan in providing space and free movement, the buildings being made up of simple geometric forms having carefully considered scale and proportion. The accepted format of the station – originally modelled on the domestic dwelling – was abandoned in favour of a purpose-designed structure suited for its function in both layout and appearance. Holden wrote in 1944:

> Ruthlessly analyse your motives. Eliminate everything which does not fulfil a definite and necessary function. (Holden, 1944)

Ticket halls became extensions of the street, sheltering the facilities necessary for the transition between street and train. New technology in the construction of steel and concrete frames gave planners a much freer hand and saved in building costs, while the development of plate glass made it possible to introduce much bigger windows – an important factor given the climate of Northern Europe. Brick was seen as a traditional building material, and one that imparted a sense of warmth, while conveying the functional nature of the building. A limited range of materials ensured a homogeneous appearance, which could later be adopted by other Underground architects.

These stations were intended to be innovative rather than in keeping with the prevailing neo-classical style, and must have looked odd alongside the 'tudor-bethan' style of the speculative housebuilders. The Underground thought nothing of demolishing outdated stations that stood in the way of progress – the concern for 'heritage' was not as it is today. Continued experiments with different materials were undertaken to improve the appearance and wear of surfaces, and items such as poster displays were planned into the overall design both as decoration and with commercial value in mind. Holden's attention to detail, and the thought given to both the needs of the day and future requirements, ensured that many stations remain virtually unchanged and still function properly after more than half a century.

Good design was good for business. By the example it set, the Underground was gradually able to change the travelling public's attitude to railway stations, which had in the past often been shabby and inhospitable places. Pick saw the chaos that would ensue if the effects of the modern world were to go uncontrolled, and he was aware of his responsibility to manage the changes within his sphere of influence. Sir Nikolaus Pevsner has said that Pick saw in every detail a 'visual propaganda', and he used this not only to promote the Underground but also to improve the environment for the public as a whole. Charles Holden brought the (Underground) railway station to the forefront of modern architecture; this achievement is unequalled by any other English railway company on such a scale before or since.

After completion of the first experimental station at Sudbury Town, 1931, a run of stations followed based on the box form of ticket hall. Perhaps the most well known, and Holden's own favourite, was that at Arnos Grove. Holden followed the European example of making stations focal points in the urban environment, with surface transport networks enhanced to feed the line. Southgate was one of his most perfect schemes, where the corner site was utilized to provide a shopping parade and bus lay-by behind the circular station building.

In a report on the Royal Institute of British Architects' visit to the Piccadilly line the writer noted:

> the consummate skill that has been shown in the solution of every problem ... That the directors of the Underground Railway should have so correlated every part of their organization that everything from a poster or a doorknob to a complete station should so clearly express *Underground* [their italics] is an achievement of which they have good reason to be proud. (*JRIBA*, 1933, p. 28)

Buildings were adapted for different locations, Boston Manor and Osterley (both 1934) having Dutch-style lighting towers to suit the housing of the area

Fig. 15.4 Osterley, station on the Piccadilly Line, 1934, is one of Charles Holden's more mannered Underground stations, employing a high tower with Dutch finial to advertise the railway in an undistinguished housing area. (D. Lawrence)

and yet be easily found by travellers. At South Harrow (1935) broken-down volumes gave greater flexibility in handling the two station levels created by the railway overbridge.

A second New Works Programme for 1935–40 brought the opportunity to improve lines hitherto neglected and increase the system to tap or generate further growth of the suburbs and potential development areas. Northern and Bakerloo Line services would be extended, and the Metropolitan Line modernized. Holden's office was now heavily involved with the University of London buildings, and work was farmed out to other architects. After difficulties with the cost of Uxbridge, Frank Pick discovered this, and in typically volatile form threatened to put future commissions elsewhere. Holden was subsequently able to resolve the situation, but buildings of this period such as Uxbridge and East Finchley lack the coherence of the earlier works. Stanley Heaps completed St John's Wood during this period, and this is one of the few locations where the escalators still retain their original bronze uplighters.

By 1938 London Transport was concerned by sluggish increases in traffic on the extensions, and speculated that their expansion plans might be too optimistic. Frank Pick stated that:

> Progress which is not self remunerative, and appearance which does not enlarge custom, are luxuries not to be afforded. (LPTB, 1937, p. 3)

204

It was proposed to use simplified, plain block structures for future station developments, with a life expectancy of 25–30 years. In the event the Second World War put a stop to new projects. Pick retired prematurely from the London Passenger Transport Board in 1940 and died in November 1941. The expense of consulting architects could not be justified under wartime conditions, and the arrangement with Adams, Holden and Pearson terminated in 1942. The Underground's own staff architect, Stanley Heaps, retired in 1943.

Projects were restarted at a reduced level after the war. Extension of the Central Line east and west includes works of interest by architects commissioned on behalf of the main-line railways whose metals London Transport were to take over: John Murray Easton – Loughton, Oliver Hill – Newbury Park, Brian Lewis and Frederick Curtis – Hanger Lane, Perivale and Greenford.

A length of new tube under the Eastern Avenue included the last three Holden stations: Wanstead, Redbridge and Gants Hill. Redbridge was more or less according to the pre-war design, but Wanstead was less fortunate; economics forced Holden to adapt the brick shell of a building erected to serve a wartime factory operated in the tube tunnel. The Underground management had wished to build a 'Moscow'-type subsurface concourse at one of their new stations since 1936, when the first part of the Moscow Metro was opened. At Gants Hill the aim was realized, with the lower escalator landing enlarged between the platform tunnels to form a spacious and brightly lit area.

Thomas Bilbow succeeded Stanley Heaps and supervised the reconstruction of White City station, gaining a Special Architectural Award at the Festival of Britain. A series of minor works then followed in connection with the Festival, and the complete redevelopment of Notting Hill Gate in 1959. It was during this period that the once ubiquitous 'bathroom' tile, now failing extensively on the Victoria Line, came into use. Many young architects left the railways during this period as they saw their vision of a post-war utopia eroded by economic and bureaucratic obstructions. For those that remained, a lead in design was taken from airport planning. Toward the middle of the 1950s authority was given for the construction of a new deep-level tube that would become the Victoria Line, the first completely new tube through central London for over 50 years. London Transport undertook to design the Victoria Line wholly 'in house', under the direction of the London Transport Design Panel, with members including Chief Architect Kenneth J.H. Seymour and Misha Black (later Sir Misha, whose organization Design Research Unit acted as consultants to London Transport until the early 1980s).

The project was completed in stages between 1968 and 1971. Except for Blackhorse Road, station works were mostly below ground, which limited the architectural possibilities. A uniform scheme of platform finishes was adopted throughout the line, with light grey tiles to provide a neutral background for posters, and signage selected as a standard colour, which would be easy to replace if damaged. Grey appears to have been the suggestion of Sir Misha Black; it has since been said that it gives the stations a somewhat clinical and drab appearance, but the designers themselves commented:

Fig. 15.5 The 1950s was not memorable for London Underground station architecture, so South Ruislip, 1959–61, an Underground and British Railway interchange, is particularly worthy of inclusion for its unique ticket hall. (British Rail)

the stations may be criticised for appearing visually unexciting, but we consider that preferable to a transient popularity without lasting qualities. (Seymour and Black, 1969)

Pastels were used in ticket halls, and accents – orange or yellow – identified obstructions such as columns. Mosaic tesserae and brushed metal trimmings added some richness and variety. Graphic designers and artists produced tile panels for the seat recesses, which related in some way to the surrounding area.

Sydney Hardy began restructuring of the architect's department when he was brought in from British Rail after Kenneth Seymour retired. Modelling the organization along private sector lines, he sought to improve cost efficiency under the constraints of continuing budget problems. An extension to Heathrow Airport was designed at this time, based on Victoria Line styling but with more extensive use of colour and plastics in the decoration. Signage at Heathrow Central carried experimental pictograms for the benefit of travellers unable to read English. The Jubilee Line followed in 1979. As with the Victoria scheme, new works were mostly below ground. There was a further move away from austere design, with brightly coloured finishes for platforms and ticket halls, and full-length murals at Charing Cross.

Finance was promised to London Transport for the refurbishment of facilities neglected during the Victoria and Jubilee line works. The *Station Update Policy Report* of 1979 considered proposals for the improvement of Central and Bakerloo line facilities, and the following year Sydney Hardy and his staff drew up the *Initial Design Strategy for the Rail System*, a report that set out to address the state of decay on the Underground and the means of dealing with it in a comprehensive station modernization programme. The writers

commented on the 'visual chaos' that had resulted from the piecemeal alterations and addition of equipment such as security cameras and 'off the shelf'
light units, with little consideration for the environment or compatibility with
other fittings. Vandalism and litter added to the state of decay after years of
little maintenance. A design strategy was felt to be essential to link the
disparate elements present on the system and reconcile the various departments
involved in station refurbishment, who often worked without consulting each
other. New guidelines were to be established, which would facilitate the better-
coordinated management of new projects. The aims were to improve passenger
confidence, maximize use of the Underground and available resources, and
improve the environment for both passengers and staff.

A grant was won from the Greater London Council (GLC) and a team of
architects and consultants established to start projects. The grant was then cut,
and the final award had to be stretched as far as possible, so the decision was
made to spend the money where it would have the most visual effect. This
meant that central stations received decorative platform schemes, but that ticket
halls and entire stations further out were neglected. An emphasis was placed on
the local identity of the station over the identity of the organization as a whole
– this practice has since been reviewed. After consultation with the Arts
Council, artists were commissioned to produce decorative schemes for individual stations, and later in the decade competitions were held for students at the
Royal College of Art. Amongst works of this period, Tottenham Court Road,
Paddington and Embankment all won awards. Terminal 4 station at Heathrow
Airport (opened in 1986) was designed by London Transport architects in a
restrained style looking forward to the minimalist approach of the 1990s, with
reconstructed marble as the predominant material. This station is unique in that
the underground concourse immediately adjoins the single platform.

Looking back to the 1970s it will be seen that much has been done to rectify
the poor state of affairs and halt the decline of the system. There is, however, a

*Fig. 15.6 Heathrow
Terminal 4, Piccadilly Line,
1986, is representative of the
minimalist approach taken to
Tube platform design in
recent years. (D. Lawrence)*

great deal still to be done, and there remain problems in the application of new works. Platform refurbishments were completed with varying degrees of success, but for reasons of cost stopped at the platforms, and upper levels would continue to deteriorate. To save time new works were applied over old. The difficulties of introducing modern railway technology into outdated and inadequate station buildings at low cost, and the implication of revised fire precautions, resulted in original ticket windows, tiling, signage and fittings being removed, despite protests from conservationists. Replacement of almost all the bronze escalator uplighters on the system by lighting engineers, who saw them as inefficient (increased lighting levels were required for safety) and dirt-collecting, is one such example. Lack of coordination highlighted in the 1980 *Initial Design Strategy* was still apparent, particularly where the rebuilding of ticket halls for the installation of Underground ticketing system equipment was carried out separately from the modernization schemes.

It is now policy to create a calming visual environment of neutral colours and rationalized signage. Reduced budgets are available for decoration, and there has been a shift away from giving stations an individual local identity towards a single corporate style. That ticket halls and platforms may be entirely devoid of ornament is perhaps a questionable improvement, but some of the subtle detailing of recent works adds points of interest. Office developments on station sites have increasingly been promoted to assist the financing of public projects, Hammersmith and Angel being recent examples.

Both staff architects and consultants now prepare briefs and undertake design projects. An independent design manager is responsible for proposing guidelines to maintain high levels of quality within an overall vision of the direction developments should take.

Through the pressure of both internal and external agencies the Underground has recently become more aware of heritage, and refurbishments are now carried out with more regard for the existing features. Policy is to leave sites alone where they are still safe and functional, restoring original elements where necessary. Pleasing all interested parties is not an easy matter: conservation pressure groups, design managers, architects and external consultants all have their own view on what is required, and perhaps their own agendas. It is true that rules for conservation are hard to apply, as each case has individual circumstances, but the link between good intentions and actual works is where things can go wrong: the very act of design can have unsatisfactory results when it imposes the designer's own ideas on the work, founded on inadequate research and attention to detail. Furniture, equipment and finishes can be unsympathetic to the structure and space, dominating instead of complementing the character of the environment. Designers may make too many assumptions about the authenticity of the features they have been empowered to replace or add to, and need to maintain a constant awareness of the past when responding to present needs. Encouraging a sense of 'ownership' amongst the staff of a station has been one way of educating for care of assets. Clear identification and promotion of historically important sites and dialogue with local groups would further establish civic pride and reinforce the need for a community response to the actions of authorities.

Mention must lastly be made of activities by other agencies on behalf of the London Underground that run counter to official policy, primarily the removal of signs from 'listed' stations in an over-zealous attempt to raise money through disposal of assets. This does nothing to enhance the reputation of the Underground as guardian of its heritage, held on trust for succeeding generations of citizens. The complex nature of the organization and budgetary pressures often lead to conflicting interests. A notional overall responsibility is no substitute for the accountability of individuals who have an informed and sympathetic awareness for the structures in their care. It remains to be seen whether funds allocated for the modification of imposed services and decoration at listed buildings is sufficient to return them to a condition appropriate to their status as examples of architectural heritage.

Select bibliography

Anon (1863) The Metropolitan (Underground) Railway. *Builder*, **21**, 10 January, 23.

Anon (1933) A visit to the Underground stations on the Cockfosters line. *Journal of the Royal Institute of British Architects*, **40**, November, 28.

Barman, C. (1950) *An Introduction to Railway Architecture*, Art and Technics, London.

Heaps, S. (1927) The design of stations, *TOT Magazine*, February, 36.

Holden, C. (1944) Aesthetic aspects of civil engineering, unpublished paper, 26 April.

Lawrence, D. (1994) *Underground Architecture*, Capitol Transport, London.

Leboff, D. (1994) *London Underground Stations*, Ian Allan, Shepperton.

London Transport (1979) *Station Update Policy Report*, Internal report, Department of the Chief Architect, London Transport.

London Transport (1980) *Initial Design Strategy for the Rail System*, Internal report, Department of the Chief Architect, London Transport.

LPTB (1937) *Report of the Second Conference of the London Passenger Transport Board*, LPTB, London.

Rasmussen, S.E. (1934) *London: The Unique City*, Jonathan Cape, London.

Seymour, K.J.H. and Black, M. (1969) Notes on the Design of Stations on the Victoria Line, unpublished report. March.

Stand, P.M. (1929) Underground. *Architectural Review* **66**, November, 218.

Underground (1926) *The Morden Extension and the Kennington Loop*, Underground, London.

Part Five

Engineering Structures

Gregory Beecroft

How British Rail Property Board manages the closed-line estate

The closed railway line running through the fields is a familiar part of the countryside. However, who owns these lines, and how are they managed? I shall describe what British Rail's closed-line estate comprises, some of the special problems it presents, and how we deal with them.

The first thing to say is that most closed lines are no longer owned by British Rail. We now have well under 1000 miles (1600 km), or about 10% of the total. Those sections that we do retain are mostly those with major liabilities, such as tunnels, which nobody else wants.

Some parts of closed lines are readily disposed of, especially station buildings, houses and goods sheds. Many people find a former station building especially attractive as a home or business location, particularly if railway features survive. We rarely have such buildings available for disposal, and most that come onto the market are private sales, with premium prices due to the railway connection.

Large buildings can cause problems if they are not immediately suitable for alternative use, but we normally leave conversion to the new owners. Major terminals are a special case, successful conservation schemes including the Exhibition Centre at Manchester Central and the Sainsbury's supermarket at Bath Green Park. However, many city centre sites, for example Nottingham Victoria and Glasgow St Enoch, have been entirely redeveloped.

Most station sites on closed lines sell readily for redevelopment, unless in Green Belt or subject to other town planning difficulties. Frequently, only the street name in a housing estate may indicate that there was once a railway on the site. So, disposal of the stations is rarely a problem, but what about the track beds themselves? Whenever possible, we try and dispose of lines complete to bodies such as local councils or the Forestry Commission, who often purchase them for use as footpaths or bridleways. Valuable work has been done by

Sustrans, with British Rail Property Board and local councils, to create cycle routes along old lines. Problems mainly arise if a council would like to purchase, but does not have funds to pay the market value of the land, or if a planning zoning is placed on the line that prevents sale. We can sometimes find ourselves having to hold on to track beds for many years, because of proposals for new roads, rapid transit schemes and so forth. Most railway reopenings have involved preservation societies. While such sales can be complicated to deal with, we generally welcome them as a means of disposing of an entire railway in one transaction.

If there is no purchaser for the full length of a line we have to resort to piecemeal disposal, though this is less satisfactory. More individual sales are needed, and we run the risk of being left with unsold sections that nobody wants. The nature of the estate is such that sales are normally to adjoining owners, though free-standing development opportunities may be available in urban areas. However, embankments and cuttings may not be attractive to adjoining proprietors, though cuttings can be of value for tipping. In remote areas there is often little interest in track beds, though some long enclosed ones have been re-examined for footpath or steam railway use.

Individual sales in country areas are almost always to adjoining owners, with the track beds reverting to agriculture or becoming farm roads. A noteworthy exception is the use of several miles of the Cambridge to Bedford line for the Cambridge University Radio Telescope.

The hierarchy of disposal that I have described for track beds, of selling complete if we can to a council or preservation society, and then turning to adjoining owners, is followed for several reasons. Not only does this minimize the number of sale transactions and maximize the chances of preserving the formation, but there are important legal considerations also.

Fig. 16.1 Turvey Station building, Midland Railway, last used by passengers on the branch line from Bedford to Northampton in 1962. It is one of many hundreds of stations put to alternative use by new owners, in this case as offices. (G.D. Beecroft)

Bridges

Most railways feature numerous bridges and other works, and most of these had to be maintained by the railway company. The principal exceptions are trunk road bridges, and over-line bridges of roads that were built after the railway was constructed. The importance of maintaining railway bridges and similar structures is such that a statutory obligation to do so was placed on railway promoters, for the protection of the public, by the Railway Clauses Consolidation Act 1845 and its Scottish equivalent. British Rail is still required to comply with these Acts in respect of closed lines, and does not automatically lose its obligations by selling a structure.

A highway authority or another statutory railway, such as a preserved line in possession of a Light Railway Order, can take over our Railway Clauses Consolidation Act obligations, but a private individual certainly cannot. You will immediately see the attraction to us of selling to councils and railway preservation societies! Limited disposal of statutory liabilities is possible if we sell to an adjoining owner, principally the obligation to fence the railway – which does not go away when the line closes.

Bridges carrying public roads are by far the most serious liability that we have on closed lines. They usually carry traffic much heavier than was envisaged when the line was built, and the consequences of any failure could be catastrophic. We are still responsible for about 1000 such bridges, many of them on lines that are otherwise entirely sold. Needless to say, all have to be inspected at least annually, and maintenance bills can be quite large.

We are presently facing the prospect of 40-tonne lorries crossing these bridges from 1999. Fortunately, from our point of view, the highway authorities are responsible for footing the bill for checking and, where necessary, strengthening our bridges. It should not be assumed that large lorries are confined to main roads; vehicles conveying agricultural produce from farms can be particularly heavy, and just about anybody up a country lane might want to take delivery of a load of ready-mix concrete. We do at least have the option of filling in or removing weak bridges. This is usually cheaper than reconstruction and effectively eliminates our maintenance obligation.

Although bridges carrying public roads are a special responsibility, they are only a small part of our total bridge stock, which is about 5000 structures. Bridges over public roads are less of a liability, as they carry no load. The main difficulties are trespass and vandalism, particularly trespassers falling off, or pushing coping stones and parapets into the road below. Restricted-headroom bridges are susceptible to being hit by road vehicles. The consequences are much less serious than bridge-bashing on operational railway lines, but structures can be damaged or seriously weakened. We rarely have immediate reports of such incidents, however. The culprits usually get away undetected, and we find the damage later. Not all bridges are old; some under-line bridges were built quite recently for new roads, but still require periodic inspection. Quite often, former railway bridges are removed, particularly steel- or iron-decked ones, where the spans can be readily lifted out. However, Railtrack remains responsible for the abutments, unless these are demolished and the embankment sloped back.

Fig. 16.2 The road from Wakes Colne to Bures crosses over the former Colne Valley line on a brick arch bridge. The track bed has reverted to agriculture, but British Rail Property Board still meets the expense of inspecting and maintaining the bridge. (G.D. Beecroft)

Fig. 16.3 The portal of Catesby Tunnel on the London Extension, Great Central Railway, 1897. Disused since 1966, the 1 mile 1100 yard (2.6 km) tunnel is still cared for by British Rail Property Board. (G.D. Beecroft)

River bridges generally present the same features and problems as those over public roads. However, we have to be aware of the effects of scour action. In recent years a number of operational railway bridges have been undermined by water action, and have collapsed. There is not the same degree of risk on a closed line, but any failure could dam the river and cause flooding, or debris could cause injury and damage downstream. We do not just manage bridges, but also the remains of them. Old piers and abutments all require checking.

Tunnels

Tunnels and retaining walls are a specialized problem, not least because they are the most difficult structures to dispose of. Apart from a few with ornamental portals, or those with particular technical or historic associations, it is unusual for tunnels to have much heritage value. People rarely want to preserve them for their own sake, and alternative uses are very limited. Filling in tunnels is extremely complicated and expensive. We are responsible for about 200 closed tunnels, with a total length of 80 miles (130 km), and I see little prospect of our ever being rid of them.

Some disposals have been possible. The Woodhead Tunnels are owned by National Grid and are used as a cable route. It was possible to sell Warden Tunnel, near Bedford, because the purchaser owned all of the land above and around. However, this is a very unusual situation. Far more typical is Catesby Tunnel, on the Great Central Railway's London Extension. Operational for just 67 years, it extends for almost 2 miles (2.6 km) through the Northamptonshire hills. Not only do we have the bore itself to care for, but the five ventilation shafts as well.

Miscellaneous liabilities associated with closed lines include a few sea defence works and the causeway to Roa Island, Barrow-in-Furness, but these come rather outside the scope of 'railway heritage'.

216

Viaducts

If one mentions railway heritage in connection with closed railways, most people will think of the viaducts. They are the most prominent structures, and the most attractive. We have 50 listed viaducts, a very small proportion of our total stock of structures, but as the prime examples of railway heritage owned by British Rail Property Board, they receive a disproportionate amount of our time. This is not just because we recognize the need to give the viaducts special attention, but because they are of particular interest both to the general public and to those professionally concerned with railway architecture, engineering and history.

A few viaducts have been preserved as part of steam railway lines. Avon Viaduct, also known as Birchill Viaduct, on the Bo'ness & Kinneil line near Edinburgh is an example. British Rail has also gifted Imberhorne Viaduct, East Grinstead, to the Bluebell Railway for its northern extension. A possible future steam railway project involves Chelfham Viaduct, on the former Lynton & Barnstaple line. This narrow gauge railway opened in 1898 and closed in 1935, so the viaduct has been out of use for almost 60 years, after an active life of just 37. British Rail, established in 1948, has never run a train over this structure, but still has to care for it. We should be more than pleased to be able to pass the viaduct on to a new railway company.

However, we are encouraging preservation schemes for individual viaducts in their own right. As an example, Leaderfoot Viaduct, in the Scottish Borders,

Fig. 16.4 Bennerley Viaduct carried the Derbyshire extension line over the Erewash Valley near Ilkeston, Great Northern Railway, by E. Johnson, 1878. The railway closed in 1968, but the viaduct survives as one of the few remaining metal trestle bridges in Britain. Some repair works were carried out by British Rail Property Board in 1994–5, but it is hoped that comprehensive restoration will follow transfer to a preservation trust. This scheme is being supported financially by English Heritage and Railway Heritage Trust. (G.D. Beecroft)

is being transferred to Historic Scotland. The future of this viaduct and others in the Borders led to a Scottish Viaducts Committee being established. This comprises representatives of British Rail Property Board and other organizations with an interest in the viaducts, including the Scottish Civic Trust and local authorities. The committee has been extremely helpful in promoting interest in the viaducts, so that preservation schemes can be set up. Following the success of the Scottish committee, an equivalent one was established for England and Wales.

Largo Viaduct in Fife provides a typical example of the type of preservation scheme we have been able to promote with the committees. The local community wanted to keep the viaduct, as an important part of the local landscape, so it was gifted to the local council by British Rail Property Board. We also provided an endowment to cover future maintenance costs.

A similar scheme was promoted in Cumbria, when Smardale Gill Viaduct, built in 1860 to designs by Thomas Bouch, was transferred to the Northern Viaducts Trust. Prior to the transfer, comprehensive renovation work was undertaken, funded jointly by British Rail Property Board, English Heritage and the Railway Heritage Trust. The Property Board has also paid a capital sum to the Northern Viaducts Trust to cover future maintenance. In this case it was possible to transfer the viaduct to the Trust freehold, as there were no public roads or other rights associated with the structure. In other cases we are having to grant long leases, so that British Rail can ensure that its Railway Clauses Consolidation Act obligations are fully met. Conversely, it has been possible to sell a few viaducts to private individuals, because of particular local circumstances.

A similar scheme is well advanced for Lambley Viaduct, on the former Alston branch. Repair work, jointly funded by British Rail Property Board, English Heritage and the Railway Heritage Trust, started in spring 1995, and is due to be completed in 1996. The structure is being transferred to the North Pennines Heritage Trust, and will carry the South Tyne Trail footpath. A trust is being established for Bennerley Viaduct, near Ilkeston, a wrought-iron trestle structure. This structure illustrates an interesting question about direction of resources. There were several large metal viaducts on British railways, of which Bennerley was among the least attractive and least impressive. In retrospect, it is a pity that the resources now to be devoted to Bennerley could not have been used to preserve Belah Viaduct, a dramatic trestle structure in an impressive Pennine setting. Unfortunately, the railway over Belah viaduct closed in 1962, when we were less conscious of our railway heritage, and it was demolished not long after.

What should we preserve?

The question that we now need to consider is, how much of the railway heritage do we preserve, and what do we prioritize? British Rail Property Board does not have limitless resources, either to keep structures ourselves, or to fund trusts to take them over. How does a viaduct, conserved mainly for its landscape value, compare with structures of little aesthetic worth, but of great historical or technical interest? Both of the viaducts committees have done valuable work in setting priorities, but viaducts have to compete for resources with other structures.

We have priorities other than conservation, notably safety. A viaduct may be an attractive structure in a dramatic setting, but in terms of safety would have to take second place to any public road bridge requiring repairs. We are fortunate that most of our structures were well built, and are tolerant of limited maintenance, so we have been able to set priorities based on attending to those in worst condition first. We are also encouraged to devote resources to conserving a structure if there is local interest in its future. By 'resources' I am referring to staff time as well as money, for the Property Board is quite a small organization, and disposal of closed-line structures is a specialized activity.

To summarize our approach to the management and disposal of closed lines: we shall continue to seek to dispose of closed lines intact whenever possible. It is in everyone's interests for us to do so. Heritage structures will be particularly prioritized for conservation work if this can be associated with a locally based, continuing preservation scheme compatible with our statutory obligations. Most importantly, resource constraints will prevent us from achieving all that we would like. As a starting point, we must maintain a constructive relationship with all those professionally concerned with conservation of the railway heritage. Hard choices may need to be made, for we cannot preserve every-thing, at least not straight away.

Charles Blackett-Ord

The challenge of disused railway viaducts

After a rural railway line is closed and the track is lifted, the evidence for its former existence slowly disappears. The trackside fences are removed, and the track bed is returned to agricultural use. Embankments become a source of fill material and are levelled. Cuttings are filled with waste. It is the structures that are the most enduring, and isolated bridges are sometimes the only clue that a railway once passed over them. Viaducts are the most dramatic remnants of disused railway lines. Some are widely known because of their scale and location. Low Gill Viaduct on the edge of the Yorkshire Dales National Park must be noticed, if not fully appreciated, by many travellers on the West Coast main line or the M6 motorway, as they approach the south end of the Lune Gorge. According to the observer's point of view they are either useless masses of masonry, which constitute a liability to their owners and a danger to the public, or important monuments to past engineering achievement.

Closure of railway lines that have been found to be uneconomic has been occurring throughout the century, but the greatest rate of line closure followed the recommendations of Dr Beeching. Much damage was done in the years immediately following the Beeching report of 1963, when attempts were made to remove as much as possible of the evidence of railways immediately after their closure. However, since then appreciation of the cultural and historical importance of the railway heritage has increased dramatically. After the withdrawal of services from a line the track was immediately lifted, and the land-holding was sold. In rural areas this was generally to neighbouring landowners, once again linking ownership of land divided in the nineteenth century. The major structures, including bridges, viaducts and tunnels, were not so readily saleable, so they remained unrealizable assets in the hands of British Rail.

Maintenance on these structures all but stopped. They were still inspected by railway engineers, and reports were filed, but only repairs that were considered

Fig. 17.1 Low Gill Viaduct, Cumbria, built 1861 on the edge of Yorkshire Dales National Park. It is situated at the south end of the Lune Gorge in Cumbria, where the Ingleton branch line from the Midland Railway at Settle joined what is now the West Coast main line. (E. Ryle-Hodges)

essential because public danger was involved were carried out. The cost of demolition was usually prohibitive, and could not be recouped in the value of salvaged materials. Where bridges crossed over public highways they were often destroyed because of the liability for the safety of the public.

As well as bridges carrying the track itself the railways owned bridges carrying roads over the track. These too were destroyed and turned into embankments so that ownership could be transferred to the highways authorities, who prefer a simple embankment to a bridge that would require regular maintenance. Understandably, highways departments were not willing to take over bridges that would leave them with a future maintenance responsibility.

Successive line closures have left British Rail with a large number of disused viaducts in their ownership. As the viaducts' importance came to be appreciated by the public, they were listed, almost without British Rail noticing. This gave the viaducts statutory protection, and imposed a responsibility on their owners for repair and maintenance. British Rail has thus been placed in the unfortunate position of owning a large number of redundant structures, which make no contribution to its business of providing a transport system, and it has insufficient resources to be able to divert funds into maintaining disused industrial monuments. In modern parlance, disposal of the viaducts would be regarded as a decommissioning cost, but this was not appreciated at the time of closure of the line.

In a number of cases British Rail, like building owners sitting on a negative asset, applied for listed building consent to demolish viaducts, but these applications tended to be unsuccessful. As a result, in the absence of any incentive to provide long-term maintenance, the condition of most of these structures is continuing to deteriorate, and in due course they will become unsafe and beyond repair.

A public relations exercise in 1991 by British Rail Property Board, the railway body responsible for disused viaducts, highlighted the problem by advertising viaducts for sale for £1. Only in a few cases has this offer been taken up, even though a substantial endowment could be negotiated towards current and future repair costs. Some examples of viaducts that are most likely to have a safe future are discussed later in this chapter.

The Civic Trust set up the English and Welsh, and Scottish, Viaducts Committees to address the problem of disposal of disused listed railway viaducts, and these committees have acted as catalysts for progress on some of them.

Alternative uses

During the 1980s and 1990s conservation has become inextricably linked with commerce, and 'heritage' with education and entertainment. The repair and maintenance of historic buildings now has to be seen to provide some sort of return, either in the form of a commercial use or as some form of tourism development programme. Historic houses and even cathedrals are shown to a paying public as a means of providing income for the building's upkeep. Less obvious attractions, such as agricultural barns and railway stations, have now to provide an economic use to justify their existence, even if this use entails substantial alteration and near-destruction of the features that are intended to be preserved. Barns are turned into houses in the name of conservation, but what is actually conserved in the end is not always clear.

The concept of a new use for a historic building or structure has become rather overstretched in the current economic and political climate. If a monument is sufficiently old, such as Hadrian's Wall or a ruined castle, a new 'use' does not seem to be necessary except perhaps as part of a profit-making 'heritage development', which is more an exploitation than a use. Viaducts are in the same class in terms of usability, but they have not been able to avoid entirely the alternative use syndrome, which is a pity because, like Hadrian's Wall, ruined castles, lime kilns and drystone walls, their place today is as features in the countryside as much as individual monuments. It is now generally appreciated that a well-engineered railway viaduct in a dramatic landscape can complete many a rural scene in the same way as a folly or eye-catcher could enhance a Baroque landscape a century before the railway era.

The most obvious uses to which disused viaducts can be put are for pedestrian or cycle paths, or possibly for roads. However, more imaginative schemes have been put forward by Stephen Weeks and his Monumental Trust Ltd. The trust has looked into acquiring a number of viaducts from British Rail with the intention of placing static carriages converted to holiday residential use on them. An engine would be set at their head. The carriages could each provide about 500 ft^2 (45 m^2) of holiday letting, with panoramic views. The idea of placing an engine as well as the carriages on the viaduct is to give to the distant viewer an impression of the continued existence of a working railway. Unfortunately the trust has had difficulty persuading planning officers and planning committees of the advantage of its proposals. Although the idea could provide an income towards repairs and maintenance of the structures, it introduces numerous additional considerations, such as services and car parking. Many viaducts are in remote areas, and access to them is often only available along the track bed. In many cases this has already been sold off, and access is barred. In some places key under-bridges have been removed.

Viaduct design

The geometry of masonry viaducts could be complex. Unlike short bridges, viaducts were frequently built on a curve. Sometimes the gradient changed in the length of the viaduct. The reason for this becomes apparent when the topographical constraint on the construction of railways is considered. The design criteria of large-radius curves and gentle gradients required extremely careful alignment design if expensive earthworks were to be avoided. However, once a viaduct or a tunnel was found to be unavoidable these constraints of topography were removed at once. It is virtually no more expensive to build a viaduct on a curve than to build it straight, so the opportunity could be taken to change gradients or change direction at will.

Curved or skew arch structures have extremely complicated geometry. The stones forming the arch ring of a skew arch, if the coursing is inclined and not horizontal, are all different, and the railway engineers, or more probably mathematicians, had to provide elaborate formulae for calculating the shape of each stone according to its position in the arch. A curved viaduct can have either cylindrical arches and tapered (on plan) piers, or rectangular piers and truncated cone arch barrels. In some cases the piers were completed before any of the arching was started, and a reassessment of the geometry was made at arch-springing level, leading to outward- or inward-leaning spandrels.

The superstructure of masonry viaducts was either of the solid or hollow spandrel type. In the hollow type the deck and rail track is supported on parallel sleeper walls built up off the arch barrel, with voids between them. This arrangement has the advantage of removing any outward thrust from the fill on the spandrel walls. It also simplifies the drainage arrangements. The piers were usually solid, but in some cases were hollow, as at Lambley Viaduct, on the Haltwhistle to Alston Line in Northumberland. Great lengths were taken to ensure sound foundations, and these are recorded as being founded tens of metres below ground level in areas of poor ground or in river beds.

The main causes of structural decay in disused viaducts is vegetation growth, which can become established within a year or two of any lapse of maintenance. Saplings easily take hold, particularly in wooded areas, and within 20 years their roots can present a serious problem as they erode soft mortar joints and prise apart the masonry.

Originally the deck or the arch barrel extrados was waterproofed. This was normally done with puddled clay, but later bitumen was used. The clay was particularly prone to failure. Doubtless it was not always correctly placed and puddled in the first place, but the problem often appears to be one of drying out during long dry spells, leading to cracking. An additional mechanism for decay could be the decomposition of the clay from water soaking through limestone ballast.

Once water penetrates the structure it washes out the lime mortar, leaving the characteristic white streaking that can be seen on so many masonry structures. Another problem is one of freezing of saturated masonry, which leads to expansion and decay of the stonework. Further damage can be caused by drainage spitter pipes, which were intended to drain the structure above the waterproofing layer. These often discharged water down the outer surface of the masonry, leading to saturation and erosion. Work on renewing or redesigning the waterproofing of a viaduct is an essential part of any long-term repair programme, particularly as these structures are often at high altitudes in exposed conditions, where freeze thaw action is extreme.

The masonry arch was the commonest type of railway viaduct until the 1860s or 1870s, when fabricated girders were introduced in both wrought and cast iron. In the 1880s the use of cast iron in structures was discontinued because of its brittleness and unpredictable tensile strength, in favour of steel, which by the turn of the century was being used in lattice girders and trusses.

Viaducts with a future

Outwood Viaduct, which was built in 1844 on the Bury to Rawtenstall line, is an example of a structure originally built in timber on brick piers. The superstructure was converted from timber in 1881 to one of cast iron made by Handyside & Company of Derby. The line was closed in 1966, and there is now a possibility of its forming part of an urban walk or cycleway.

Outwood Viaduct is particularly complex to analyse structurally because it comprises six parallel iron arch rings in five spans between skew brick piers. The sleepers were laid directly onto the ironwork, with cast-iron transoms to distribute the load between the arch rings. Complex deflections occur as loads move across the deck, loading different points on each adjacent arch. Longitudinally the arches are designed to be continuous from one span to the next and to act as a continuous beam, but fractures have reduced the structure to a series of independent spans. Although the fractures now allow arch action to take place in each span, the flexibility of the structure does not provide sufficient restraint at the piers, so that thrust on the piers makes them deflect horizontally as a moving load crosses the viaduct. The problems of the movement of the piers and the fractures in the ironwork were of considerable concern while the viaduct was part of an operational railway, but they are much less important, to the point of insignificance, if the structure is to be used only for pedestrians.

The repairs now required to the viaduct mainly involve the provision of a deck as a replacement to the temporary timber one, which was constructed as a safety measure when the line was closed.

An almost ideal reuse of a viaduct is the diversion of one carriageway of the A689 road over Newton Cap Viaduct in County Durham. The work involved providing a new, slightly widened, concrete deck to give enough width for a two-lane carriageway. Some of the superstructure has been lost, but it would be hard to question the appropriateness of the alternative use. The aim of the engineers, Bullen Consultants, was to design a widening scheme with minimal increase in the self-weight of the viaduct. The existing construction was masonry with brick arches. Transverse reinforced concrete support walls at

5.2 m centres were built monolithic with reinforced concrete saddles over the arches. The level of the deck was raised by about a metre, which left 2–3 m headroom within the interior to provide access above the arches. The new 450 mm thick concrete slab is 257 m long, and continuous over the full length of this viaduct. It is fixed near the centre of the viaduct and supported elsewhere on sliding bearings. Thus a 140-year-old viaduct has been adapted using modern materials into a structure providing a modern use to current standards.

Lumb Viaduct near Haslingden was built in the 1840s of stone with brick arches. The stone parapet wall was taken down by British Rail to prevent further vandalism after it was damaged by pieces of stone being thrown off the structure. The masonry from the parapets now forms a sapling-covered heap in the centre of the track bed. It is intended that the viaduct should be open for public access. The key issue concerning the repairs is whether to rebuild the stone parapets, which would require about 30% new stone, or whether to provide a new replacement railing of a design appropriate to a listed structure.

Both Outwood Viaduct and Lumb Viaduct are destined to form a public amenity provided by a local authority. In the case of Smardale Gill Viaduct in Cumbria, already referred to by Gregory Beecroft, the Northern Viaduct Trust

Fig. 17.2 Smardale Gill Viaduct, Cumbria, South Durham & Lancashire Union Railway, by T. Bouch, 1860, showing pier masonry before repairs. (C. Blackett-Ord)

225

Fig. 17.3 Smardale Gill Viaduct after repairs. (E. Ryle-Hodges)

was formed under the Chairmanship of Gavin Martin. This was the first private trust to take on a disused listed railway viaduct, and the project has been set up as a model for others to follow.

Smardale Gill Viaduct was repaired in 1990–91 with extensive stitching, masonry repairs and the provision of a new deck at a cost of £350 000. The viaduct became a cause for concern in 1985, when masonry started to fall from one of the piers. As is common with structures of this type, the failures were initiated by defective deck drainage arrangements, so that the piers became saturated and the stonework was damaged by frost and leaching out of the mortar.

One of the major constraints on carrying out repair work was the viaduct's location in a Site of Special Scientific Interest and in a County Nature Reserve. The presence of nesting birds within the structure and of butterflies on the track at one end limited the access, and affected the programming of the work. Fortunately the different conservation interests worked well together, and solutions were found to the problems that arose.

A further interest in Smardale Gill is the proximity of the quarry from which the original stone was obtained, together with the haulage tracks, which can still be clearly seen. It was not considered appropriate to reopen the quarry for the new stone that was required for repairs, and the nearest available geological equivalent was used instead.

The new deck is of asphalt with granite chippings, with two longitudinal drainage gratings running the full length of the structure. An open drainage system was used to facilitate maintenance, and this was possible because the viaduct has a longitudinal gradient. All the drainage could therefore be taken to one end and discharged into the beck. The original spitter pipes have been left

in position. Now the viaduct has a new-looking deck and a painted handrail. Some visitors regret the absence of vegetation growing on the structure, but for a long future life with as little maintenance as possible, an element of sanitization is inevitable. It has become a popular attraction for walkers, as it is very close to the coast-to-coast long-distance walk, and it complements the dramatic surroundings of the nature reserve.

Another viaduct that is now being repaired at a cost of over £600 000 for future use as a public walkway is Lambley Viaduct in Northumberland. This viaduct carried the single track of the Alston branch of the Newcastle to Carlisle railway over the South Tyne river. The eventual owners will be the North Pennines Heritage Trust, which has been in existence for a number of years, mainly involved with repairs to old mine workings. In this case the repairs are being implemented by British Rail Property Board with grant assistance from the Railway Heritage Trust, English Heritage and the European Union.

Water saturation has been the main problem with Lambley Viaduct. It had been pointed with a hard cement mortar, which was bursting off in strips, and

Fig. 17.4 Lambley Viaduct, Alston branch of Newcastle & Carlisle Railway, Northumberland, 1852. (E. Ryle-Hodges)

227

extensive stone decay has been occurring on the arch imposts. The deck is being made waterproof and a handrail provided. Some stone is being replaced, and the whole superstructure is being repointed using a pure lime mortar. The original structure was, of course, built with lime mortar, and the more recent cement pointing has done nothing but harm. The repointing in lime of some 3000 m^2 is the largest repointing contract in a traditional material for a considerable period. The use of this material does, however, introduce limitations compared with current practice, and it was necessary to break the work into two seasons to avoid the risks associated with using lime mortar in the winter.

Disused viaducts have become a liability to the railways, but they are an asset to the landscape, appreciated by the growing numbers of people who use the countryside for recreation. It was the railways that brought more people into and through the rural landscape in the nineteenth century, and their part in the social and economic history of the country cannot be overestimated.

There are now a number of examples of disused viaducts that have been repaired for the public benefit, with public money. The resources available are inevitably limited, but the possibility of funding from the Heritage Lottery Fund may be in time to prevent terminal deterioration of many more. Viaducts deserve such investment, as some of the finest symbols of the skill and enterprise associated with railways.

Index

References to illustrations are given in the form of figure numbers in **bold**, listed in sequence after the text references.